FARCE

Brian Rix first retire... years as an actor-m... ...enting and appearing in farce, in order to concentrate on theatrical management in London and New York. It was not the happiest of experiences, and after three years he answered an advertisement and was appointed Secretary-General of MENCAP – the Royal Society for Mentally Handicapped Children and Adults. In most people's minds the change was breath-taking. And so it was. And so it is, for now Brian Rix has set it down on paper.

For his work in the theatre and the world of mental handicap Brian Rix has been honoured many times. He was appointed CBE in 1977 and knighted in 1986.

Not bad for a Yorkshire lad who simply wanted to be a successful actor. Which he was – and is.

For Brian Rix has gone back to his first love, the theatre. He is chairman of the Arts Council of Great Britain Drama Panel, and in 1988 returned to the stage in a new production of John Chapman's classic farce *Dry Rot*, in which he first appeared – albeit in a different role – in 1954.

Farce About Face – the sequel to *My Farce from my Elbow*, published in 1974 – is an account of the tumultuous years since in the life of Sir Brian Rix.

BRIAN RIX

Farce about Face

FONTANA/Collins

First published by Hodder & Stoughton in 1989

First published in 1990 by Fontana Paperbacks
8 Grafton Street, London W1X 3LA

Printed and bound in Great Britain by
William Collins Sons & Co. Ltd, Glasgow

Dedication

To Elspet, our extended family and our many friends.

To people with a mental handicap and their families.

To members of the Great British Public and the media, for your, often, surprising degree of support and help. Oh yes, and to the East Acton Pogo Stick Dance Association who once rang offering an undisclosed evening's entertainment on MENCAP's behalf if I would attend. I wish I had.

Thank you, one and all, for your affection, your understanding and your interest. I hope this second part of my autobiography, from birth to bus-pass, will give you some laughs, some wry smiles and some tears along the road.

LIFE, A THEATRE
Robert Bland

This life a theatre we well may call
Where every actor must perform with art
Or laugh it through and make a farce of all
Or learn to bear with grace his tragic part.

BRIAN RIX, *Barnes, London*
April 1990

Contents

PROLOGUE

"Kismet"   3

ACT 1

Scene I   "I Have Been Here Before . . ."   21
Scene II   "Love's Labour's Lost"   40

       Intermission   47

ACT II

Scene I   "Anything Goes"   55
Scene II   "All's Well That Ends Well"   90

       Intermission   125

ACT III

"A New Way To Pay Old Debts"   133

EPILOGUE

"The Relapse"   303

Yet another FAREWELL
PERFORMANCE!   332

Envoi to the Paperback Edition   335

Index   338

Illustrations

Brian Rix aged eleven.

Hornsea, 1938. Brian Rix playing cricket in the garden.

Brian Rix with his wife Elspet Gray on their wedding day.

Jonty, Jamie and Louisa Rix with Elspet and Brian outside York House in the 1960s.

Brian with Shelley about the same time.

Brixham. The morning of Jamie's wedding, 1980.

Shelley at Barnes, 1988.

Familiar Faces at the Whitehall Theatre.

Cartoon of *Reluctant Heroes*.

Outside the Whitehall Theatre, soon after the opening of *Chase Me, Comrade!*

Dry Rot, 1954 and 1,000 performances later!

Cartoon by Stanley Franklin commemorating Brian Rix's retirement from the theatre in 1977.

This is Your Life, 1977.[1]

Brian Rix with Ray Cooney in the Cooney-Marsh offices.

The Victorian theatre at Normansfield.

The Gateway Festival at the Royal Festival Hall. 1981.[2]

The opening of the Rix Toy Library at Normansfield.

Elspet Gray with Dr Norman Langdon-Down and Lady Brain at Normansfield.

The MENCAP Annual International Art Exhibition, 1980.[3]

The Summer Fayre at Normansfield, 1988.

The launch of the Bruce Forsyth Gold Classic.[4]

Filming for *Let's Go* and presenting the programme on television.[5]

Queen Elizabeth the Queen Mother opening the MENCAP headquarters in Golden Lane, 1981.[6]

Prince Philip talking to Brian Rix, 1984.[7]

Brian Rix receiving his honorary degree from the Open University.

Louisa's wedding day, 1981.

Brian Rix by his swimming pool at Barnes.[8]

Elspet and Brian, summer 1988.[9]

The launch of the *MENCAP Famous Faces Collection*, 1983.

Glenys Kinnock and Brian Rix launching the 'Community Carers' Campaign, 1987.

Brian Rix outside Buckingham Palace after his investiture ceremony, 1986.[10]

Brian Rix, 1981. His official portrait as Secretary-General of MENCAP.[11]

In the dressing-room at the Lyric Theatre, Shaftesbury Avenue, 1988.[12]

On stage in the 1988 revivial of *Dry Rot*.

Elspet and Brian's granchildren, 1988.

The family at Barnes. Summer 1988.

Brian Rix walking with Elspet on holiday in Wiltshire, 1988.

Acknowledgments

[1] Christopher Smith
[2] Jeffrey Smorley
[3] NSMHC
[4] David Howe
[5] BBC
[6] Islington Libraries
[7] British Petroleum Co. PLC
[8] Topham Picture Library
[9] Photo by Graham Wood. Camera Press (*The Times*)
[10] Clive Howes
[11] MENCAP
[12] Color Features

The illustrations are from the author's private albums. The publishers have attempted to trace copyright owners. Where inadvertent infringement has been made they apologize and will be happy to make due acknowledgment in any future edition.

Prologue

"Kismet"

And as he journeyed, he came near Damascus: and suddenly there shined round about him a light from heaven . . .

And the Lord said unto him, "Arise, and go into the city, and it shall be told thee what thou must do."

And, according to the Acts of the Apostles, that's what happened to Saul (later St Paul) when it came to his conversion.

And, according to my wife – Elspet – that didn't happen to me (later Sir B.) when it came to mine.

And you couldn't call it a conversion, anyway. More a different course of action. And it would be presumptuous of me to claim that I have any connection whatsoever with that particular Saint, or any other, for that matter, or that I was anywhere near the road to Damascus at the time, or indeed, that the Lord had anything to do with it.

But I was journeying on the road to London, in Fore Street, Brixham, to be precise, being driven by Elspet, in her Renault 5. Furthermore, the light that shined about me was somewhat clouded o'er by a West Country drizzle, but it was enough to read an advert on the appointments page of the *Guardian*, telling thee (and me) that the National Society for Mentally Handicapped Children required a new Secretary-General. The date of this singularly non-ecumenical event was Wednesday, August 15th, 1979 – quite a few years later than Saul's dramatic fall to the earth. About 1,900 years later, to be more precise.

How did I come to find myself in that position –

scanning the *Guardian* pages for a job which would appear to be the very antithesis of everything I had done up to then? Well, it's a long story. Much of it was recounted in my earlier autobiography *My Farce from my Elbow*, originally published by Secker and Warburg in 1975, but I shall assume that many of you did not avail yourselves of such saucy material at that time – either in hard or paperback – nor did you swell my public lending rights, so it will be necessary for a little regurgitation. New readers start here . . . Previous ones move to page 40, unless you need a little memory jogging, that is . . .

I was born one cold and frosty morn, on January 27th, 1924, in my mother's bedroom (my father's too, come to think of it. Where did he spend the night?) at our impressive semi-detached house, Gairloch, in the largest village in England, Cottingham, East Yorkshire. Sorry if I've had to dress that up a little, but I was the youngest of four children – and always had to exaggerate somewhat to create any impression whatsoever. When your brother is already away at boarding school, and your sisters can both read and write, it's difficult to be the one always bringing up the rear. The gift of the gab, and a general air of confidence (only assumed, I can assure you) became my particular forte. It has stood me in good stead on many an occasion since – but it's also landed me smack in the middle of the mire just about as often.

I left Cottingham as a very small child and, strangely enough, I didn't see the house where I was born again until immediately after my mother's funeral, some fifty-one years later. My brother, Malcolm, and I had just left the crematorium and he was leading me back to the London road, as I was uncertain of the way. He suddenly stopped his car and I juddered to a halt behind him. He got out, pointed up to the house and there, with cold February mists swirling around, I saw the windows of the room in which my first squawls had been heard so long ago. It all seemed a bit eerie, adding to the gloom of the occasion.

My childhood, under the watchful eye of Allie, my nanny, was reasonbly happy. When I was four we moved to a succession of large houses in Hornsea, a charming little east coast seaside resort. Oh dear, here I go again . . . Hornsea is an unremarkable place, as cold as charity, with an east wind that would make even a brass monkey cry for help. Furthermore, we moved to *two* large houses, not a succession, and there I spent my formative years with a mother who was mad on amateur theatricals and a father who was mad on cricket but earned his living, with his two brothers, as a ship-owner in Hull. Out of loyalty, he also built the scenery for my mother's productions and thus allowed himself to become embroiled in the fatal attraction of the theatre – an attraction which proved irresistible to his two younger children, Sheila and me. The two elder, Malcolm and Nora, were made of sterner stuff and escaped the lure of the greasepaint.

In the meantime, school had to be suffered, and suffered it was by me, except when I was playing cricket or camping about as the lead in my prep school plays. My old headmaster – Bickie (Dr G. H. Bickmore) – was besotted by both endeavours, so until the age of thirteen, I was pretty happy with my lot. Bickie was even alive to comment on this only last year, when at the age of ninety he was visited by three of his favourite old boys to reminisce about those permanently sunny days. Then, for me, came the abyss. Boarding school. How I hated it. I'm sure it wasn't Bootham's fault for, as a Quaker school in that most civilized city, York, it had all the right ingredients. It just didn't suit me. Perhaps it was because I was pitchforked into the cricket 1st XI in my first term, with boys much older than I. Perhaps it's because I suffered an accidental orchidectomy during a hernia operation when I was nine, which caused much bullying. Or, more simply, perhaps it was because I was, frankly, a precocious pain in the arse. Whatever the reason, I loathed my boarding days – and used every ploy I could to get away.

Get away I did, before taking my entrance exam to Oxford, where my father was determined I should go. Not for any academic reason, but simply because he wished his youngest to get his cricket Blue and be able to put Oxon after his degree. I defied all this splendid logic and, as the Second World War was on, managed to get myself attested as PNB (Pilot, Navigator, Bomb Aimer) in the RAF. But then came the fatal pause. I was deferred for ten months. Ten months! The thought of sitting any further exams never crossed my mind. It was hey-diddle-de-dee, an actor's life for me – and I was off with Donald Wolfit on tour, when he played King Lear for the first time, which was followed by a season at the St James's Theatre, six weeks of ENSA (Entertainments National Service Association, colloquially known by the long-suffering troops as Every Night Something Awful) and, wonder upon wonder, further deferment. Repertory with the White Rose Players at Harrogate filled in that time, but then, inevitably, came the RAF. But not before I'd had an antiquated operation for sinus trouble and that, together with the demand for pilots lessening each year (the war in Europe was coming near to a close), ensured that my dreams of glory in the skies faded all too fast. Just as well, I imagine, otherwise I might not be here to tell the tale.

Instead of climbing into the skies, I descended into the bowels of the earth for a spell down the mines as a volunteer Bevin Boy, a further few months in the RAF as a medical orderly instructor, founder of the station Dramatic Society and Captain of cricket, followed by demob in October 1947 at Padgate – calling in to see my sister Sheila playing in *East Lynne* twice-nightly at Warrington. She was then Sheila Rix. Now she uses her married name, Sheila Mercier, but is probably better known to millions

6

as Annie Sugden, the doughty heroine of *Emmerdale Farm*. What's in a name, anyway?

By the time I was demobbed, most other young actors had already been back on the job market for at least a year – so I recognized it could well be something of a struggle to re-establish myself. Not that I was established anyway, but you know what I mean. When I'd joined Wolfit in 1942 any fledgling actor who could walk on to a stage was almost certain of a job. It was a fact of life that if you were too young for military service, unfit for military service, or what was euphemistically known as temperamentally unsuited for military service, you were in great demand on-stage. But by 1947 things were very different.

However, Donald Wolfit had demonstrated an activity which appealed to me. He was not just an actor, but an actor-manager. That's what I could become. And that's precisely what I did become and remained in that precarious occupation for exactly thirty years. I must have needed my head examining. I mean, what sane person would undertake a working life of choosing the plays, raising the money for the plays, playing the lead in the plays, finding a theatre for the plays and sometimes directing the plays? Mind you, raising the money at first was not too difficult. I borrowed £900 to be precise – from my father and Uncle Bertie, chipped in a hundred quid of my own, hired a theatre (which was *not* a theatre), assembled a company and we were off.

On Easter Monday, March 29th, 1948, the curtain went up at the King's Hall, Ilkley, and half of it promptly came down again. It was one of those old-fashioned curtains which swagged up in two halves to each side of the proscenium arch and the rope holding up the right-hand half was about a hundred years old, and disintegrated. The actors were gathered round a desk in the middle of the stage and realized they couldn't be seen by many of the audience, so solemnly pushed the desk to the left-hand side of the set. That's where I had to make my first entrance, through a door that opened on-stage but which was now incapable of movement – for the desk was jammed up against it. So, in a state of blind panic, I dashed round to the window at the back of the set and made my first grand entrance as an actor-manager through this, the only opening I could see. As you can imagine, such a method was greeted by considerable laughter for, apart from anything else, the window was shut, but having no glass in it allowed me to sneak through. Then again, I received a round of applause – not because anyone knew me, but simply because of my courage, I imagine. You see, the play we were doing was the old American farce, *Nothing but the Truth*, and the first act takes place in a New York skyscraper, twenty-eight floors up . . .

You could say that unfortunate opening was but a taste of things to come. Ilkley was a disaster. By the end of twenty-eight weeks that original £1,000 capital had been swallowed up in a loss nearing £3,000. My father and uncle were getting distinctly nervous. I was terrified. But then fortune smiled and I was offered a season at Bridlington. Now Bridlington is a pleasant seaside resort, about fourteen miles north of Hornsea and fourteen miles south of Scarborough. It has a successful summer season which runs through July and August. *We* opened there in November. Furthermore, because of the gales which lash the seafront, we couldn't be in the proper Spa Theatre but, instead, had to perform inland at the Grand Pavilion, which was more suitable for chorus lines of about 150 spread across the vast proscenium opening, dominating this singularly inappropriate theatrical venue. However, we persevered, and in spite of the nor'easters and the lashing rain, we managed to produce a pantomime – *Babes in the Wood* – which made enough money to keep us limping on until the summer, when we transferred to the Spa.

But that year of 1949 was vital to me. In the first place,

I met Elspet, who was auditioning for another company I was opening at Margate in January. You must admit, I was a glutton for punishment. Two winter seasons in two summer resorts! No wonder the young are considered to be foolish and headstrong. Anyway, I fell head-over-heels for Elspet and found her a job under my wing, as it were, in Bridlington. There, romance blossomed, and we married on August 14th in the same year. It must say something for east coast resilience – we've been together ever since. And that, in spite of the fact that although we have been married for nearly forty years, we have had many a cross word. We have had so many, in fact, that people knowing us are amazed we are still together. We maintain it is because of our differing opinions that we are!

Our differences really started before marriage. The first little minefield to be negotiated was very tricky – the date of our wedding, followed by the location of same. Let me explain . . .

When I first met Elspet I behaved like any hero out of *Peg's Paper*. As I say, I was bowled over. Of course, those heroes were always fine and upstanding. I had a hangover. Nothing daunted though, I pressed my suit, proposed marriage, and was rejected out of hand. However, I am not a stubborn Yorkshireman for nothing and shortly afterwards I was enjoying the perks of marriage without any of the problems. It seemed to be the ideal arrangement, but Elspet's opinion, was, as ever, different from mine. We were in the bath at the time when Elspet suddenly sat bolt upright (the resulting tidal wave nearly made marriage a fruitless exercise for I bottomed heavily on the plug chain) and declared that our nuptials must be solemnized at the earliest opportunity. In those pre-marital days I never argued vocally, only achieving my objectives by stealth, so the date was fixed with unseemly haste. Unseemly, inasmuch as Elspet's father was in India and unable to attend the wedding. I pointed out this omission to my future helpmeet but again her opinion was diametrically opposed to mine. "If we wait for Daddy," she said, "if we wait for Daddy" (I like that phrase, it is redolent of hockey and lacrosse and Kashmir) "we'll have to hang about for another eighteen months and we won't be together then." And so it came to pass we were married, sans Daddy. We sent him a recording, though.

The venue for the ceremony caused considerable bad blood between the opposing families. Elspet's mum just wanted to get us married cheaply, efficiently and with the minimum of fuss. She wasn't a Scots Presbyterian for nothing. On the other hand, my lot (including me) wanted a full white wedding in our local church. My lot won. The score now read fifteen all, and Elspet and I emerged, toothily, from *my* church on *her* date.

That is how it has been ever since. What theatres should we visit? Where should we park? Where to spend Christmas Day now the family are no longer at home? Should we live in the country? Does life exist outside Barnes? What about Wiltshire? And so on, and so on. The list is endless. So what is so good about all this discord? Well it keeps us talking, for one thing, and in marriage that is half the battle. Look at the next married couple you see in a restaurant. The chances are they will open their mouths only to order the food, shovel in the food and ask for the bill. The rest is silence. Surely they would be better off chatting, even if only to complain about the soup being too hot or the coffee being too cold, or the food stains on the waiter's jacket, or what-have-you. That is our theory anyway, and if you see Elspet and me in a restaurant we are always chattering away. The content of our chatter sometimes leaves much to be desired – but what the hell, we are *talking*. Furthermore, we still like each other and that must be a bonus in any marriage. We are very lucky.

And luck, too, played its part in the second vital occurrence in that Bridlington season when I stumbled

10

across an extremely funny play, *Reluctant Heroes*, which had been doing the rounds of various managements for some four years, but no one had had the sense to see its possibilities. I did! We tried the play out in front of the Spa Theatre audience in July and broke the house record. I was certain I had found my way into the West End with Colin Morris's hilarious piece – all about conscription – which was still very much a part of all our lives. National Service had just been extended to two years, thanks to Monty badgering Prime Minister Attlee, and anyone else he could pressurize.

So, in February 1950 Elspet and I, with Wally Patch, Dermot Walsh, Larry Noble, Colin Morris, John Chapman (who was my understudy and wrote my next Whitehall farce, *Dry Rot*) and a few others (the cast kept changing in the smaller parts), began our marathon tour which eventually brought us to the Whitehall Theatre on September 12th, seven months after we'd started. We were the natural successors to *Worm's Eye View* which had occupied that theatre for some five years, but even then we had to wait patiently in line whilst another play, *The Dish Ran Away*, disgraced the Whitehall stage for a few limp weeks before it collapsed and died, simply because the management of the Whitehall couldn't believe that one so young and inexperienced as I had a genuine bargain to offer. But I had, and *Heroes* ran for four years. But it was a close-run thing. Although the Whitehall management had heard of our play they still wanted to see it before committing themselves. We were at the Theatre Royal, Nottingham, so I had to transport the Whitehall house manager from a meeting in London to the East Midlands, to see the five o'clock matinée. It was in the days before motorways and I inadvertently ended up in Leicester! However, a kindly speed cop saw my plight, put us on the right road, and we arrived at the stage door of the Theatre Royal two minutes before the curtain was due to go up. Everybody's nerves were torn to shreds, including the Whitehall plenipotentiary's, but in spite of this and a very tiny audience, good old Nottingham came to our rescue and *Reluctant Heroes* was greeted with glee and gaiety by those hard-working few sitting out front, surrounded by rows of wood and plush.

The Whitehall house manager came round afterwards beaming from ear to ear. "It'll be a smash," he said. We were IN! Thank you, Nottingham, for making it all possible.

Actually, Nottingham has always been kind to me, in one way or another. My first girlfriend came from there. I have no intention of embarrassing her or her family by naming her. It could be that she prefers that episode of her young life to be well and truly closed and relegated to the past. In any event, it was nearly fifty years ago . . . Let me say she was a very pretty girl, I was a fairly pretty boy; we might well have made a lovely couple – but we didn't.

The second occasion I had good luck in Nottingham came when I first visited the town as a junior member of Donald Wolfit's company way back in 1942. It was also the occasion which hinted at near-disaster. Anyway, first things first – my first fan letters (all two of them) arrived at the Theatre Royal's stage door. I mentioned this in my previous autobiography *My Farce from my Elbow*, and named the two ladies concerned. To my amazement, I received another letter from one of them – over thirty years after her original one – and I found this a very pleasant reminder of those far-off, courteous days when a first fan letter certainly gave great encouragement to a callow, inexperienced actor, who was me. If she reads this book, maybe I'll get another . . .

The unpleasant memory of the Theatre Royal, Nottingham, happened at the same time. I was "off", which meant missing an entrance and this is an actor's principal nightmare, apart from the worse one of finding yourself on-stage without knowing your lines! Now the stage door of the Theatre Royal used to abut the stage door of the old Empire and I had wandered over during our matinée of *King Lear* to ogle at all those lovely dancing girls gracing the Empire's stage in that week's production of *Chu Chin Chow*. I was so gob-smacked by all the noise and music and chat, apart from those diaphanously robed ladies in the chorus, that I overstayed my welcome and arrived back on-stage at the Theatre Royal to find I'd missed my one and only speaking entrance, as Curan a courtier, by some five minutes. I do not have to exaggerate for your benefit the fire and brimstone which Mr Wolfit (it was before his knighthood) heaped upon my quaking head. It was a lesson well learned and a misdemeanour never to be repeated.

Of course "off" stories are legion in our business. In 1947 Elspet was in *Edward, My Son*, and saw Dame Peggy Ashcroft change into a ghastly red wig and blowzy clothes to denote the passage of time and her downward descent as an alcoholic, one scene and one interval ahead of time. The audience were justifiably bemused as to why this incredible change had taken place in what was, of course, the same day in terms of the act being performed.

A great friend of mine, Tim Manderson, was once playing the Duke in *The Eagle Has Two Heads* in the totally unsuitable and cavernous Kilburn Empire. It was a part which appeared at the beginning and end of the play. He used to climb up to his dressing-room after his opening scene and read a book until it was time to go down for the final scene. On this occasion it was a bad matinée and it was decided to cut one interval. This information was not conveyed to my chum, who was off by ten minutes – or rather would have been, if a perspiring, puffed-out assistant stage manager hadn't panted up to his dressing-room and managed to push him on only five minutes late. The half-dozen people in the audience were almost wakened by the sight of a suave courtier, the Duke, an officer and a gentleman no less, hurling himself on to the stage to meet his Queen, pulling on his riding boots, doing up his flies and buckling on his sword all at the same time.

Elspet once did it to me in the middle of a television, *Jane Steps Out*. She had changed at the wrong moment and was in a nightdress instead of an evening dress. In those days, tellys were live. Elspet was supposed to interrupt my kissing Ann Firbank. She was two minutes twenty-five seconds late and it was the longest kiss in the business, practically causing apoplectic fits amongst all guardians of the nation's morals who were watching. When Elspet finally did arrive on the scene, she had to play the entire remainder of the act facing front; she had scrambled back into her evening dress — but did not have time to do up the zip at the back! Oh, we saw life in the raw in those days — if you know what I mean.

I'm sorry if that was a somewhat circuitous route to tell the Whitehall/Nottingham/*Reluctant Heroes* saga — but I think it filled in one or two other gaps as well. However, in spite of our apparent success and good notices for *Heroes*, we were having a bit of a struggle for, after all, we were unknown in London and up against stiff opposition in the laughter stakes — led by *Seagulls Over Sorrento* and *The Little Hut* — not to mention *Worm's Eye View* itself, which had transferred to the Comedy. It was the BBC which came to our rescue — for the first, but not the last time. They offered me a fifteen-minute radio excerpt on the Light Programme, and that quarter of an hour of the beginning of Act I did the trick. Incredible, isn't it? In spite of the counter-attraction of the Festival of Britain, we were up and running.

Then in May 1951, just before that radio excerpt, Elspet announced she was pregnant. She played a small part in the film of the play, and then retired to await the happy day. Our earnings from the film — all of £750 — allowed us

14

to pay the key money for our first two-bedroomed flat in Holland Park, one room for us, the other for the baby.

She was born, after a forty-eight-hour labour, at 2.30 a.m. on Monday, December 3rd, in the Westminster Hospital. She was a funny little thing, like all newly born babies, but she seemed beautiful to us. We were in raptures. Elspet's father roared with laughter as she stuck her tongue out at him. She seemed to stick her tongue out rather a lot . . .

Elspet was a little worried. "They don't bring her to me as much as I'd like," she complained. "Do you think there's something wrong with her?"

"Don't be silly," I said, "all the babies seem to be kept away from their mums, except for feeding times."

But the early warnings had been sounded. Elspet remembered her strange feelings during pregnancy. Often she had thought the child she was carrying was not a normal child. She was, in the event, correct; but everyone was loath to tell us. It was the maternity sister, Sister Gilbert, who finally persuaded the gynaecologist, Mr Searle, to reveal the facts. "He'd like to see you in Harley Street at six o'clock tomorrow evening," she said in an off-hand way to me.

My reaction was understandably nervous. "What for? And why Harley Street? Why can't he see me here?"

She calmed me down: "It's just a routine interview he likes to have with *all* new fathers – away from the hurly-burly of the hospital."

So I reported this to Elspet and her fears multiplied, but I battened down my own feelings and attempted to encourage her. My fears, however, dragged side by side with hers and as I stepped into Mr Searle's consulting-room I had only to look at his face to know the worst.

It's laughable really. Actors perform these parts better than their actual counterparts. Mr Searle behaved like the newest drama student.

"Do come in . . . Do sit down . . . Do have a cigarette."

I came in, but I neither sat down nor had a cigarette. I was a non-sitter and a non-smoker in those situtions. A non-smoker at all times, anyway.

"Have you heard of mongolism?" was his first question. Well that was one way of putting it. Direct and to the point. Our daughter was a mongol. My stomach went through the consulting-room floor and has never, really, recovered its rightful place since. "Have you heard of mongolism?" "I have to tell you your son has been killed in a car accident." "Your husband was a brave man." Jesus Christ! It's only in moments such as these that you realize the inadequacy of the spoken word. Afterwards you recognize that the poor devil stumbling and stuttering before you is as mortified and horrified at explaining the disaster as you are at receiving it. But that's the way we do it and what other way is there?

What indeed? I wrote those lines for my first autobiography, one cold, wet January midnight in 1974, huddled over my desk in my room at the Angel Hotel, Cardiff — weeping the while at the memory. My miserable stay in South Wales was occasioned by appearing in pantomime at the New Theatre, but we ran into Edward Heath's three-day week and the whole thing was a damp, unpleasant farrago. Perhaps that's what made my unhappiness all the greater, but the majority of parents are easily transported back to the shock of those first numbing words, when you learn your child is not as other children. Mongolism has now been dressed-up as Down's syndrome, of course, but the pain and grieving remain the same.

And so it was, when I first saw the advert in the *Guardian*, I only had to read it to Elspet — who was driving — for us both to realize that this was the way ahead for me. But first I had to get the job. It wasn't as easy to become the Secretary-General of MENCAP as I thought. And why did I want the job at that particular time, anyway? After all, Shelley had been around since 1951. I told you, it's a long story . . .

Act I

"I Have Been Here Before . . ."

As you might expect, life went on after Shelley's arrival. Following a cursory inspection and some negotiations, off she went to a private home, where she remained for the first five years of her life. That was the norm in those days. If you had the resources, however limited, the advice you received was to thank your lucky stars, put your mentally handicapped son or daughter in private care and get on raising the normal members of your family. As Shelley was our first, we couldn't do the raising bit, but we did follow the rest of that advice, proffered, I must add, by the medical profession. Of course, if you were less well endowed, you had no option other than to follow the certification and "asylum" route or – more generally – you kept your handicapped offspring at home. It was an horrendous time. No wonder the first group of parents had started to band together. Without that Association of Parents of Backward Children – now the Royal Society for Mentally Handicapped Children and Adults (MENCAP) – we'd still be in the Victorian era.

But Elspet and I didn't know about such an Association – very few did – so we took the easy way out and paid for Shelley's upbringing. When she was five we were lucky enough to be offered a place at Normansfield for her, just across Richmond Park from our house, and there she has lived ever since, visiting us at regular intervals. Normansfield was then considered to be the jewel in the crown of the newly developing health service for, until 1949, it had been *the* private home for people with a mental handicap and the patient list reads like pages torn out of *Who's*

Who. Even after the NHS had taken the place over, the clientele were generally selected from the same upper-crust background so, as actors, I suppose we were lucky to have been considered. Even so, Shelley had to be certified – for she was entering a state hospital – and the memory of that dreadful process, conducted by two LCC women doctors, will remain with us always. At least that degrading step was removed soon after Shelley's admission but, again, it was parental pressure which brought about its demise.

What was so special about Normansfield in the first place? It was founded in 1868 by Dr John Langdon-Down as an institution for the mentally handicapped sons and daughters of the well-to-do, who generally placed their offspring there, endowed them generously, and then pretended to the world at large that they had died. Mind you, those with no money, too, often ended up concealing the fact from their immediate neighbourhood and their unfortunate children would be kept hidden away, in curtained back rooms and exercised (if at all) when darkness fell. We were even less sympathetic then, than now, to anyone who was in some way different or disabled, and the shame and horror of having produced such a child descended like a miasma over everyone's head, forcing them into unimaginable half-truths to hide the grisly facts from anyone who might be interested or simply curious.

Quite frankly, it wasn't so different in our day. My father, a kind and gentle man, wept when he heard about Shelley – but never mentioned her again to the day he died. He didn't want to upset us, but he also considered it a blot on the family. Perhaps understandably, for he had been born in 1885, just when Langdon-Down was really getting into his stride, and Victorian shibboleths abounded. The good doctor was an amazing man and even though he got things a bit wrong, he was still years ahead in his "treatment" for those he housed. He was wrong, inasmuch as he named his patients "mongols" – and, in turn, believed that mongols were a throw-back to early man. But such an error is forgivable, for we only discovered the actual cause of the condition less than twenty years ago. Up to then, the guilty twenty-first chromosome was an unknown factor. It certainly was when our daughter was born. I was asked if I had VD, or was drunk at the time of conception. No wonder people used to hide them away.

Old Langdon-Down was advanced in his thinking on many other counts, too. To begin with, the numbers living at Normansfield were small in comparison to the asylums and colonies which housed the rest of the so-called "idiots". Then again, he introduced schooling for his residents – and remember the state considered mentally handicapped children ineducable until the 1970 Education Act came into force in April 1971. Nowadays, Riding for the Disabled is a thriving and deserving cause – but Langdon-Down had his excellent stabling and horses in operation about ninety years before anyone else. Furthermore, he built a unique and beautiful Amusement Hall, which housed a splendid Victorian theatre, simply because he believed such "remedial activities" would enhance the lives of those in his care. He was right, but no one else took much notice. Out of sight, out of mind was the thought for the day – and it's taken a long time for such thoughts to turn in the direction of community care. And even that phrase is open to question as being only a phrase, not a widely supported concept.

I would like to dwell for a moment on that Amusement Hall, which is one of the finest examples of a fully equipped private theatre in Britain. Its stage is a unique working model of a kind once common but now, alas, extinct. Its collection of one hundred pieces of painted "stock" scenery is of national importance – as are the machinery and effects. There are even some of the screens from the original D'Oyly Carte production of *Ruddigore* dating back to January 22nd, 1887, when it was produced at the Savoy Theatre, some eight years after the Normansfield Theatre itself was built. A superb magic lantern, with slides that actually move, was also discovered there – and remember, all this was for members of Victorian families who had been discounted and discarded. No wonder mongolism is now referred to as the Langdon-Down syndrome. Dr John deserves that accolade, at least. Furthermore, he left a valediction which is still relevant today: "We have to provide the highest possible culture, the best physical, moral and intellectual training – to open out fresh realms of happiness for those who have the strongest claims on our sympathy."

And, strangely enough, we have an opportunity to follow that philosophy with the old Amusement Hall. A group of us have come together to try and turn it into a sophisticated National Arts Centre for Disabled People. I was asked to write the Foreword in May 1987 for our complex application to the powers-that-be, in which I pointed out that the Attenborough Report on Arts and Disabled People had been published some three years earlier. This, in turn, was followed by the formation of the Carnegie Council to monitor the Report's effectiveness.

At the same time, the Arts Council of Great Britain issued a code of practice to enable arts organizations to meet the needs of people with disabilities and put together a Monitoring Committee, of which I am Chairman, to oversee all this activity.

I went on to stress that disabled people still did not have a home in the Greater London area. A centre where all art forms could be pursued; integration, in the widest sense, take place and desirable therapies made freely available. The National Arts Centre for Disabled People at Normansfield would provide such a home.

In spite of my final plea that over the years the arts have prompted some of the finest achievements of the human spirit and that it would be splendid if some of those achievements could now arise from Normansfield, reflecting on the ideals of its founder, Dr John Langdon-Down, using his beautiful and unique Entertainments Hall as the centre-piece for such an enterprise, I have to report a singular lack of success. The local arts bodies are not too keen, nor are disabled people themselves – believing it would create another ghetto. Wrong, in my opinion, as this could be an arts centre that would be an example to all as to what proper facilities and access should be like. But there we are . . .

Of course, Shelley's arrival pushed Elspet and me in the direction of a number of charities which were just beginning to emerge, connected with mental handicap – particularly the Friends of Normansfield, of which I am now Chairman. The founder was a certain Stella, Lady Brain, the widow of the late Lord Brain. But then Stella, like us, had a vested interest. Not only was she a Langdon-Down herself, being the granddaughter of Dr John, but she was brought up at Normansfield (her father being the joint Medical Superintendent there) with her brother who suffered from the condition now named after his grandfather – in other words, he was a mongol. On the other hand, Stella's cousin Norman (another Langdon-Down) was also brought up at Normansfield, for *his* father was the other joint Medical Superintendent. Norman went on to become a doctor himself and, in turn, the last Medical Superintendent at Normansfield. You could say the *family* had a vested interest! You could also say, with absolute certainty, that they had an abiding and compassionate interest in all the goings-on at Normansfield and the creation of a very active League of Friends was an obvious step forward, in line with the growing custom at that time. So Elspet and I were roped in, willingly I might say, and an incredible fund-raising drive began to provide many essential extras: a fully equipped school (remember this was fifteen years before the 1970 Education Act); a holiday home at Selsey Bill (now sold – but in those days people with a mental handicap were not welcome in normal holiday places); a club house, shop, boutique and swimming pool (all still in constant use); a toy library (now a recreation centre) and, more recently, housing in the community. No wonder we had difficulty in keeping our friends. We were always selling them tickets.

But our lives were still in the theatre. Not the one at Normansfield (we discovered its real worth about ten years ago), but that splendid little playhouse at the opposite end of Whitehall from the Houses of Parliament and under the eternally watchful gaze of Lord Nelson.

1952 brought an extraordinary world première, as far as I was concerned. The first ever television excerpt from a West End play – and it was *Reluctant Heroes*. I had been negotiating with Cecil Madden at the BBC for some two or three months plus, of course, Equity and the West End Managers and then – bingo! – on May 14th the first act of our good old army farce was presented on the only television channel available at the time, the good old BBC. Oh yes, and it was introduced by good old Brian Johnston, except, in those days, he didn't really qualify for that epithet. The result was staggering, even more so than the fifteen-minute radio excerpt we'd done the year before. Remember, the film of *Heroes* had already been made, and was hellbent on becoming the most successful comedy movie of the year, so plenty of people had already seen the piece, for the play, too, had been running on tour and in the West End for over two years.

But that excerpt – phew! That was something else! From May 15th – and right through the summer and autumn – queues formed every day down Whitehall around lunchtime, as theatregoers struggled to find a few seats in an already over-booked theatre stretched to its limits, with seventy-six people standing at every performance. West

26

End Managers swallowed their pride in dollops and hustled the BBC, like old whores, to get their productions on the screen. It was amazing. One day, I was outside the charmed circle; the next, its leader. Well, not exactly its leader – more its favourite prodigal son. I don't think I ever came any closer. Jonah Barrington, writing in the now defunct *Daily Graphic and Daily Sketch*, summed it all up, pretty well I think:

> Thank you, Brian Rix! This far-sighted twenty-eight-year-old actor-manager has broken down years of prejudice and suspicion by allowing, for the first time since the war, a West End play to be televised from a West End theatre.
>
> And what fun *Reluctant Heroes* was, and how splendidly photographed and how Mr Rix has cashed in since, through overwhelming box-office takings.
>
> No viewer, I suggest, minds only seeing part of the play; that adds to the excitement. The appetite is whetted and both sides, viewer and promoter, benefit.
>
> So what about it, Messrs Jack Hylton, Emile Littler, Bernard Delfont, Val Parnell and other members of our TV-shy West End Managers' Association?

Well, as I said, that lot were hard at it, selling their wares. Unfortunately, the concept of the excerpt was never accepted by the television purists. Their argument was simple: "It's not true television, it's bad news for the vast majority of the home audience, for they can't get down to London to see the show anyway and it's supporting those unmentionable commercial theatrical managers." The fact that the majority of BBC executives and actors and studio managers, at that time, came from the commercial theatre never seemed to occur to them. It made life very difficult. Now, of course, the television excerpt is a thing of the past, but both BBC and ITV go in for mind-boggling

27

award ceremonies instead, bringing out the very worst in the sycophancy and false humility which stalk hand-in-hand with the film and theatrical world on such occasions. This vacuous vainglory is even perpetrated in the world of television with awards which must make nepotism seem unreal by comparison. Not to mention Oedipus.

But the first-ever showing on the screen of Act I of *Reluctant Heroes* had great repercussions. It led, eventually, to a seventeen-year contract with the BBC and that can't be bad, at least for the salesman concerned, and that huckster was me . . .

Not that it was all that easy. The BBC Controller at that time, Cecil McGivern, had religious principles which made it difficult for him to accept farce on Sundays. Indeed, our very first full-length television production, *Postman's Knock* by Philip King, had to be transmitted live from the Whitehall on a Tuesday in October 1952, after the normal evening performance of *Reluctant Heroes*. It was hugely successful, in spite of starting around 9.30, but it nearly killed all of us who were trying to do two shows, virtually for the price of one. We had to wait until ITV started in earnest, with *Sunday Night at the London Palladium* cleaning up the majority of the audience, before Cecil McGivern swallowed his religious scruples – said a few more Hail Marys no doubt – and allowed Whitehall farce on his virginal Sunday screens, with an appropriately entitled *Love in a Mist* by Kenneth Horne. So began my seventeen-year contract, renewed every three or so years, leading to over seventy full-length farces being transmitted from the Whitehall or Garrick Theatres (originally they were live, recordings came later) plus a couple of series, too – *Dial Rix* and *Six of Rix* to make up a century of laughter. But the television purists didn't like full-length theatrical productions on the screen any more than they'd liked excerpts. The two Cecils, Madden and McGivern, never commented. You just can't win . . .

Meanwhile, back at the ranch, the Whitehall farces proper continued to flourish. In 1954 came *Dry Rot*, succeeding the apparently unstoppable *Reluctant Heroes*. Like *The Mousetrap*, I believe *Heroes* could have gone on and on – but the difference between me and Sir Peter Saunders (who presents *The Mousetrap*) is simple. He is a manager, who never has to go on – whilst I had to go on – and on – and on – and on. Eventually, ennui took over, and a new play had to be found. Students of Whitehall and Garrick farces will note that the runs got shorter and shorter. That's because my boredom threshold was following a similar pattern.

Of course, *Dry Rot* was immensely successful too and with John Slater, Basil Lord, Larry Noble – plus me – in the cast, we had a mixture of favourites from both *Reluctant Heroes* and *Worm's Eye View*. Furthermore, the author, John Chapman, had been my understudy in *Heroes* so knew exactly how to tailor his play for the reigning incumbents. Again we did an Act I television excerpt, and again we made an early film during the run, with Ronnie Shiner and Sid James taking over from John Slater and Basil Lord. Many people remember Leo Franklyn in the Cockney bookmaker role played by John and Ronnie, but Leo only joined us in 1956. In spite of all this exposure, and all the cast changes, we just rolled on and on. As I said – we were unstoppable.

In 1955, an important occasion had occurred in our household. A second daughter, Louisa, was born and great was our rejoicing, for parents with a handicapped child are always fearful at any subsequent births. I suppose she'll always be someone rather special to Elspet and me, but there will be those who think that's not acceptable. After all, Shelley was still around and it was our fault she wasn't at home. As I said, you can't win. 1958 brought another John Chapman production, *Simple Spymen*, and another child, a first son, Jamie. Both events were a great success, I am happy to say. And so was another happy occasion, in 1960, with the birth of a second son, Jonathan. We were nothing if not prolific. And in the meantime, the television productions from the Whitehall continued their popularity, and so did the plays at the theatre. We were rich. Well, not rich exactly – but at least pretty well off – and our lifestyle reflected our success. Each Sunday, after a television production, I'd take the entire cast and staff out to dinner. Every one hundred performances or every Christmas or every excuse imaginable provided a reason for another spot of roistering. It was all lovely and only the Tax Inspector made it seem a little difficult – but even he was lenient. You could entertain more lavishly until Jim Callaghan became the Chancellor in 1964. Then you could only entertain foreigners. That is, until 1988. Now Nigel Lawson has even taken that perk away. All those mythical Americans we used to dine . . .

But, strangely enough, our audience was almost entirely homegrown. Foreigners generally didn't find us funny, probably because they couldn't understand the lingo, the puns, innuendos, topical jokes – all very difficult. Of course, filthy French farce has always been different from its British counterpart. Your classic French compote (of the Feydeau or Labiche variety) generally shows you a gallant French officer in his long johns, chasing some blowzy French hussy into her bedroom (or a bedroom at the house of assignation) the moment the curtain goes up. Furthermore, we learn pretty fast that the officer's wife is having an illicit liaison with at least half her officer husband's regiment, whilst her greatest love has some grotesque physical defect and suffers from chronic halitosis, etc, etc, etc.

Now your typical English farce has none of that. The plot develops steadily from a base that would have been accepted by Oliver Cromwell – and if sex is involved at

all, it is generally managed so maladroitly by the anticipating adulterers that the question of a successful conclusion
is never, but never, envisaged. Furthermore, we no longer
allow deafness, old age or the cloth to be objects of fun, so
it's all down to good old double-meanings or simple,
straightforward buffoonery. And for some maddening
reason, our critical friends will always try and find favour
with the French variety of farce rather than the English
variety. Yet I'll bet we've had a greater number of successes
this century, which have travelled happily round the world,
than any of your old ooh-la-la lot put together. Ben
Travers, Vernon Sylvaine, John Chapman, Ray Cooney,
Colin Morris, Michael Pertwee, Philip King – to mention
only the ones I was interested in – have provided more
laughs, for more people, in the theatre than probably any
other bunch of writers in history. But where are the blue
plaques on their houses? Mind you, some of that lot are
still alive, so maybe memorials would not be too
welcome . . .

As if to underline my point, the next play I presented, in
1961, was perhaps the most innocent of all but, conversely,
the most successful. Seventy-six people stood for every
performance for eighteen months and only the dreadful
winter of 1963 had any effect on the box-office. But even
then we survived. Well, for another eighteen months when
– once more – boredom set in and *One for the Pot* came
to an untimely end.

You might think that was hard luck on the actors and
the authors. Well, so it was, in a way, but as most of them
were the same, in one capacity or another, it made very
little difference – except to their royalties. For instance,
when *Spymen* came off in 1961, John Chapman was
already established as a television writer and was busy
with other things. Colin Morris, who wrote *Reluctant
Heroes*, had long since gone to the BBC as a highly
acclaimed documentary writer, whilst innumerable other

actors had turned writers in their sojourn at the Whitehall, or on tour, and were busy elsewhere. Offhand, I can think of Clive Exton, Donald Churchill, Charles Dyer and the late Philip Levéne. But there must have been others. However, two I *can* remember were Ray Cooney and Tony Hilton. Tony had toured for me in *Heroes* whilst both he and Ray toured in *Dry Rot*. Ray then came into *Simple Spymen* for the London run, but as he was only on in Act I and at the end of Act III he had plenty of time to kill. Instead of filling in the pools or watching telly or playing cards, he and Tony had worked hard on writing a play – and that play, simple as it was, was *One for the Pot*. But all good things come to an end.

Incidentally, it was during *Pot* that I did my first *This Is Your Life*. Lest you think that sounds a bit grand – it is! I was done again a second time (BBC the first time, ITV the second) in 1977 when I had retired from the stage and gone into theatre management. But to learn more about that you'll have to turn to Act II of this book, when all will be revealed.

And so in 1964 came *Chase Me, Comrade!* the last of the original Whitehall farces, as it turned out. Again it was by Ray Cooney (without Tony Hilton) and for the first time I was able to play straight, without a North Country accent. Mind you I'd done that, too, in *One for the Pot* – but only as one character. The others had been Yorkshire, Irish and French. But in case you find that hard to follow, I'd better explain that in that particular play I played four brothers, who had been brought up in different countries, never mind different parts of the country. How I got on and off was the evening's main attraction. Many plays have twins in the cast. *One for the Pot* was the only one, as far as I know, with quads – all played by one actor, me.

In *Comrade* however, I was able to play from start to finish in my normal, public school accent. But as I spent half the time impersonating a naval commander, or a defecting Russian ballet dancer, or a talking tiger-skin, my accent had to be strangulated somewhat, even then. Ray Cooney swears the play was inspired by his seeing Rudolf Nureyev crossing Trafalgar Square. Up to then Ray had been toying with a play about an escaped convict. That convict now turned into a ballet dancer – and the play pirouetted to a triumphant success. On my wall is a picture of me in Elspet's open car (a Facellia) outside the Whitehall stage door, with the cast's children clambering all over the tonneau. My goodness, we were a fecund lot. But the posters behind us proclaim our grip on Whitehall:

"Comrade Rix Does It Again", Felix Barker, *Evening News;* "The Audience in Agonies of Helpless Laughter", Philip Hope Wallace, *Guardian*. But perhaps the supreme accolade: "The Greatest Master of Farce in my Theatre-going Lifetime", Harold Hobson, *Sunday Times*. Oh yes, Harold deserves his knighthood all right. And his CBE.

But, in spite of all that acclaim and box-office success, my days at the Whitehall were numbered. Why? Quite simply, because I wanted to buy the place and the owner, Felicity Cooper, kept wavering. We would all arrive at the offices of Price Waterhouse, to discuss terms, and Felicity would just as suddenly flounce out, avowing that she'd now changed her mind. This charade went on for some time, so I decided that the only way to force the issue was to leave, prove that I was both a fixture and a fitting at the Whitehall – and watch Ms Cooper come reluctantly to the decision to sell before she lost any more money. My ploy worked. Only too well. Felicity sold all right – but not to me. She went to the highest bidder, Paul Raymond. Not renowned for losing his trousers perhaps, but better known for many an unconscious stirring within those male garments, caused by his unclothed girls and sexy magazines. A far cry from the valedictory message delivered by Ronald Bryden, of the *New Statesman* and the *Observer*, which followed me to my new home, the Garrick Theatre, just as I was leaving the Whitehall:

> There they are: the most robust survivors of a great tradition, the most successful British theatrical enterprise of our time. Curious that no one can be found to speak up wholeheartedly for them – no one, that is, outside enthusiastic millions who have packed every British theatre where they have played. It's particularly curious considering the current intellectual agitation for a theatre of the masses, a true working-class drama. Everything, apparently, for which Joan Littlewood has struggled – the boisterous, extrovert playing, the integrated teamwork, the Cockney irreverence of any unself-conscious, unacademic audience bent purely on pleasure – exists, patently and profitably, at the Whitehall. Yet how many devout pilgrims to Stratford East have hazarded the shorter journey to Trafalgar Square to worship at the effortless shrine of the thing itself? How many Arts Council grants have sustained Mr Rix's company? How many *Evening Standard* awards went to *Dry Rot*? How many theses have been written on the art of Colin Morris, John Chapman or Ray Cooney? The time has come, surely, to fill the gap.

So, I crossed Trafalgar Square, to the Garrick Theatre, where a larger stage and auditorium encouraged me to try and change things, inasmuch as I went in for a repertoire of farce, rather than the single play in a long run. But it was a disaster. I couldn't afford the money on advertising to make my new policy clear and the public were convinced that I was doing short runs of plays, with each new play entering the repertoire being the one that was now on permanent show. As the plays changed weekly, houses dropped alarmingly and after six months we had to continue with the last play in the repertoire season, *Let Sleeping Wives Lie*. Of the other two, *Stand by Your Bedouin* went into cold storage, never to see the light of day again (but as its original title was *Bang, Bang Beirut* that's fairly understandable) whilst *Uproar in the House* transferred to my old home at the Whitehall, where it limped along for quite some time, but never playing to the business it deserved. Its authors, Anthony Marriott and Alastair Foot, went on to even greater things with *No Sex Please, We're British*, but I always thought their first play – *Uproar* – was just as funny. However, repertoire put the mockers on it.

Let Sleeping Wives Lie, by Harold Brooke and Kay Bannerman, ran for two years on its own, with a splendid cast headed by Leslie Crowther, Derek Farr, Leo Franklyn, Elspet and me. Anna Dawson and Andrew Sachs were also well to the fore – and it has always amazed me how many good notices Andy collected before anyone took the slightest interest in his capabilities. You know him best, I'm sure, as Manuel in *Fawlty Towers*.

In 1969 *Wives* finished, after a very happy and successful run, and I then went on to my first Michael Pertwee farce, *She's Done it Again,* based on an earlier farce, *Nap Hand* by Vernon Sylvaine and Guy Bolton. *Nap Hand* was bombed off in the early days of the last war, but it was still a very funny idea – culled from the Dionne Quins. In those days fertility drugs were unknown and the possibility of live quins being born was very remote. The Canadian Dionne girls were an exception and Vernon and Guy had written a play where a couple of cousins pool their respective new-born twins, borrow another baby and proclaim to the outside world that one mother has produced all five. Michael and I felt the plot stood up very well and the first night seemed to prove our point, as did the notices:

Derek Farr, Leslie Crowther, Elspet Gray and me in
Let Sleeping Wives Lie, Punch 1967

I have no doubt at all about what has been the
principal theatrical event of the week. The Master is
back again, and London can once more be gay.
Michael Pertwee's farce, *She's Done It Again,* is the
funniest in which the great Brian Rix has ever
appeared. There are dificulties in the way of com-
municating a proper sense of its delicious and deliri-
ous qualities. But what looks feeble and hackneyed on
the page glows with glorious life in the Garrick
Theatre – Harold Hobson, *Sunday Times.*

It is easily the funniest show I have seen this year –
Irving Wardle, *The Times.*

Almost continual laughter at the Garrick Theatre last
night – John Barber, *Daily Telegraph*

A furiously funny frolic – Weston Taylor, *News of the World*.

The lark's on the wing, Brian Rix in his element and all's right with the world – Felix Barker, *Evening News*.

How can you go wrong with notices like that? Well, we did – and the result was the shortest run I'd ever experienced. We opened in October 1969 and closed at the end of May 1970. I shall never understand why. We took the play on tour, where it played to absolute capacity, but the audience just wouldn't come to the Garrick.

As if to reinforce the point, my next production at the Garrick, *Don't Just Lie There, Say Something* – also by Michael Pertwee, with additions by me – opened to almost total press silence, due to a newspaper strike, and yet we overcame this drawback, and power cuts in the middle of quite a number of performances, to achieve another two-year run. How do you account for such irrational behaviour? If you know the answer, you could make a fortune as the Old Moore of the theatrical world. But I fear your prognostications would be just as haphazard as those in the *Almanac* or those surmised by theatrical managers. Like homing pigeons, audiences seem to have an unerring sixth sense which leads them to the plays they want to see – and keeps them away in droves from those they don't. They certainly never solved the problem, for my next play, *A Bit Between the Teeth* – again by Michael Pertwee with embellishments by me – was just as funny as its predecessor, *Don't Just Lie There*, but never really hit the jackpot, except on tour, when it played to enormous business, just like that earlier "failure", *She's Done It Again*. And again the notices were good. Here's John Barber in the *Daily Telegraph*:

In *A Bit Between the Teeth*, Michael Pertwee has reduced bedroom farce to its barest essentials – a cast of five, a mountain of misunderstanding, and a London flat with nine exits and entrances. But come in a bit closer.

Of the five characters, two are superbly resourceful comedians – Brian Rix, the bespectacled knight of the woeful countenance himself, and Jimmy Logan, who can wag his jaw like an irate rolling-pin.

Add two shapely undressed girls, and the obligatory copper, and you have the indispensable basics for updated bed-to-bedlam Feydeau.

But if the ingredients are few, they have been stirred with alarming ingenuity, and the result is very funny indeed. The show is a riot of comic confusion, with never a dirty joke or leering innuendo. And the director, Wallace Douglas, whips it along at a stunning pace.

The secret of its success is that the plot is built on panic. Mr Rix, a prim-and-proper jeweller with a stammer, discovers to his horror that his married philandering partner has used his car, and his name, on a date with a girl. But the vehicle disappears, and the girl with it.

So the police descend on Mr Rix – who just happens to be hiding his partner's pretty but rain-soaked wife, who just happens to have taken off her clothes to dry.

I cannot explain how husband and wife are kept apart, nor the girl in the pantry, the cat in the fridge, the tin of exploding beans, nor lines like: "What was the Countess de Le Touquet doing with Diane's handbag in the back of the stolen car?" But I promise you, they make a kind of insane sense, granted Mr Rix's one fatal lie to the law.

As never before he is struck scarlet with shock, paralytic with fright, rigid with moral disapproval.

Mr Logan bullies him superbly, a man to bluff you matily into digging your own grave.

Donna Reading and Vivienne Johnson are delectable and Peter Bland's policeman is a triumph of cunning bewilderment. I admit the fun slackens, especially towards the end. But I laughed and laughed.

Maybe the fun did slacken a bit, but Mr Barber still laughed and laughed, and so did the audience.

And there my first book ended. With a question mark hanging over everything. *A Bit Between the Teeth* had finished its successful tour, and there was I, in 1976, contemplating my thirty-fourth year in the theatre, my twenty-ninth year as an actor-manager, with considerable trepidation. Added to which, I had recently joined forces with Duncan Weldon and Louis Michaels of Triumph Theatre Productions, and my good friend and trusted General Manager, Gilbert Harrison, also transferred to Triumph as the company's Administrator. This union meant, inevitably, more touring, summer seasons and pantomime – that was Triumph's strength at the time – and the thought of this, the thought of more and more touring, the thought of trying to find new ways to make people laugh, the thought that I might well be on the skids, all added to my disquiet. That, and the fact that my original mentor, my mother, had recently died (my father having died ten years earlier), and our family were rapidly growing up and leaving home made everything seem uncertain, to say the least. But I had one last go.

On August 26th, 1976 – twenty-six years after my first appearance at the Whitehall Theatre – I strode on to that same stage again in *Fringe Benefits*. Well, not striding exactly, but clattering down the stairs in a comic wet suit and flippers. You could say I was stumbling into deep water without a dinghy and certainly without a paddle. There's no business like show business . . .

SCENE II

"Love's Labour's Lost"

Barbara Kinghorne, Jane Downs and me in
Fringe Benefits. Punch September 1976.

It's a time of theatrical anniversaries. The National
Youth Theatre is twenty this year, and Brian Rix
returned to the Whitehall Theatre for the first time in
ten years. So did I, and it hasn't changed much,
neither the theatre nor the play. This time it's called
Fringe Benefits and it's written by Peter Yeldham and
Donald Churchill. But that, if they'll forgive me saying
so, is irrelevant. A Brian Rix farce is Brian Rix and no
one else, be it writer, supporting actor or director.

When he is off stage there's a perceptible drop in
the heat of the audience reaction. They still laugh but
guffaws subside to titters and the other actors, bowing
to the inevitable, "vamp till ready". Once Rix is back

on stage, all is well and the laughter floods back. It's as if the audience gets anxious if he's not there, like children left at home while Mum pops up the road to the shops. Indeed, the whole thing is so cosy I half expected a conjuror to come on after the interval.

Ah, but Rix is a conjuror, producing laughs where you least expect them, dealing adequately with the jokes, but drawing out the words of a perfectly ordinary speech, like Kardomah filling the stage with flags, in a way that is delightfully funny. He's even better when he doesn't use words at all, but just uses sounds. Indeed, as he constantly teeters on the brink of being found out in some indiscretion or falsehood, he spends most of the evening bleating like some goat, moaning in despair or emitting a high-pitched giggle of near hysteria when it seems inevitable that he's done for.

The straightforward stage business is, as you would expect in farce, crisply handled, beautifully executed, and in *Fringe Benefits* is surprisingly original. There is a moment that is quite perfect, when Rix hides a telephone in his trouser pocket, finds there's a hole in the pocket and spends an agonized few minutes with his friend Jim (Terence Alexander) on his knees chatting to his kneecap, before the instrument is painfully extracted.

Terence Alexander makes an excellent foil to Rix and, in fact, I can't remember seeing a better. He collects his own laughs, unselfishly helps the others to get theirs, and behaves like an absolute brick throughout. Jane Downs as Rix's wife, Isobel, manages the tricky role with care and finesse, bringing a nice note of mischief to what could be a stereotype. The rest of the cast do well too with the rough and tumble of entering and exiting, nearly being caught, hiding, and generally behaving in the daft way that's expected of

41

farceurs. I commend you to the performance of Richard Latham as Dickie, the randy plumber posing as a TV repair man, who, at the end of a long and rambling speech by Rix which totally fails to explain the presence of two lightly clad young women to Rix's wife, says plaintively, "Excuse me, am I still the TV repair man?"

If you like farce you'll enjoy *Fringe Benefits*. If you like Brian Rix you'll adore it. Admittedly, you know how it'll all come out from the moment the curtain goes up. It has the inevitability of a bullfight, but were it a bullfight I would have no hesitation in rewarding the ears and the tail to Rix.

I apologize for quoting Barry Took's *Punch* notice in full, but as it is the last one to appear before I gave up acting, I'm sure you'll allow the indulgence. I only wish I could report on the play's unqualified success. Alas, I cannot.

Although much had been rewritten by Ray Cooney (the play was presented by his management, mine and Duncan Weldon) and was directed with great expertise by Wally Douglas (who had directed so many of my productions) and in spite of considerable press coverage at my return to the Whitehall, *Fringe Benefits* never really took off. I could blame the play, the weather, the lack of tourists, all the usual rubbish trotted out by disappointed actors or managements, but there was still a nagging feeling in the pit of my stomach that some of the blame must have lain at my door. Unhappily, this self-doubt was reinforced by some lengthy correspondence between my very old friend and colleague, Michael Pertwee, and me, correspondence which verged on the unpleasant and was certainly unpalatable as far as I was concerned. And yet . . . and yet . . .

We were actually having a bit of an up and a downer over a new play of Michael's and my part in its origination.

This came to a head because Michael had decided to do the play without me (and with hindsight, who can blame him – I was in *Fringe Benefits*) and a lot of unfriendly words were written between us. However, Michael finally put the boot in with this damning paragraph:

I cannot get away from the belief that, regardless of the play, you now have a strictly limited West End appeal. Taking this particular play we would again be in exactly the same situation as you are at present. Despite other good roles the main star part would be yours. There is no room for another real star name. Thus, like the present play, it would succeed or fail entirely on your own personal appeal. The faithful Rix would come. The people who do not like Rix would stay away. I am only stating a personal view but unhappily this is what I think.

Unhappily, it was also what I was beginning to think, but nobody likes to hear half-suppressed fears expressed so openly. Nevertheless, it added fuel to the fire which had already been lit by an agent, Richard Stone, when he voiced the view to one of his clients – my wife, Elspet, as it happened – that her previous television appearances with me were "the kiss of death anyway". As my contract with the BBC had lasted for seventeen years that was certainly some lingering death. But actors, contrary to popular belief, are remarkably insecure creatures and two such statements about my qualities certainly rocked me back on my heels.

Incidentally, in spite of my Dracula-like attentions Elspet was doing pretty well at that time, having just finished a most successful *Catweazle* TV series, and was now playing one of the leads in *The Crezz* – a Thames television soap about the middle classes which, though excellent, never took hold like *Coronation Street* or *Crossroads*, or even that farming epic, *Emmerdale Farm*, which was by then reaping a rich harvest, with my sister Sheila as Annie Sugden, the matriarch of all the Moors and Dales she surveyed, or so it seemed.

So Michael's words sank in and about that time along came friendly, jaunty, ever-optimistic Ray Cooney with an offer I could hardly refuse. He gave me the opportunity to escape from thirty years as an actor-manager – finding the plays, the actors, the directors, the money, the theatre, etc, etc – and offered me a role of quite a different kind. He and Laurie Marsh had gone into partnership as Cooney-Marsh Theatres and were looking for a Theatre Controller, someone who could place productions in those theatres and, at the same time, be responsible for their overall management. I would *not*, repeat *not,* have to take the weight on my shoulders by performing every night. All I would have to do was to find others to do it for me. It sounded all too easy and I fell.

Other changes were taking place in our lives, too. There's a marvellous story which tells of three men of the cloth discussing when life begins. The Catholic believes that life begins at conception, the Anglican is convinced it happens at the quickening, whilst the Rabbi merely comments that "life begins when the kids have left home and the dog's died". Well, that roughly is what had happened to us. There we were, in our vast Roehampton home and large London garden, with only one son in regular need of a bed – and that need strictly limited because Jonathan, too, was in his last year at St Paul's and about to go a-roving. Furthermore, our marvellous old golden labrador, Hickory, *had* just died; Elspet and I were rattling round our family home, without a family (except for Sunday lunch) and with a fortune going down the drain in upkeep, heating, gardening, rates – you name it, we paid it. So we decided to move, found ourselves a super Victorian house in Barnes, and journeyed the one mile there, accompanied by the removal men and our much-loved "daily" Molly Holman, at the beginning of December 1976. Now we all know the trauma of moving – but this, coupled with everything else that was going on in my life, made me seek change. Whether it was for the better or not would remain to be seen.

In the meantime, I went to the end of *Fringe Benefits*, which finally came off on Saturday, January 8th, 1977. It was to be the last time I set foot on a stage, as an actor, for eleven years and nine months – and I'm glad to report that the occasion was noted by quite a number of newspapers, including this leader in the *Sunday Express*:

THANKS

It is sad that Brian Rix should be quitting the stage. Some trumped-up intellectuals – the sort of people who seem to prefer that plays should disgust and harrow – may have looked down on his farces. But the audiences who came by charabanc did not.

Brian Rix brought pleasure to millions. He belonged to the ancient tradition on the English stage of healthy vulgarity. And behind it, strange as it may seem, there was a kind of innocence. For who else but an innocent in these permissive days would regard it as slightly shocking for a man to lose his trousers and show his striped underpants?

That brought a lump to my throat, I can tell you, and for the first and last time I was sad when the curtain finally came down on that Saturday night. Always in the past I knew what I was going to do next and there was always the thrill of anticipation. Now, I was venturing – not into the unknown, exactly – but into an entirely new field, theatre management, pure and simple. I was somewhat apprehensive, to say the least.

Oh, just for the record. I'm happy to say that Michael Pertwee and I have remained the best of friends ever since that acrimonious exchange of letters. As the years went by, I came to sympathize with his view even more. That, and the fact that he has an absolutely lovely wife, Maya, and a super family, would have made it very difficult for us to remain distant. On the other hand, Richard Stone and I still circle each other a little warily. Or rather, did. Since Roy Kinnear's tragic death, we've become much closer. Richard represented Roy – and he and I became involved in the memorial service. It's difficult to be distant in the face of such overwhelming sadness.

Finally, the last word – on that last night – in the *Evening News*:

What will he miss most now that he is leaving the stage? Without doubt, the sound of laughter and joy from the audience, he says.

And, do you know, I never missed it at all. We're funny creatures, aren't we?

Intermission

Lest you have no desire to fight your way into the bar during the entr'acte, I thought you might prefer a little divertissement, so let me recount a cricket story. After all, cricketers and actors have a great deal in common. As I've already mentioned, I'm not just a cricket watcher, I actually played the game. For Hull in the Yorkshire League, for the MCC, for the Stage and the Lord's Taverners. I *do* know my off-cutter from my off-drive.

One freezing February morn, some years ago, I dressed in long johns, thick woollen socks, vest, polo-neck sweater, flying boots and anorak. The purpose of this over-dressing was not some polar expedition but merely preparation for a hard day's rehearsal of a new play at the Haig Hall, Parson's Green, where the central heating had failed.

In no other industry would this be possible (we *are* known as the entertainment industry) for the workers would be out in droves at the drop of a thermometer below the official toleration level. Actors – never! Equity could scream and shout (and quite rightly) but actors would ignore their union for one very good reason – fear. Not the fear that some other actor will jump into the job, but the fear for oneself, the fear that on the night you will not be ready and able to face an audience.

So it is with cricketers (and, to a lesser extent, most other sportsmen) for in the coldest months of the winter they don sweaters and socks and vests and underpants in an effort to keep the cold at bay so they can practise their beloved game in the indoor nets. They then proceed to wear much the same clothing during the freezing months of April and May when all sensible people should still be in front of roaring log fires watching telly.

Now the cricketer is not necessarily worried that he will be unprepared by April and May – he's gone through all that cooling-up process in the winter. No, he simply knows that if he wants to play the game to which he is devoted, he will have to do it under *any* conditions, other than complete darkness or torrential rain.

The same can be said of the actor. He leaves his freezing rehearsal room and arrives in his freezing theatre – for often the heating has failed there too. All the additional hazards such as mugging, transport cuts and possibly no audience at all he also faces, if not with equanimity, at least with dogged determination for, long ago, he learned this was the way of the world.

There are many other similarities between the actor and the cricketer. Both are individuals trying to do their best for themselves, as individuals, within a team framework. Both are subject to playing to bad houses or good houses – to audience antipathy or approbation. Both are rejoiced in or reviled by the critics. Both can be star performers one day and bit players the next. Both have to face the horrors of auditions, whether it be reciting lines from a play on the stage to an auditorium filled by an impresario, an author and a director or to an equally minute selection committee who turn up to see your performance on the square on the very day it probably all goes wrong. Both have longer playing lives than most other sports or professions and both the actor and the cricketer enter their particular bloody silly way of earning a living because they can think of no other career more rewarding in terms of personal pride or job satisfaction.

So, we have a lot in common – and in some mysterious way our union has become consummated, for actors love being seen with cricketers and vice-versa. Charity cricket games are organized together, actors help out at benefit matches. They scream ribald remarks from the Tavern or proudly don their MCC ties and act as officers and gentlemen when the occasion befits. Complimentary tickets are given away so that cricket teams can sit in theatres. Cricketers invite the actors back to the pavilion dressing-rooms. Oh, it's a marvellous world of give and take, and one which seems to give great pleasure to both parties.

I think it was Emmott Robinson who once ate vast quantities of pease puddin' and beans so that the next morning at Headingley he could "try an bowl t'buggers out – but if that's no bloody use – ah can fart 'em out".

When I followed cricket to Jamaica the local reporter on the *Daily Gleaner* bestowed on me the accolade of being "London's best known fart actor".

From this you must gather that actors and cricketers aren't so much hand in glove – they are cheek to cheek . . .

After that, you'll no doubt be much relieved to know that the bar bells are ringing and the curtain is about to go up. Please take your seats for Act II.

Act II

"Anything Goes"

It is difficult to write about life under Cooney-Marsh without seeming grumpy, vindictive, pompous, vain or just plain stupid. And I'm not referring to Ray Cooney or Laurie Marsh personally. Actually they are still very good friends of mine. Ray Cooney, you'll remember, wrote *One for the Pot, Chase Me, Comrade!* and *Stand by your Bedouin*, whilst Laurie was then the Chairman and powerhouse behind Classic Cinemas, which he had built up into a considerable chain of small, well-operated theatres. Eventually he was taken over by Lord Grade, when that particular mogul was riding high in the film industry. But then, along with other films, came *Raise the Titanic*, which, for the second time in its life, was a disaster. However, before that, Laurie had scrambled into a lifeboat and was well clear of Lew's undertow. No, in 1977 Laurie was fighting to keep his theatrical theatres open, and that was no easy task.

You see, it was the theatres, and the producers they attracted, which caused the problems. So many of them went bust. The producers, I mean. I counted no less than ten when I was going through my 1977 diary, many of them managers who should have known better. But optimism is endemic in the theatre – and that applies to almost everyone, whether producers or bricks and mortar – in other words, owners. Even Sir Peter Saunders (he of *Mousetrap* fame) has had his failures. Not many, I'll grant you (after all, how many managers have seen one of their productions supersede the Tower of London as a tourist attraction) but he has had the odd stumer, for all that.

This generally happens when you are allowing other people's productions into your theatres. You can never be absolutely certain what you are getting until the first night. But if you have to *persuade* people to occupy your theatres, as well as generally cutting their rents halfway through a run to keep them going, or you have to put on your own productions just to stop the places from going dark, and these productions are somewhat dicey too, then you've got problems.

We had problems.

Well, you've only got to look at the polyglot theatres we ran. The Regent (near Broadcasting House), the Broadway (in Kilburn), the better known Duke of York's and the Ambassadors as well as, eventually, the Astoria (in Charing Cross Road and once a cinema), the Shaftesbury (also in the West End) plus, for a short time, the Trafalgar in New York. Oh, yes. And Ray also had a private arrangement with the Savoy Theatre, but we really didn't become involved in that until I had left the company.

I shall touch on each of the theatres, and their particular difficulties, in turn. Then, in that ghastly modern jargon, follows an examination of the infrastructure interface – meaning I'll tell you a few more interesting tit-bits. But first, a word about my job.

I became a director and Theatre Controller of Cooney-Marsh Theatres at the beginning of 1977 and for one week I was going to the office every day and then wandering down to the Whitehall in the evening to do the last few performances of *Fringe Benefits*. It wasn't a particularly long walk, for the office was at the Duke of York's Theatre in St Martin's Lane, which is only across Trafalgar Square from the Whitehall. The office I occupied at first wasn't really mine, for it still belonged to Ray Cooney. However, he was away skiing, so for some weeks I sat behind his desk, until we hired larger premises just up the road, overlooking St Martin's Court, which houses the Albery and Wyndham's Theatres. One of my abiding memories of the view from this office was seeing all the down-and-outs congregate in the Albery exit doors drinking their lethal cocktail of sweet sherry and meths. This tragic spectacle happened every day, as regularly as clockwork, at 11.30 a.m. By mid-afternoon they had all collapsed or gone across the road to seek the warmth of the kitchens – lying on the grilles or near the extractor fans – which backed on to all the restaurants in St Martin's Lane itself. I could only think there was a Rowton House or a Sally Ann nearby – there was in Covent Garden – because the numbers never seemed to decrease. It's incredible to think that such scenes as I witnessed were far more common-place when the Albery and Wyndham's were built – but even today they are bad enough and a constant reminder of our failure to cope with society's outcasts.

A Theatre Controller is just that. No, not an outcast (although you often feel like one), but a controller of theatres. I was responsible for overseeing all the myriad tasks which have to be performed to keep a West End theatre going: licences, booking the plays, negotiating the contracts, library deals (i.e., ticket agencies) which must not run counter to the agreements reached between the Society of West End Theatre (SWET) and the Library Committee. After all, it would be only too easy for a theatre manager to negotiate a separate deal with a ticket agency, whereby you give that agency a bigger percentage to sell your tickets than any of your rivals. That way madness lies. Madness also lay for me in the catering world. I tried to open up as many of the theatres as possible at lunchtime, to attract local office workers into the buildings, but it was a thankless task and one which really came to a head when Laurie asked me what my penetration of ice-cream had been during the previous week. At first I thought he was being rude or funny – but then realized he was deadly serious. My penetration had only reached 42 per cent, whereas his Classic Cinemas were pentrating as much as 75 per cent. I can only think that we sold softer ice-cream than they.

But of course, it is a different world – cinema and theatre. In the cinema the product has been made for you by someone else. All the projectionist has to do is put the reels on in the right order and the production is the same at every performance. There is plenty of time to concentrate on the sale of popcorn or ice-cream or sweets or chocolates. But the theatre is live, and as such, things can fluctuate or go wrong so much more easily. I don't think Laurie quite believed that when he teamed up with Ray – but he soon learned the hard way.

The theatres, of which I was Controller, were a mixed bunch indeed. Two of them had been brought to the party by Laurie – and both had been cinemas – the Regent and the Broadway. Ray chipped in with the Duke of York's and the Ambassadors, for he had done private deals with the owners, Peter Saunders and "Tinker" Jay, whilst the Astoria was still under reconstruction but, as an ex-cinema, it was probably Laurie who had more to do with its acquisition and understanding, gained, no doubt, from all the cinemas he had altered for the Classic chain. As I say, Ray also had some deal or other with the Savoy, whilst the Shaftesbury was not acquired until the end of 1977, with the Trafalgar, in New York, coming on stream in early 1979. It was my lot to control this hotch-potch for three years – for that was the length of my contract. By the time it expired, it seemed much longer.

The Regent was actually the old Regent Cameo-Poly Cinema at the Polytechnic in Regent Street. When I joined Cooney-Marsh Theatres all was reasonably well there, for it was housing Harold Fielding's production of *Let My People Come*, which was a sort of down-market *Oh, Calcutta* – if such a thing is possible. Once the dirty mac brigade, plus the flashy foreigners, had had their fill, audiences dropped off and we were back with a theatre on our hands which was quite impossible to let – hyperbolize its assets, come what may. Putative tenants took one look at the auditorium shaped like a football field, with a tiny circle stuck at the back, and realized it might be all right for indoor cricket nets, but it was a dead loss as a desirable theatre. You could even imagine Dennis Lillee, at his most aggressive, being able to take his full run up – with room to spare – such was the length of the stalls from stage to pit. And that stage! It was really a shelf with a cast-iron balcony running across the back wall, mounted by a spiral staircase, under which you ducked to enter two or three tiny little dressing-rooms. Well, they weren't dressing-rooms really. More like broom cupboards. In fact, they propably had been broom cupboards when the Poly was using the place for its rightful role – that of a lecture theatre. Rumour had it, though, that this non-theatre had once been used for opera. I bet they never mounted *The Ring*.

You may well ask, why didn't we let the Poly go back to being a cinema, at which it had been fairly successful? A good question. The snag was that Classic Cinemas, through Laurie Marsh, had let the building as a theatre for live performances, and so we were restricted in our use of the place as a cinema. Furthermore, the real landlords, the Poly, also had some sway over the use of the hall. Altogether it was a dog's dinner. I mean, look at some of the shows which were *our* tenants . . .

Perhaps the unhappiest, from all points of view, should go first into the frame – *Little Willie Junior's Resurrection*. I will repeat that. *Little Willie Junior's Resurrection*. It was described as "a dramatic new musical experience". It was certainly that. Never have I cringed so ashamedly in the back row of any theatre as I did on that particular production's first night. Everything that could go wrong did, but in truth the show just didn't transfer well from the States. In fact, it didn't transfer at all. Except in one particular aspect. All the vituperation which was heaped on the show the next morning by the critics included some reference to the landlords, Cooney-Marsh, or – in one particular case – to me. We were reviled for letting such rubbish darken our doors. The truth is we were lucky to get *any* rubbish to darken our doors at the Poly, but we tried to keep that awful truth quiet. After all, we had rent to pay, too.

Oh, and that particular critic who had a go at me had to apologize and the newspaper sent a donation to the Friends of Normansfield. He was Nicholas de Jongh and the paper was the *Guardian*, but I think I was lucky. If I had been Mr de Jongh, I believe I would have written a far ruder notice, but perhaps of not such a personal nature. And, talking of rudeness, *Little Willie Junior's Resurrection* was never called that in the Cooney-Marsh office. But its new title might have stood up quite well in *Let My People Come*.

There were not many other productions at the Regent, thank God. After *Little Willie* it acquired a somewhat oppressive air of gloom and producers approached us with even greater trepidation. No, actually, they didn't approach us at all – we went on great sweeping recces for *them*. Unfortunately, the professionals had become very adept at keeping their heads down, although one or two producers didn't quite escape, but I bet they wished they had. Linda Thorson was in *The Club* – if you know what I mean. Marti Webb and Brian Protheroe starred in *The Great American Backstage Musical* and David Mamet's plays *Duck Variations* and *Sexual Perversity in Chicago* no sooner came than they went. With titles like that, are you surprised? We were hopeful about Stephen Berkoff's *East* – which went west in a matter of weeks; very disappointing. That, and the fact that Stephen was perhaps the most vocal – I was going to say strident – of all the producers I met, particularly when it came to requesting the inevitable reduction in rent, made life difficult, to say the least.

Finally, we managed to do a deal with Classic and the Poly. We secured the right to show a film, but as that film was *Gone with the Wind* it had a dramatic effect on the box-office, and it went on for some time before our rights ran out. Then it was gone with the wind for us – and gone with the wind for them. We managed to end our tenancy, and another fringe theatre was no more.

I keep writing "we" or "us". Of course I'm referring to all of us at Cooney-Marsh – those who worked in the production or theatre offices – but I'm really meaning my PA Joanne Benjamin, who joined me some three weeks after I moved into the office. Without her loyalty, support and affection I think I would have found it almost impossible to last out my three-year contract. There's none so lonely as a theatrical manager when things are going wrong. With me, it was difficult to count the days when they were going right!

Now the Broadway was totally different from the Regent, inasmuch as it was extremely comfortable, had plenty of room backstage and even looked like a theatre. There was only one snag. It was at the bottom of Kilburn High Road and audiences there are more prone to enjoying the odd Guinness or a jig or two in the local pub, than supporting a toffee-nosed theatrical enterprise down the road. But at least we had a regular income: every Sunday Indian films were screened almost from dawn to dusk, and the company, Shiv Films, did all the donkey work and just paid us the rent.

Shiv was run by an extremely polite Indian and his charming family, but I don't think they made a fortune out of the deal, even though it looked as though the entire population of the Indian subcontinent had foregathered, if you went past the building on a Sunday. Again, the problem was that the Broadway was really another Classic Cinema renamed and that's what people thought about it. On the other hand, it *had* been a theatre once – nothing less than the famous Kilburn Empire – and Laurie had sandwiched the auditorium of the new theatre between the circle and stalls of the old one. It was an extremely ingenious creation, but more than ingenuity was needed to keep the place open as a live theatre. But we tried and nearly pulled it off. Yet another case of "if only".

Just twenty-eight days after joining Cooney-Marsh, I had visited the Roundhouse (itself a converted locomotive workshop) to see Lindsay Kemp in *Flowers*. I was knocked out. Not by the all-pervading scent of incense, but by the production which I knew must be an attraction if I could only get it to the Broadway. After all, both Roundhouse and Broadway were off the beaten track, but the old train shed was packed. I reckoned that if folk would go to one place to see Lindsay, they'd almost certainly go to another. In the event, I was right. Unfortunately, Lindsay had signed contracts to go back to Australia and his burgeoning season at the Broadway had to close. A sad loss for us all – particularly us – for we had invested much of the capital in the production and only a really lengthy season would have seen it back. Alas, that was never to be and Lindsay, with his extraordinary company, went back to a country which treated him like minor royalty. A funny lot – in the Land of Oz. You'd have thought all that mime and music and transvestism would have been at odds with their macho image. Not a bit of it. They lapped it up – even more than our audiences at the Broadway, who certainly didn't look like your average West End theatregoers in any shape or form.

After that minor flurry of success, it was back to hawking the place around to any likely punters. We could have become the home for the temporarily unhoused Mermaid, which was rebuilding, but Sir Bernard Miles

(Lord Miles to-be) was discouraged from making any speculative moves by his Governors – as was Michael Croft who ran the National Youth Theatre. He, too, was looking for a temporary home, as asbestos had been found in his usual venue, the Shaw Theatre, but his financial straitjacket would not allow him to experiment with a different location. The BBC nearly took the place for all their late-night chat shows – Parkinson and the like – but they were offered better terms elsewhere and buzzed off to the Greenwood Theatre, leaving us "if onlying" yet again. Amateur shows came and went; Camden Council ran a panto, *Puss in Boots*, and my PA, Jo Benjamin, arranged for Young Variety to present a production called *The Vamp*, which was visited by HRH The Duchess of Kent, but it was all to no avail. We simply couldn't get a regular rent-paying tenant.

So, it was back to Classic with a request to let us reopen the place as a cinema, even though that was against the lease. Seeing the plight we were in, they agreed – after all, Laurie has a foot planted firmly in both camps and it was his money we were losing. Now we found ourselves meeting film bookers, certainly a new experience for me. And you know, we didn't do too badly. A season of Clint Eastwood films got us off to a good start, but after a while Classic decided they could do the job better than Jo and me (which they could) and the Broadway melody, never very tuneful as far as we were concerned, came to the end on a very flat note. Now the place is shuttered, bolted and barred, its great days as the old Kilburn Empire long forgotten, and its dreadful days as the new Broadway Theatre even less worthy of recall.

I think you might find it useful if I described how theatres are rented out in the West End. Generally, freeholds or long leases are acquired by bricks and mortar managements, sometimes individual purchasers such as the late Louis Michaels (the Haymarket), or sometimes conglomerates such as Stoll-Moss who own most of the theatres in Shaftesbury Avenue, and more besides. They seek to find producing managements who have plays or musicals they wish to present, and these managements pay a rent and a contra (which covers all the cost of staff, electricity, heating, etc) until they fall below the "break-figure", a figure agreed on at the signing of the contract, below which you must not fall for two consecutive weeks or you can be given notice or give notice. That's the general pattern, but there are many variations. You can go into a theatre on a percentage deal, eg: 65 per cent of the box-office to the producing manager, 35 per cent to the owner, or you can do a "four-wall deal" (which they fancy in New York), when you rent the shell of the theatre and pay for everything else, but putting in the staff you need, rather than taking the one you are given. Other factors come into play: the time of the year (are there more plays than theatres?), the lack or surfeit of tourists, the location and size of a theatre in relation to the amount of money it can take at the box-office to pay for a particular production, the need sometimes to nurse a production, because there is nothing else in the offing and so on and so on. It's a complex business, but it's a general belief that the bricks and mortar do better than the producers. At least that used to be the belief − but there are an awful lot of wealthy producers about these days. The rising costs of maintaining a theatre have taken the top off many a landlord's profit. But at Cooney-Marsh we didn't see too many profits either way, in those late 1970s. Even at an established theatre like the Duke of York's.

The Duke of York's began life as the Trafalgar Square Theatre in 1892 (a strange coincidence, considering *our* Trafalgar Theatre in New York nearly eighty years later), but changed its name only three years after opening. Most of Barrie's plays first saw the light of electricity here −

including the original production of *Peter Pan* – but it had many plays and artistes appearing there until it was closed because of enemy action at the beginning of the last war. However, it was eventually repaired and Michael Pertwee's father, Roland, had a play of his on there – *Pink String and Sealing Wax* – just before the theatre's longest run, Ralph Lynn in *Is Your Honeymoon Really Necessary?* which ran for 980 performances from 1944 until the dreadful winter of 1947. I remember that particular play with great affection, it being the first time I had ever seen the great Ralph Lynn on stage, and even though he was an elderly man, the skill and timing were as impeccable as ever. I also had reason to be thankful to the play itself, for I subsequently presented it twice on television, such was its success. I played Ralph's part, of course, and I could always hear his voice over my shoulder. Perhaps that's because he made the speech at a dinner I threw to celebrate the passing of the old Aldwych farce team's record of ten years seven months and four days in one theatre. Ralph's speech was probably one he had given for nearly half a century – with minor adjustments (he started by pulling out his notes, which were a laundry list) – but it was enormously funny and I shall always be glad I had the opportunity to hear him at close quarters. He and Ben Travers and Robertson Hare and Winifred Shotter were there at the party, too. Lovely people, all.

That was in 1961. Sixteen years later the Duke of York's had been bought by Peter Saunders but Ray Cooney had engineered that he would be responsible for its running – paying Peter a suitable rent, of course. I think it was always imagined that Peter would one day sell the theatre to Ray, but by then some harsh words had been exchanged between them and Peter decided to sell his theatre elsewhere. He didn't have far to go. Sir Richard Attenborough was an old friend, having started off *The Mousetrap* all those years before, and was keen to buy the theatre for

Capital Radio (of which he was Chairman), spending a great deal on the building to remove the pillars which blocked the view, instal radio studios in the old balcony and generally restore the theatre to a pristine condition long forgotten. Sir Peter closed the deal with Sir Richard (the Independent Broadcasting Authority giving their approval) and plain Mr Ray C. was out. Since then, Capital have acted as hosts to one or two reasonable productions and one or two stinkers – which is about par for the course, and certainly follows the pattern we established 'twixt 1977 and 1980. One of the better productions recently was a revival of Alan Ayckbourn's *How the Other Half Loves*. I know, because daughter Louisa was very good in it.

When I arrived at Cooney-Marsh, the Triumph production of *A Bedfull of Foreigners* with Terry Scott and June Whitfield was still going strong at the Duke of York's, so there was little I had to worry about. I just had to spend sleepless nights wondering how to fill the Broadway. However, Terry and June eventually left, and although David Jason had taken over from Terry, business slumped and the production came to an end. Mind you, I hasten to add that David was only just beginning to become a favourite on television (in *Only Fools and Horses*), so it wouldn't be fair to blame him for the play's withdrawal. But that's the difficulty of taking over. If all goes well, very few people know how successful you've been, for there are generally no notices to boost your ego or inform the public at large of your amazing achievement. If all goes badly, very few people come near the building but *everyone* in the business knows you've been a flop. In such a no-win situation, it is not surprising that actors are extremely dubious of stepping into another's shoes.

So, Jo Benjamin and I were out shopping for a Duke of York's client. We found one – in fact we found three in succession – and each one was adjudged successful, both financially and artistically, which can't be too bad an average. In each case we were only the landlord, the productions being mounted by others. Number one opened on June 15th, 1977, and was an extremely interesting version of *Hedda Gabler* with Janet Suzman and Ian Bannen. It ran to very good business throughout the summer, but was always destined to be a limited run. Long before the end, we were hunting around for a successor. This turned out to be a revival of J. B. Priestley's *Laburnum Grove* with Arthur Lowe. I remember seeing the old boy – J. B. – slumped in his box, glowering at all and sundry throughout the first night. When it was over, he lumbered to his feet and delivered a lengthy and eulogistic speech about the play we had just seen, in particular, and about his West End productions, in general. Those of the older generation will remember that they used to be presented by the London Mask Theatre, under the direction of J. B. himself, with Ronald Jeans and Thane Parker. At one time the Mask company was stationed at the Westminster Theatre and was extremely successful after the last war with *Nightmare Abbey* and *Carrington VC*. I don't think Mr Priestley mentioned any of that, but he did prattle on about *Dangerous Corner*, *I Have Been Here Before*, *Time and the Conways* and *Johnson over Jordan* – all far better plays than the one we had just seen. In fact it would have been a completely unmemorable evening but for Arthur Lowe's performance, which was certainly worth a few pounds of anybody's money. Unfortunately, the great British public didn't think so. The play squeezed its way through the winter of 1977, ending in February 1978. Then came the big one.

As I write these words, there has recently been a great deal of justifiable fuss at the return of Sir John Gielgud to the West End stage, for the first time in ten years, in *The Best of Friends*. I'm proud to say that I had something to do with his previous productions, *Half Life* by Julian

Mitchell, which transferred to the Duke of York's from the National Theatre on March 2nd, 1978. I had been negotiating with Peter Stevens (then the National Theatre's General Administrator) since early January. But negotiations nearly ended in disaster. I'd better explain.

Peter Stevens and his then side-kick, Jules Boardman (responsible for marketing at the National) had been visiting my office for some time to try and hammer out a deal. At last we agreed terms and went out, with Laurie Marsh and girlfriend, to celebrate at the Ivy. Laurie's girlfriend, who was wearing quite a well-filled, low-cut gown, sat between Peter and Jules. At a critical moment, just as Peter leaned forward to speak across this splendid cleavage to Jules, the proud owner also leant forward to speak to me sitting opposite her. In an effort not to come into collision with the good lady, Peter put out his hand to steady himself on the table at the precise moment the waiter put down the little primus stove to flambé the next course. This turned out to be Peter's hand. The waiter reacted just like Manuel in *Fawlty Towers* – not like an experienced garçon at the Ivy – and picked up the nearest ice bucket, hurled away the bottles gathered therein, and plunged poor Peter's hand, arm, sleeve and all, into the freezing water. Excellent first-aid, no doubt, but not so good for Peter's dignity, or suit. Steam arose, as might be expected, and then all tried to pretend that nothing untoward had happened, as only the English can. It was several days after that before Peter would – or could – sign the contract between us. It was his signing hand he'd flambéed and he simply refused to hold the pen with his teeth. Oh, and by the way, Peter is now fully recovered, and moved on to pastures new in show business, whilst Jules Boardman, who nearly ruptured himself trying to control his laughter, is the Managing Director of Ticketmaster and therefore responsible for many of the computer print-out tickets you now get at theatres, as opposed to the old method, which led to so many double bookings. Jules will kill me if I say things don't seem to have changed much — so I won't.

John Gielgud would only do a limited season, naturally enough, so by the end of the summer we were hunting around yet again. This time our luck ran out and we entered into a period which Jo Benjamin described as our rep. season. I travelled up to the Edinburgh Festival in the August and put together a number of comedy shows, which came down to the Duke of York's as *The Lunatic Fringe*. Actually they were very good. I can't remember who they all were, but in that season at the Duke of York's, as well as in a subsequent one at the Shaftesbury, I know that *Instant Sunshine* appeared. So did the Questors Theatre Company in Michael Green's *The Art of Coarse Acting*, whilst a very talented bunch of doctors and nurses from Addenbrooke's Hospital in Cambridge appeared as *Irreversible Brain Damage*. As we charged £2.50 for any seat in the house, all the artists' families and friends could come quite often, which resulted in more than average business, I'm glad to say.

This Festival season was followed by another limited run, presented by an imaginative agent, Richard Jackson, which could have gone on much longer: *An Evening with Quentin Crisp*. This extraordinary man, who had made his name with *The Naked Civil Servant*, which was the story of his life, just stood on the stage and told, again, the story of his life. The audience was enthralled and the place was packed. Immediately after this he went to America, I believe — but I shall always remember the way he held that audience in the palm of his hand. Not something you learn at your mother's knee — but a charm and a personality you consciously or subconsciously hone as the years go by.

Next came a thriller, *Spinechiller*, written by two authors from the States with the unlikely names of Stockton Briggle and Robert Fishko. To continue that thought, it was presented by Joe Clapsaddle – and I honestly believe a plot based on the names, Briggle, Fishko and Clapsaddle would have stood more chance than the unspine-chilling *Spinechiller*. In spite of having Sian Phillips and Paul Daneman in the cast, all was lost the moment the notices came out and a very dark theatre ensued – with a lot of rent being uncollected too, if you follow my drift.

We were now into 1979 and getting desperate for another long run. We certainly didn't fulfil our ambition with the next production: Mike Margolis presenting his wife, Anita Harris, in a one-woman (well, almost) show. Now Anita is a very kind lady, with a pleasing voice and a pleasant personality, but her one-woman show was not destined to rival Sarah Bernhardt's singular tour de force. Mind you, as a one-legged person in later life, Miss Bernhardt might have found it difficult to emulate one of Miss Harris's great coups de théâtre: that of roller-skating round the Duke of York's stage whilst singing a pop song. The critics were not amused and another show folded its tent and stole away into a West End Saturday night.

But then our luck changed with two of our own productions, or rather Ray Cooney Productions. Neither would normally be considered as typical of Ray's choice, nor mine for that matter, and in truth, they weren't. They had been found by Anne Rawsthorne and I, in turn, had found Miss Rawsthorne. I'd better explain.

Anne is actually a distant relative of mine by marriage. We shared a common uncle: in other words Bob Somerscales came from Anne's side of the family and married my mother's sister, Grace. Bob was an artist of considerable talent, but nowhere near as well-known as his father, Tom, who was described as "the second best marine artist of his day" – hardly an accolade he would have enjoyed. For those of you who know anything about marine art (I don't), his most famous work is "Off Valparaiso". But that's all by the way. I was merely trying to explain that I had known Anne for a very long time, since childhood, in fact.

Coupled with this fascinating family history is the coincidence that Anne married an old friend of mine from my days in repertory at Harrogate. His name was Tim Manderson. Actually it's Miles Manderson, but old friends call him Tim, because that's his first name. Well, Timothy actually. But there we are. You've met Tim before, in the Prologue as the dilatory actor who was off in *The Eagle Has Two Heads*. Tim had long left the theatre and by 1977 was the highly successful Chairman of a hire car company, Miles and Miles Ltd. Oh well, I may as well go the whole hog and finish the plug. Maybe I'll receive one or two free chauffeur-driven rides in gratitude. Tim started the business when he was a stage manager at the Westminster Theatre during the Mask Theatre's run there after the war, to which I've already referred, and as he couldn't afford a car personally, he decided to make it pay for itself by plying it for hire. It was never a mini-cab (they hadn't started in those days) but a smart limousine with a dark-suited, suitably capped chauffeur at the wheel – generally Tim himself or one or other out-of-work actors. Tim always used to drive the car on Christmas Day, because no one else would, and then come on to our house for the evening, with Anne, to enjoy what was left of the day with our kids, for Tim and Anne are godparents to all of them. Tim looked a picture, clad in his dark demob suit and his black demob shoes and always counted out the tips he had received to amuse the gathered clan. It was quite obvious that his clients were not imbued with the spirit of Christmas. They had probably spent all their money before the great day, and Tim was generally left with a handful of fly buttons, farthings and bottle tops.

Anyway, the business prospered. Tim gave up the profession – by then he was in charge of BBC Ealing studios – and Miles and Miles now run a large self-drive fleet and probably the biggest chauffeur-driven car operation in London. The great thing about them is that they are never late and if there is an odd occasion when they slip up, you always get a bottle of champagne as compensation. Well, I do anyway. The snag is, they've only been late once, as far as I am concerned, so I haven't exactly laid down a stock of vintage bubbly. Anne, on the other hand, had continued in the theatre, and in 1977 was General Manager with a West End management about to close. I suggested she should join Ray Cooney Productions. Ray thought this was a great idea, so Anne moved over, and began the endless search for plays worthy of production. Never an easy task.

Ray promptly made Anne a director. I was one already, but the numbers steadily grew over the months, as Ray seemed to like appointing them. Once when Peter Saunders rang up to speak to Ray, he was greeted by a voice he didn't recognize on the switchboard, although the operator, who had recently joined the company, knew him. She identified herself as Michèle Noble, the daughter of Larry Noble who had been with me for so many years at the Whitehall, to which Peter responded by asking her how long she had been with the company. "Ten days," said Michèle. "Oh," responded Peter, "hasn't Ray made you a director yet?"

Apart from the plethora of directors there were three PAs who stood by us through thick and thin. Jo Benjamin I've already praised, whilst Anne was joined by the indefatigable Sally Vaughan and Ray continued to enjoy the steadfast support and loyalty of Jacki Harding, who left the company for a short while to go into the TV series *Mind Your Language*, but returned when that finished and is still with the Theatre of Comedy, Ray's creation, to this day. Quite honestly, I don't know what we'd have done without that trio. Life in the theatre is uncertain and chaotic enough, but they managed to keep the three of us more or less sane and sober and generally going in the same direction. Not always, mind you, for Ray is an imaginative man and can turn a carefully thought-through plan on its head after a night's sleep, whilst Anne would become bogged down in the minutiae of management and I was trying to fill all the holes in a very leaky bucket. Jo, Sally and Jacki, however, succeeded more often than not in their attempts to bring matters to a fruitful fulfilment.

Anne was just very good at picking plays. The two she found for the Duke of York's were both successes, critically and financially. One went on as our swan-song before the theatre closed and was rebuilt by its new owners, Capital Radio. This was *Clouds* with Felicity Kendal and Tom Courtenay, whilst *Duet for One*, with Frances de la Tour and David de Keyser, was the highly acclaimed production following *Rose* which reopened the Duke of York's after its refit. Anne was also responsible for finding *Bodies* by James Saunders, with Dinsdale Landen and Gwen Watford, which was presented at the Ambassadors (next on my list of Cooney-Marsh theatres) and Brian Clarke's *Whose Life Is It Anyway?* with Tom Conti and Jane Asher at the Savoy. In addition, she saw to the successful mounting of *Chicago* at the Cambridge, *Not Now, Darling* at the Savoy, *They're Playing Our Song* at the Shaftesbury and *Elvis* at the Astoria. Quite an impressive list, I think you will agree. Eventually, though, she and Ray parted and Anne went on to Lord Miles at the Mermaid, and when that closed she became General Manager of the famous theatrical firm, H. M. Tennent Ltd, from whom she has recently retired. Not bad for the daughter of a coal exporter, brought up at St Anne's-on-Sea, near Blackpool. Unexpected, anyway.

So, having been sold to Capital Radio, the Duke of York's passed out of our hands, but we still had the Ambassadors. This delightful little theatre housed *The Mousetrap* for over twenty years, before it moved next door to the St Martin's Theatre, and during the last war Herbert Farjeon presented those famous revues, *Sweet and Low*, *Sweeter and Lower* and *Sweetest and Lowest*. However, by the time I joined Cooney-Marsh, Ray had made a deal with the lessee, Tinker Jay, to take the theatre off his hands for a lengthy period. Tinker rather liked this for, although his father had built the theatre just before the First World War, he was a businessman (something to do with chromium plate, I believe) and a keen yachtsman, so the thought of running a West End theatre was hardly a priority. By letting it to Ray Cooney he could enjoy the best of both worlds: the excitement of first nights and the exhilaration of yachting, well away from the West End. Unfortunately, he had to attend rather too many first nights.

The problem with the Ambassadors is its size. Although it's a dear little theatre, the operative word is "little". It seats 453 people and, in this day and age, that's not many. Even the Duchess Theatre is bigger. So, unless you have an inexpensive production – preferably one with a small cast – you can be in serious trouble. We were generally in the latter condition, for the productions we were able to find were really all too big.

I inherited Nigel Patrick and Phyllis Calvert in *Dear Daddy*, but by the time I stepped into the office this was running out of steam. Then came a musical (we must have been barmy – or desperate), *Something's Afoot*, which was a musical version of Agatha Christie's *Ten Little Niggers* (or, as it's called nowadays, *Ten Little Indians*). Agatha Christie was on the scene again for the next production, *Who Killed "Agatha" Christie?* with James Bolam and Gerald Flood, but for the life of me, I can't remember a single thing about it, except that those two actors made up the entire cast – ideal for the Ambassadors. After that came the aforementioned James Saunders's *Bodies* and then, as I was leaving the company, another two-hander, a revival of Anthony Shaffer's *Sleuth*. And that, truthfully, is all I can recall. Very dull, I fear.

So let's turn to the Astoria Theatre in Charing Cross Road. Once a pickle factory, I believe, it was indeed in that condition when I first saw it. After its bottling days, it had been turned into a huge cinema, almost opposite the Dominion, and was now facing the well-publicized Centre Point – still without tenants, if I remember rightly. Laurie Marsh had negotiated an under-lease from the Rank Organization, who were in turn lessees of the British Shoe Corporation, and he and Ray Cooney were busy tearing the heart out of the huge building to turn it into a theatre. In this they never entirely succeeded – not a true theatre anyway – but it became a marvellous venue for a pop concert-type production. For this I must pay tribute to Laurie himself, who had a wonderful eye for theatre alteration, coupled with his architect, Donald Armstrong, and with technical assistance from Ian Albery, the fourth generation of his family to be running Wyndham Theatres Ltd. Ian subsequently broke the chain, for his theatres were taken over twice and he resigned, to become the Managing Director of the Theatre of Comedy, another Cooney creation, in 1988.

But as the months went on, into mid-1977, and the building work came nearer and nearer to its close, we were no nearer to finding the first production to grace this new theatre's boards. Possible tenants came in, took one look at the vast auditorium, and vanished. Actually the auditorium wasn't all that big – it simply looked it, being on two levels only, with the circle (having been a cinema) seating more than the stalls. The total capacity was just under 1,500 people, but even so, that's still an awful lot of bums to put on seats. Then, one day, Ray Cooney had a rush of blood to the head and dreamed up the idea of *Elvis*, to commemorate the late pop idol's life.

To be fair, I think Ray had been harbouring the germ of

an idea ever since he had seen the New York production of *Beatlemania* which had Beatles look-alikes belting out their songs against a backcloth of still and moving pictures, but *Elvis* was better by a long chalk, in my view. So, Ray hired Jack Good to put together the production – and he was inspired. Those of you who followed pop music in the early days of black and white television will remember the *Oh Boy* programmes, which were devised and produced by Jack, but since then he had moved to Sante Fe and had to be persuaded back. He was – and the result was marvellous. A great rocking production, with P. J. Proby, Shakin' Stevens and Tim Whitnall playing the three ages of Elvis, which took London (or, rather, the pop fans) by storm – ending up winning the *Evening Standard* Drama Award for the Best Musical of 1977, and ensuring that the Astoria's first ever production, as a full-time theatre, was enshrined in theatrical history. Would that happy situation had continued. But it didn't.

Portentously, on Good Friday, April 13th, 1979, Anne Rawsthorne came to me and said she was having a spot of bother with P. J. Proby who was behaving somewhat eccentrically, shall we say, during the performances. Would I help her warn him that such eccentricity was unacceptable and if he didn't return to his original, brilliant, performance as directed by Jack Good, he would have to go. I'm never very good on these occasions, but along I went, and the warning was delivered.

On the day following, Saturday, at the first house, Anne was again in front and was slightly staggered when Mr Proby addressed the assembled audience, complaining about his treatment the previous day, black Friday. She immediately rang for me to come along to the theatre to do the necessary and, cursing that my annual Easter chore of preparing the garden furniture and cleaning the swimming pool had been interrupted, along I went. Together we faced P. J. with the fact that his contract was being terminated and I must say he took it very well and gave a splendid farewell performance. But he had to go – and go he did. The show never really recovered.

That, in spite of another excellent performance from Bogdan Kominowski, who took P. J.'s place. I suppose P. J.'s propinquity to Elvis had given the show an added dimension which all Bogdan's good looks and ability could not achieve. *Elvis* slowly slithered into the also-rans and eventually closed. It was resurrected for a tour abroad at a later date, but all that is in the infrastructure interface, so please wait with patience.

What made this whole affair so doubly sad was that we had launched a revamp of the old TV series *Oh Boy* at the beginning of 1979 to fill the Astoria on Sundays. These concerts were presented in conjunction with Capital Radio (broadcast by them), through the good offices of John Whitney, then Managing Director of Capital, later Director-General of the IBA, and using most of the *Elvis* cast, plus others, directed by Jack Good (once more prised back from Sante Fe) and lastly a young producer, Richard Leyland, with an eye on an eventual TV production. In the event, this happened when Central Television bought the package but, of course, the great talent of P. J. Proby was by then no longer available to us. Dear oh dear, what fools we mortals are. We so often shoot ourselves in our own flat feet. Mine are full of bullet holes.

I must tell you the story of a trip to Sante Fe, when Ray Cooney, his wife Linda and I went over to discuss all manner of musical matters with Jack Good: *Elvis*, *Oh Boy*, and a new idea for the life story of Bing Crosby, which never came to anything. An alternative, *Music, Music, Music*, was suggested by Jack, but that never came to anything either.

Anyway, after Jack, Ray and I had banged our heads against a brick wall for three or four days, Jack's wife Margit (she was born in Germany and christened Margrit, but the priest missed out the second "r" so Margit she remains) suggested that we repair to the nearby Indian Reservation, which encompassed holy ground. We pointed out that it was now 4.30 in the afternoon and the Reservation closed at 5.00, but Margit persisted. We clambered into the VW van and lumbered off.

At the Reservation gates we were greeted by a somewhat startled Red Indian gatekeeper, who pointed out that the whole place, spirits and all, closed up at five o'clock and it was now ten minutes to. Margit was German in the extreme. "We will be back by five o'clock precisely," she declaimed – and we were off.

It seems to me that all Red Indians must have been four feet tall or squatted permanently on their hunkers, for the ruins on the holy ground indicated rooms of four foot two inches by four foot two inches (4'2" x 4'2" – for those of you who find numerals easier to follow) with no room to stretch for a reasonable-sized dog, never mind a human.

By now, dusk was falling and it was extremely cold. I glanced at my watch. "Oh my God," quoth I, "it's ten past five."

"Have no fear," responded Margit, "those Indians will wait for us."

They didn't. The whole place was firmly secured to keep us in and to keep all intruders out. Even though the living had to adhere to normal working hours, there was no intention of the spirits being disturbed during the night watches – though they might have been working in twenty-four-hour shifts. So there we were. Secure within an Indian Reservation. The great American Dream locked irredeemably outside.

We contemplated the heavily bolted gate. No way. We inspected the barbed-wire entanglements which bordered it. Even worse. We were stuck. And all we had to live in (or sleep in) was a clapped-out old Volks with enough holes in the body to let the icy blasts blow through it like a cullender. We could well freeze to death on a New Mexican hillside.

It was no use rounding on our hostess, Margit, with accusations of Teutonic arrogance. It was no good cursing the Red Indian gateman for being a lazy, good-for-nothing bastard. We might join the spirits in this place if we didn't do something pretty fast.

Ray and I returned to the VW. We inspected what was laughingly known as the tool-box, and came forth with a jack and a tyre wrench. Placing the jack under the left-hand side of the gate, we literally forced the hinges apart, by the simple expedient of jacking the gate up and wrenching the metal away as it gradually succumbed to fatigue. We could now swing the gate open, using the central post as the fulcrum.

But Indian Reservations have strange guardians. As we delighted in our ingenuity and the gate came swinging free, we saw the biggest bull you could imagine, glowering at us, with head lowered, from the free ground. We hastily leaned the gate back and convened a council of war.

We decided that Margit would edge the VW up to the gate, Ray and I would swing it ajar, Linda would open the back doors of the van, Margit would block the opening as best she could and Ray and I would sprint for safety – leaping into the van as it swept through the jacked-open gate.

It worked! But as we drove through, Running Bull decided to charge, ending up inside the Reservation. Ray and I leapt out of the van, propped the gate up against its original post and, breathing a collective sigh of relief, we drove off into the freezing night air to the nearest bar and several tequilas.

We wished we could have been there in the morning. The Red Indian gatekeeper arriving – unlocking the central part of the gates – trying to swing them open – the left-hand gate falling on his foot and Running Bull charging him, all at the same time.

That'll teach the Red Indians to cross a German Squaw.

As *Elvis* was closing, I was approached by Helen Montagu, Anne Rawsthorne's predecessor at H. M. Tennent, and then with Backstage Productions, to see if a revival of *Grease* would be welcome at the Astoria. It most certainly would, we thought, and on June 7th, 1979 it duly opened. Alas, we were wrong. Despite some excellent performances from a young cast, it was perhaps too early for such a 1950s pastiche to be remounted in the West End and *Grease* slithered into oblivion.

Ray Cooney was all for bringing over *Beatlemania*, which had been such a hit in the States. Those of us who were a little nervous of this felt that Ray's own creation of *Elvis* had superseded the earlier *Beatlemania* and anyway the Beatles had been the "property" of this country. Who needed look-alikes over here? Coupled with these doubts was the US management's demand for a large downpayment on the production which Ray had to guarantee personally – never a very good thing.

But Ray prevailed and *Beatlemania* had its first night at the Astoria on October 18th, 1979. It was not a success. The Beatles were originally played by four young Americans, but Equity (the British Actors' Equity Association) insisted that they were covered by four young UK artists and that the US singers would only be able to give a limited number of performances before being replaced by their English counterparts. All very reasonable really – after all, the Beatles were English. However, this added to the expense and uncertainty, and the production lost Ray a great deal of money. Sad really. *Beatlemania* had been so exciting in New York, but over here it meant very little.

By now I had left the company, but an attempt was made to shore up the Astoria's fortunes by yet another transfer of the musical *Ipi Tombi*, which Ray had brought over originally from South Africa. I believe it worked reasonably well in this, its third theatre (it started life at Her Majesty's, then moved to the Cambridge), but I wasn't around to see the returns.

I was around however, for the start of the Shaftesbury Theatre saga. Towards the end of 1977, Laurie Marsh announced that the theatre was for sale. Were we interested? Both Ray and I thought it an excellent idea for, although the Shaftesbury did not enjoy the best of reputations, we felt this could be largely ignored if the right production was found. In the event such a production wasn't forthcoming until I was just about to join MENCAP – on October 1st, 1980 – when *They're Playing Our Song*, with Tom Conti and Gemma Craven, once again placed the theatre firmly on the West End map, a position it has continued to enjoy ever since, with the Theatre of Comedy productions, the tremendous Stephen Sondheim hit, *Follies*, and, more recently, *M. Butterfly*. But when Cooney-Marsh Theatres bought the place in 1977 things were very different.

The Shaftesbury Theatre was actually the last theatre to open in Shaftesbury Avenue, on Boxing Day 1911, when it started life as the Princes Theatre, only becoming the Shaftesbury in March 1963. This change of name was an attempt, no doubt, by the then management (Sir Charles Clore and EMI) to change the theatre's image, which had become one of a somewhat polyglot nature, with innumerable revivals and transfers gracing (sometimes disgracing) the boards. The newly named Shaftesbury reopened with *How to Succeed in Business Without Really Trying*, but, ironically, that didn't really succeed either, and the first long run came in the late 1960s and early 1970s, when *Hair* went on and on, until the roof collapsed. Elspet and I went to see *Hair*. Our daugher Louisa was at drama school and making some pocket money by working as a dresser in that seminal production. As most of the cast seemed to be largely naked for quite some time, I think undresser would have described her function more precisely. And no doubt I bored everyone in sight by cracking that particularly poor joke, for quite some time. Louisa must have found it extremely embarrassing.

But *Hair* was really the last big success on the Shaftesbury stage when we took it over, and once again the spectre of an unlucky theatre haunted producing managers' minds, and by 1977 it was extremely difficult to let. As the new owners, we were lucky at the outset. A production was already in place, even though it was only destined for a short run. It was the last time Dame Anna Neagle appeared on a West End stage in a musical and it was a pity she had so little to excite the public's imagination in *Maggie*. Then followed a further selection of transfers, revivals or no-hopers: *Drake's Drum* (ghastly); *Kismet* (even the presence of Joan Diener and Alfred Drake couldn't rescue this one); *Le Grand Magic Circus* (that went down like the Big Top collapsing); *Canterbury Tales* (by now the pilgrims could hardly move for the blisters on their feet); *Dracula* (presented by Michael White who should have known better); *Boxcar Willie in Concert* (not to be confused with *Little Willie Junior's Resurrection*); *Godspell* (yet another revival, one too many); *Irma la Douce* (sorry, two too many) and the biggest disappointment of all – *Hello, Dolly*. The reason for this failure is worth a line or two.

As I shall report later, in April 1979 I had to be in New York for the opening of the Trafalgar Theatre. With that launch successfully concluded, Elspet and I flew off for a few days' holiday in San Francisco (what a beautiful city!) and then drove on to Reno to see Carol Channing in an hotel production of *Hello, Dolly*. If you've never been to Reno, you would be pushed to imagine the extraordinary nature of the town. I imagine Las Vegas is exactly the same, but bigger. As you drive in, your eye is caught by huge posters and signs advertising the hotels and casinos. It is not the quality of the hotels or casinos which count, but the size of their gambling operations. "600 SLOTS" shouts one sign, another boasts "1,000 SLOTS" – meaning, of course, slot machines. Our hotel, in which Miss Channing both stayed and appeared, struck the happy medium of "800 SLOTS" – slots which encroached up to the reception desk, with dull-eyed players gambling away their life savings (or so it seemed) on these addictive pin-ball and video-game machines. It was ghastly. Furthermore, an open railway track went straight through the middle of the town which lent meaning, as Elspet remarked, to the word "railroad", for it *was* a road, just like those carrying motor cars. We watched *Hello, Dolly* first, but after that ventured out and saw one of the huge MGM theatrical spectaculars, at one vast gambling joint or another, with about 150 in the chorus line and most of the speciality acts from England – Newcastle or Liverpool to judge from their accents. I would hate to think how much Mafia money is being laundered in that Nevada city, once famous for its speedy divorce rate, but now separating people from their money even quicker.

Hello, Dolly, in somewhat truncated form, drew many gamblers away from the slots, and we were impressed. Furthermore, we had an idea that this production, which had been touring America with great success, could come over to London, when Reno finished, to occupy the Shaftesbury. The original Dolly, Carol Channing (Dora Bryan was the "English" version over here at Drury Lane in the first production), plus one or two others, would come too. I was hopeful that, at long last, we would have a show on at the Shaftesbury which would reverse the downward trend. There were many thousands of theatregoers, we reckoned, who would wish to see Miss Channing in the role of Dolly Levi.

Well, that was my reasoning. Elspet and I drove back from Reno to San Francisco airport, via Lake Tahoe and a dreadful blizzard, to arrive just in time for the London flight, secure in the knowledge that we had a deal which would improve the Shaftesbury's image – and also guarantee a much-needed success. I had reckoned without Ray Cooney.

As I mentioned earlier, Ray is nothing if not impulsive. When I told him over the phone that things looked good with Miss Channing, he was delighted. When I got home, things had changed somewhat. To my dying day, I shall never know why Ray did it, but in the hours between my leaving Reno and arriving back in London, he had approached Toby Rowland, of Stoll-Moss Theatres, and arranged for *Hello, Dolly* to open at Drury Lane in late summer, leaving the Shaftesbury, OUR theatre, to wither on the vine. I was somewhat miffed, to put it mildly, but Ray was the boss and there was nothing I could do, except resolve that never again would I work for another theatrical management in a subordinate position, especially subordinate to someone who had once been my subordinate! Ray's action over *Hello, Dolly* and Laurie's query about my penetration of ice-cream seemed to indicate that I was in the wrong job.

I began to think seriously of seeking new outlets for my energies and shortly afterwards the Road to London, via Fore Street in Brixham, came into view with that life-changing advert in the *Guardian*.

In the meantime it was back to the drawing board, as far as the Shaftesbury was concerned. Another foray to the Edinburgh Festival, another season of transfers from the Fringe which did reasonably well and once more we were dark. But not before I had a slight spat with the critic of the *Guardian*, Michael Billington. I wrote this rather pompous letter to the Editor, which seemed to cover the ground rather defensively but, possibly, effectively:

How the West End Began to go West

Sir, I cannot remain silent in the face of Michael Billington's statement in today's *Guardian* that "the ultimate absurdity in this buy-it-and-whip-it-in philosophy" was the sight of me "nipping up to the Edinburgh Festival and plonking four of its Fringe productions into the gargantuan Shaftesbury Theatre".

Mr Billington should check his facts. After the run of *Canterbury Tales* at the Shaftesbury, another large-scale musical had been contracted to appear there. Unfortunately, the company concerned did not fulfil its obligations and I was left with a large "dark" West End theatre on my hands, for I am its Managing Director. Now, in case Mr Billington is as ignorant of this as he appears to be in other respects, a "dark" theatre the size of the Shaftesbury costs between £4,000 and £5,000 per week to run when in this condition. No suitable company could be found at such short notice to rent the theatre – not until mid-November anyway. Remembering that I had presented four Fringe shows last year at the Duke of York's Theatre, I did indeed nip up to Edinburgh and found four shows who were prepared to accept the size of the Shaftesbury as a challenge to be overcome (I think this has been achieved – all seats are £2.50 – surely a bargain these days – and the stalls have been comfortably full as a result) and we are on sharing terms – which means we have an income to offset our huge weekly expenses and the Fringe shows have money, too, to pay their way. Isn't that more sensible than allowing the theatre to languish, bolted and barred, for seven weeks? An additional plus is that the audiences actually do *enjoy* these very amusing shows, in spite of Mr Billington's view that the Shaftesbury is "hugely unsuitable".

Mr Billington was wrong in another respect. *Whose Life Is It Anyway?* was a play purchased on behalf of our company by my fellow director, Anne Rawsthorne. It was she who negotiated the deal with the Mermaid Theatre for them to present it first, for it seemed to be ideal material for that particular playhouse. Remember it ran there, commercially, until it transferred to the Savoy. The thought that Miss Rawsthorne was first in the queue of grabbing West End Managers is simply not true. Many of these same commercial Managers too, have made similar arrangements in their time with the subsidized sector, adding valuable production money to those theatres' hard-pressed budgets.

Oh, and one final point. Is it so dreadful that many plays from subsidized homes find their way into the West End? Judging by the success of those listed by Mr Billington the larger London audience seems delighted to offer support. "So-called tycoons" need that as much as the next.

"No man is an Island, entire in itself . . ."

Yours etc.

You will note that I described myself as the "Managing Director". In theory, that was the case – in fact Ray ruled the roost, as my next story illustrates. Having re-routed *Hello, Dolly* from the Shaftesbury to Drury Lane, Ray had an even greater rush of blood to the head. *Hello, Dolly* had cleaned up in its early weeks at Drury Lane for, as we had guessed, Miss Channing had a large and faithful following. But it was an old American touring production really (even the backcloths had a rather tatty look about them and hardly reached the ground – like crumpled pyjama trousers) and the audiences began to fall away. Ray now suggested it should transfer to the Shaftesbury, after all the tinsel had faded. So, it transferred. And was no good. We were dark again.

After that, I sought pastures new. But I was there for the first night in October 1980 when *They're Playing Our Song* changed everyone's luck — Ray Cooney's, Laurie Marsh's and the Shaftesbury Theatre's. It has never really looked back since. But by then, I was over the hill and far away. Laurie and Ray soldiered on, however, and eventually Laurie sold the theatre to Ray and the Theatre of Comedy. They are the proud owners to this day of what is, undoubtedly, a lovely theatre — dogged for so long by indifferent productions and lacklustre revivals. So Ray's impulsiveness paid off in the long run. It was just rather wearing if you were around at the time . . .

Finally, New York and the Trafalgar. Ours for such a short time, but a very exciting acquisition, for all that. For some years, Ray (and to a lesser extent, Laurie) had been fired with the idea of owning a Broadway theatre. The opportunity came about by a fluke (as so often happens in the theatre, or life, for that matter) because Ray and John Chapman had one of their farces presented on Broadway by James Nederlander. The farce was *Not Now, Darling* with — can you believe it? — Norman Wisdom in the Bernard Cribbins role, with an actor (now in South Africa) who used to work for me, Rex Garner, in the part originally played by Donald Sinden. Now, how those English actors, in an English farce, were expected to draw the Broadway crowds, beats me. But Jimmy Nederlander believed they could — Ray and John shut their eyes and thought of England — and the production proceeded. To die the death. But whilst over there, Ray had become friendly with Jimmy, and the seeds were sown for a Broadway theatre to be purchased, specifically to house English plays. That theatre was, eventually, the Trafalgar.

Originally called the Billy Rose Theatre (and probably several names before that) it had been going downhill for a number of years, as it was just off the main Broadway drag. Nevertheless, it was a lovely theatre in the Broadway tradition (two levels only) and had an ideal seating capacity, somewhere around 1,400. Jimmy Nederlander contacted Ray, a deal was struck, and we became the proud owners of 50 per cent of a Broadway property. Or rather, the bank did, for Laurie put up the securities. Nevertheless, it was ours. And on April 3rd, 1979, I flew over by Concorde officially to declare it open, along with Jimmy Nederlander, Tom Conti and Jean Marsh, the last two about to appear in the first production at the Trafalgar of *Whose Life Is It Anyway?* That was an incredible flight. Off at 9.00 a.m. arriving in New York some two hours earlier at 7.00 a.m., breakfast with Rex Berry, our English representative in New York, and on to the 11.00 a.m. opening. Lunch at Sardi's and back to London in time to have supper at our house in Barnes. What an adventure!

Then it was back to New York again some two weeks later, for the first night of *Whose Life*. A tremendous event, followed by a marvellous party afterwards, with the excitement of reading the notices – all good – as they came in. We were made! And indeed we were, until *Whose Life* eventually folded some months later, when Tom Conti had returned to England and the play had been rewritten to accommodate Mary Tyler Moore in the leading part. An unlikely swap – but the author seemed pleased, so who am I to argue? By then I had left the company, anyway, but I gather it was a struggle thereafter and eventually Jimmy Nederlander exercised his option and bought back the Cooney-Marsh slice of the theatre. He wasted no time in changing things. Overnight our splendid Trafalgar became the Nederlander. They do things like that on Broadway. Ever seen Bob Fosse's film *All That Jazz?* Watch the first ten minutes of an audition for a musical and you get a pretty good idea just how cut-throat is the New York scene. London is gentle by comparison. It just takes longer to get your throat cut. In the event, it is just as unpleasant.

A footnote on the Savoy. As I have said, Ray really ran this theatre as his own private fief, having come to an arrangement with Savoy Theatres Ltd. There such plays went on as Robert Morley in a revival of Ben Travers's 1937 play *Banana Ridge*. After that, Anne Rawsthorne became involved and the first prestigious success was the transfer from the Mermaid Theatre of *Whose Life Is It Anyway?* After Tom Conti left to go into the Broadway production, his part was taken over by Bill Paterson with our daughter Louisa taking over the young nurse from Phoebe Nicholls. This meant seeing the play yet again, but I still found it as moving on that night as I had at the very first. This says as much for the actors as for the author Brian Clarke. It also shows that plays like that are not easily found. When it was all over, Anne found herself casting a revival of *Not Now, Darling* with Leslie Phillips in the lead. Knowing Anne and her penchant for drama, rather than comedy, this must have been a trying experience. But all went well, with *Darling* enjoying a successful second run. But alas and alack. When it began to slip, Ray had nothing to follow and decided to keep it on.

That was where he made a financial boo-boo but, as I wrote at the beginning of this Act, optimism is endemic in the theatre and if you keep a play on just to keep a place from going dark, then you've got problems.

So, Ray, too, had problems, and by now mine were somewhat different. I was awaiting my move to MENCAP – but that is all in Act III – so back to the infrastructure interface of those years from 1977 to 1980, as I promised.

SCENE II

"All's Well That Ends Well"

The toings and froings in my temporary office at the Duke of York's Theatre were interminable during my first weeks as the newly appointed Cooney-Marsh Theatre Controller; so were my own toings and froings to others. Names and appointments keep appearing day after day in my 1977 diary and many of those names may be familiar to you for they include: Lord Delfont, Cameron Mackintosh, Duncan Weldon, Arnold Wesker, Tim Curry, Ian Albery, Joan Turner, Richard Eyre, Glenda Jackson, Harold Fielding, Sir Bernard Miles, Michael White, David Aukin, Max Stafford-Clark and Tim Rice. Others may not be so well known, for I was dealing with the management side of the theatre and not all of those make the regular theatrical headlines. Ray Cooney certainly did in early March, for he presented the biggest flop of his career at a Stoll-Moss theatre, Her Majesty's, in the Haymarket.

Fire Angel was the name of the disaster and it was a transfer from the Edinburgh Festival. A musical, based on *The Merchant of Venice* and originally called *Shylock*, it had succeeded well in Annabelle Leventon's small-scale production. Now the moguls had hold of it and it grew and grew. When it collapsed it did so in a welter of writs, acrimony and mutual distrust. It nearly bunkrupted poor Ray, for some investors arranged to put in £100,000 but, in the end, offered £1,000 instead and Ray was left holding a very expensive baby with the theatrical world revelling in his discomfiture. But that, regrettably, *is* the theatrical world when you reach a pinnacle of success and then come crashing down. Luckily, Ray seems capable of rolling himself into a ball and rebounding from all such crises, but he needed every ounce of elasticity on this miserable occasion. And I'm happy to report that Braham Murray, who had become the West End director (in succession to Ms Leventon), has gone on from success to success at the Royal Exchange, Manchester, whilst Colm Wilkinson pushed all fading memories of his singing Shylock into the background with his outstanding performance in *Les Misérables*. As for Ray – well, he bounced back into the stratosphere, with such successes as *Run For Your Wife*, *Two Into One* – and the creation of the Theatre of Comedy – but it was a near thing, I can tell you.

In spite of all the runic rumblings issuing forth from the rehearsals of *Fire Angel*, I went along to the first preview on March 22nd with some anticipation. Surely it couldn't be as bad as all that? I was soon to find out. First I had to hand over a cheque, in the full glare of television publicity, to the Spina Bifida Association. I was doing my stuff in the Circle Bar, with the cameras rolling, when suddenly a very familiar face hove into view and an equally familiar red book was thrust into my hands. For the second time in sixteen years I had been completely lulled into innocent participation as the subject of *This Is Your Life*, and the familiar face belonged, of course, to the late – lovely – Eamonn Andrews. Now to be done once is a great honour, but to be done twice is a rare privilege, and I can honestly say I enjoyed the second time more than the first, probably because I was getting used to it! I must explain that, apart from being the subject twice, I had also appeared in umpteen programmes as a contributor. Dickie Henderson, David Jacobs, Nicholas Parsons, Brian Johnston, William Franklyn, Alfred Marks, Andrew Sachs, Leslie Crowther and my sister, Sheila, all had heard stories from me which told of their many talents – and there were others, too, but for the life of me I can't remember all their names. My apologies, but unfortunately I never kept the very kind letters which Eamonn used to write to all contributors after a programme, so my list is incomplete. I think I've been on *This Is Your Life* some fourteen times in all, so you can see why I was getting used to it.

Apart from familiarity, the second programme was somewhat jollier than the first. To begin with, our children had all grown up and Jonathan was able to tell some far-fetched story about his dad, but in the first programme he'd been pushed on in a pram by Leo Franklyn, dressed as a nanny. All the other kids who had been born to members of the cast whilst we were at Whitehall were also on that first programme – there's something very moving about seeing so many children all wishing you well (which was the tear-jerking climax), quite apart from the fact you feel under an even greater obligation to their parents. I recall a picture of me, with sweat running down my forehead and tears running down my cheeks. Not a pretty sight. At least I avoided that in part two. Then again, my parents were around for the first programme, having just celebrated their Golden Wedding anniversary. They trotted on, with my mother leading the way, as was her wont, and then my father was asked by Eamonn what he thought of his son's achievements. Now you're supposed to speak the lines which you've carefully rehearsed over the last two days, but my father would have none of it. "Not bad," was his laconic reply and that was all Eamonn could get out of him, for all his prompting. I'm glad to say my mum made up for my dad's shortcomings, and prattled on about me quite happily until Eamonn had to draw matters to a close – otherwise she would have caused an over-run, and that would not have done. Elspet was a tower of strength on both occasions, firmly holding my hand and willing me not to make too much of a fool of myself in front of such a vast audience. And on the second occasion, as I say, my stiff upper lip never wavered. In fact, I laughed far too often. Nerves, I hasten to add.

Who else came on in programme two? Well, a stream of old friends and colleagues to begin with, led by Ray Cooney and John Chapman. Then came a very funny actor, Derek Royle, who had been such a success in *She's Done It Again*, portraying a doddery old Professor Hogg, a character he later developed with author Michael Pertwee into a television series, *Hogg's Back*. After Derek, a face from the old days, Larry Noble, who seemed to be a fixture at the Whitehall. Indeed, he was leaving just before the end of *Chase Me, Comrade!* to be succeeded, strangely enough, by Derek Royle. Then on walked Wallace Douglas, the director of so many of my productions, followed by author Clive Exton (he'd been Clive Brooks when he was with me as an actor) and Clive had subsequently won many awards for his television plays, apart from writing *The Crezz* which had starred Elspet and Joss Ackland amongst others. Michael Pertwee brought up the rear of this male phalanx and then came the only member of the distaff side in the first onslaught, Joanna Lumley, looking as glamorous as ever. Joanna was originally in *Don't Just Lie There, Say Something* as one of a quartet of beautiful ladies, but had gone on to greater things (well, greater exposure, anyway) particularly in the last series of *The Avengers* on the telly.

Now it was the turn of my family to appear, led, of course, by Elspet. Eventually Jamie (then at university) and Jonty (still at St Paul's) were to be seen on either side of me whilst we went through the animal impressions we used to do, whilst holidaying in Spain, and which were so lifelike we started all the dogs barking. How that came to be an integral part of *This Is Your Life* I will never know, but I shall always remember Jamie's gibbon, Jonty's chimp and my turkey, plus horses neighing, as being a very noisy interlude in the programme.

My sister Nora and brother Malcolm were next, whilst my other sister Sheila was interviewed on film at the fictional, but beautiful, Emmerdale Farm. Then she, too, joined the merry throng in the flesh, as it were. Two old school friends from Bootham followed, David Stross and Bill Turvey, my ex-dentist. Bill (real name, Brian), his wife Ann and Elspet and I have remained close friends throughout our married lives, which must say something for his expertise as a dentist, for I was always an arrant coward when it came to my visits and yet our friendship has continued in spite of all extractions and excavations.

Tim Manderson followed, telling the story of how he once knocked me down at the Opera House in Harrogate, because I would insist on whistling in the dressing-room. That, of course, is one of the better-known superstitions in the theatre and it is also extremely irritating, too. I was senior to Tim and whistled just to annoy him. At first he asked me politely to desist. I continued to whistle. He then said he would knock me down if I didn't stop. I didn't – so he did. We've been close friends ever since.

Jazz pianist Tommy Watt came on to remind me of our early days in the RAF, as well as the big band we formed together in the late 1950s. Or rather, Tommy formed – I just put up the money. We negotiated a long series of BBC broadcasts and landed a recording contract with Parlophone, then managed by the man who went on to fame and fortune recording the Beatles, George Martin. But it was a pick-up band, the players coming from other big bands – like Ted Heath and Geraldo – and eventually they complained to the BBC, and it was all over. But it was great to dream of being Count Basie – even though I can't play a note. Michael Pertwee generously praised my attitude to other actors getting laughs: in other words, I didn't mind as long as the laughs were there, whilst Leslie Crowther said that I didn't mind as long as the laughs were coming from my fellow actors – as I had a dreadful habit of trying to "corpse" my friends on stage. Absolutely true, particularly at bad matinées, and absolutely unforgivable at any time. Leslie reminded me of the lengths to which I would sometimes go, and told the tale of one performance when he and Elspet were on stage in *Let Sleeping Wives Lie*, whilst I was off-stage changing into pyjamas. "Then," said Leslie, "this monster [meaning me] brought forth a dustbin [used for off-stage crashes], stuffed a soda syphon down his pyjama pants and proceeded to pee in the dustbin, with remarkable accuracy and considerable force – for he was using the syphon, not nature." I remember the din was horrendous. "Well,' said Leslie, "that was the end of the scene as far as I was concerned – and as far as Brian was concerned. He enjoyed the joke so much he was literally crying with laughter when it was his turn to come on – and the whole matinée collapsed around our ears." Quite dreadful, and if any reader of this book was in the Garrick Theatre for that particular matinée, I can only offer my abject apologies.

Dickie Henderson brought the programme to its penultimate phase, but he was on film, being in America at the time.

His opening gag was a typical Dickie one-liner. Looking straight into camera he said: "What can I say about you, Brian, that you haven't already said about yourself?" But after that laugh, he became quite serious and described the work which I had done on behalf of the SOS (the Stars Organization for Spastics). As most of that work had been many years before, I felt slightly embarrassed at the mention, particularly as Dickie himself, as well as Elspet and Leslie and Jean Crowther, had continued to work just as hard as ever, right up to, and beyond, the date of that particular programme. Dickie reminded us all that, along with Tim Manderson, he was Jonty's godfather. When Jonty was little, he gave him a copy of the Bible and said, "When you've read that, I'll give you another present." Alas, he's no longer with us to live up to his promise, but he was a warm-hearted, generous friend when he was around and a very funny stand-up comedian. Who can forget his rogue microphone-cord act, or the wonderful would-be Sinatra trying to sing, act, light a cigarette and have a drink all at the same time, whilst balanced on a bar stool singing "One for my Baby". Wonderful stuff, as was his dancing. A great loss to us all.

And finally, that magnificent West Indian fast bowler, Wes Hall, was whisked on. Or, to give him his present full title, Senator Wesley Hall, Minister for Tourism and Sport in Barbados. How did he come to grace the programme? Well, I first met him way back in 1963 when he and Charlie Griffiths were striking terror into the hearts of England's cricketers. Our paths had crossed on a number of occasions since then, particularly in a match in Lord's in June 1973, when Wes and I joined Elton John, David Frost, Gerald Harper, Michael Parkinson, Peter Cook, Ed Stewart and Ray Barratt in a team organized by Vic Lewis to do battle with Middlesex in aid of Fred Titmus's benefit. I must report that in my fortieth year, I took 2 for 30, made 23 not out and held a blinding catch at backward point, which brought the crowd to its feet and me a bruised hand which had to be seen to be believed. For weeks I bored everyone with the story, which became more and more exaggerated as time wore on. In the end, Wes Hall had delivered the ball at about 90 mph to Mike Brearley who thumped it at about 140 mph to my right, whence I dived and came up clutching the ball which miraculously had stuck to my hand. In fact, I think the batsman was Norman Featherstone and the bowler Ed Stewart, but it makes a better story my way. And it *was* travelling at 140 mph, in either version – and I *did* catch it with one hand. So there!

When that particular match was over, I was invited into that holy of holies at Lord's – the Committee Room. I explained that my daughter, Louisa, was with me, but they decided to bend the rules and allow her to accompany me.

One of the old boys came up to her, as she sipped her sherry, and guffawed: "You know, my dear, it's a great privilege for you to be here. Normally the only women allowed in are the Queen and the cleaners." One of the great bastions of chauvinism is Lord's. No wonder Her Majesty only goes once a year.

And what about His Honour, Wesley Hall? Well, some three years earlier, Elspet and I were winging out way to the Coral Reef Hotel in Barbados in the company of Leslie and Jean Crowther. "Lucky devils" you may think, but we were going out with a solemn duty in mind: to support our ailing Test team in the Third Test at Bridgetown. Every day during the five days of the Test, small groups of enthusiasts, the four of us amongst them, left our hotels and proceeded by bumpy bus to the ground, there to cheer on the English team. We had a job on the Saturday: with 20,000 people crammed into a ground holding 14,000, a handful of English – even with loud voices like Leslie's and mine – found it difficult to be heard above the din.

We had another noisy reception of a more pleasant kind when Leslie and I did a cabaret at our hotel for the team and their supporters. Several hundred squeezed into a space normally holding less than one hundred, but they were a marvellous audience and we both found difficulty coming off that cramped cabaret floor! Next day we marched up and down the beach proudly receiving plaudits from all and sundry, and as our team went on to achieve a noble draw we felt we must have raised morale somehow. Our morale was considerably lifted too, for our guide and mentor in Barbados was the very same Wes Hall, and going round the island with him was royal progress, indeed. Thus, three years later, thanks to *This Is Your Life*, we had a chance to repay his hospitality. We took it with both hands. Wes came to stay with us for the rest of his time in London, and we had a marvellous party. All thoughts of the horrors of *Fire Angel* were driven firmly from our minds, but the reports coming in were definitely depressing.

Although I had retired from the theatre, I hadn't exactly popped my clogs as an actor. Vestigial traces still hung around. Before finally leaving the Whitehall, Barry Took (who wrote that fabulous *Punch* notice for *Fringe Benefits*) had approached me, to see if I might be interested in doing a television version of Michael Green's book *The Art of Coarse Moving*. Barry himself would be writing the script, with Michael's assistance, of course. Naturally, I would be interested, and eventually a pilot script was approved by Jimmy Gilbert at the BBC and we were off. Incidentally, Jimmy Gilbert is the man who retired as Head of Light Entertainment at BBC TV just weeks before his due date – and promptly went over to Thames Television to perform a similar function, for about treble the money. The BBC were *very* put out, but by now they must be used to it. So much so, they're inviting old defectors back. Paul Fox, late of Yorkshire Television and before that Controller of BBC 1, to name but one. Now he's returned to the fold as Managing Director, BBC Television.

But back to business. Originally, it was intended that Elspet would play my wife in the newly entitled *A Roof Over My Head*, but she was engaged elsewhere in some other telly, so Lynda Baron was brought in, and a very jolly screen marriage it turned out to be. We did the pilot in early March and then recorded the full series in July and August, with transmissions in the late summer. Not only did I enjoy playing with Lynda as my wife, but I also enjoyed the company of Francis Matthews, Dennis Ramsden, Alfie Bass and, in four episodes, my daughter Louisa, who played my giggly Scouse-accented secretary. If you think that's nepotism, you would be wrong. I promise I had nothing to do with the casting. On the other hand, I suppose I could be accused of exerting undue influence: in the last of the series there appeared an electricity board man who is billed as Jamie MacGregor. Actually, that's my elder son, James MacGregor Rix, who was earning a crust whilst still at university and before joining, in 1979, a well-known theatrical touring company, Joint Stock. This was then being run by Max Stafford-Clark, now of the Royal Court, whose father, David, was the psychiatrist who was so popular on television in the 1960s and had been in the same party as me when we enjoyed lunch with the Queen at Buckingham Palace in March 1965. But that has nothing whatsoever to do with Max or Jamie, and Jay eventually joined the BBC and is now involved in many award-winning productions on radio and TV. You may remember *In One Ear*, *Radioactive*, *The Wow Show*, *Alas Smith and Jones*, *Hello Mum*, *Colin's Sandwich*, etc – well, Jamie's name is there somewhere on the production side. Furthermore he's won (with others) an Emmy, a Sony and a Perrier Award. A bit different from being an electricity board man, walking on in the last of his dad's series. As for Louisa – well, she's in *Colin's Sandwich* too, playing Mel Smith's girlfriend, Jenny. But nothing to do with Jamie, I promise you . . . at least, that's what he tells me.

Other television activities came my way in 1977, including the pilot of the television series for people with a mental handicap, entitled *Let's Go*. This series eventually started in 1978 and finally forty programmes were produced, in which I was the presenter. It was a unique series, the first of its kind in the world, and stemmed from an earlier BBC Continuing Education series *On the Move*, with the aim of teaching illiterate people to read and write. Many people with a mental handicap took part in *Let's Go* – and apart from acting as a very useful teaching tool, the series enhanced the standing of handicapped people, showing them doing many jobs which the average Brit thought quite impossible. That, and the fact that the BBC was involved, all added to the chutzpah. Now the world has moved on, at least in this tiny corner of the globe, and a new, longer series has been produced – much more sophisticated – entitled *A Life of Our Own* and a young man with learning difficulties, Gary Bourlet, presents it. How's that for progress? The present Head of Training at the BBC, Gordon Croton, dreamed up the original idea, though, all those years ago. I think I should pay tribute to him here – and this I do gladly. I think I should also pay tribute to Messrs Cooney and Marsh, who only objected occasionally to the extent of my extra-mural activities. Mind you, without those activities I think I'd have become acutely depressed, for they reminded me that there *was* life beyond St Martin's Lane and a load of old theatres which, shall we say, were not exactly in the forefront of every theatrical manager's mind but which were, equally, my responsibility to shift. Telly, filming and executive duties made for very long hours, I can tell you, but it was my own fault for trying, as always, to fill every hole in the sieve.

All manner of theatrical correspondence used to arrive at my home, too. But in May 1977 there was something distinctly different. On the 17th of that month I received a letter from 10 Downing Street informing me, "in strict confidence", that the Prime Minister, "has it in mind, on the occasion of the forthcoming list of Silver Jubilee and Birthday Honours, to submit your name to the Queen with a recommendation that Her Majesty may be graciously pleased to approve that you be appointed a Commander of the Order of the British Empire". Would I agree? If so, please send back the enclosed form by return of post.

The form was in the post-box at the end of our road in about four minutes flat. No hesitation, as far as I was concerned. Just a little surprised, I suppose, that the honour had not been offered by that theatrical buff Harold Wilson when he was PM, but, in fact, had come from Jim Callaghan who was more interested in work for disabled people. And that was what it was for, as it turned out, although I like to think that my many years in the theatre, dispensing laughter, might have had something to do with it, too. The official Honours List was published on Saturday, June 11th – and my favourite cutting reads: "Comedian Brian Rix, star of countless Whitehall farces, gets a CBE for his fund-raising in aid of mentally handicapped children." The reason it's my favourite? Well, it appeared on page three of the *Sun*, and my paragraph nestles lovingly beneath the left breast of a certain Swedish model, Mona. When I got my knighthood nine years later Mona was no longer around to keep me company. It was quite lonely, really.

My old mate Dickie Henderson was awarded the OBE in the same Honours List, for his work for various charities. We always hoped we'd go to the same investiture too, but that was not to be. However, we all celebrated – Dickie, Gwyneth, Elspet and I – on the day I got my gong, November 20th. We were in good company that year: Sir Peter Hall from the National Theatre, Doris Speed MBE from the Rover's Return, Rolf Harris MBE from Down Under and Sir John Gielgud from the Duke of York's (he was appearing in *Half Life*), who was made a Companion of Honour. But none of them snuggled up so closely to Mona as I did.

When eventually I went to Buckingham Palace, in November, I was escorted by Elspet and younger son, Jonty, all the other kids being otherwise engaged. Poor Jonty. He was at the beginning of a bout of ill-health which carried on until after his A-levels the following summer, so much so that he spent most of the investiture closeted in the Royal loo or, rather, the one open to the gentlemen present on that day. He found it almost as charmingly decorated as the Ballroom, where the actual event takes place – and not at all Victorian, as you might expect. The investiture *does* have a Victorian air about it, though. The Queen stands on a raised platform at one end of the room, handing out the awards, with friends and relatives of the recipients in raised tiers looking on. As each person finishes, he or she comes round to the main body of the hall to take a seat to watch the remainder of the ceremony, which lasts precisely one hour. However, the Victorian air comes from a string section of one of the Household Bands, quietly playing music from Gilbert and Sullivan or *Annie Get Your Gun* or *My Fair Lady*, on a balcony overlooking the room – with the bandmaster resplendent in his red uniform jacket and conducting the while, with white gloves completing the fetching ensemble. A great day for everyone – except perhaps for the Queen, who has to stand for so long, so often, being interested and gracious to people she has never met before and whose deeds are read out to her as each and every one comes forward. On the other hand, there must be some she is delighted to meet – especially those receiving bravery awards. When I was knighted, the heroes of the Bradford football-stand fire were present. I'm sure everyone was only too aware of their great courage on that disastrous occasion.

As I have already mentioned Jonty's A-levels, let me finish the story, which continued until July 1978. I'm not sure if it's been done by any schoolboy before or since, but he passed with ease by being ill throughout, in itself an original approach, to say the least.

First of all he started the summer term with a humdinger in anyone's language, Infectious Mononucleosis, which is Glandular Fever. This he topped up almost immediately with Rubella (German Measles) and one or two allergies to the antibiotics he was receiving, requiring yet further medicines to quieten an already extremely disturbed digestive system. By now he was *really* run-down, so much so that when it came to exam time, he had also developed boils, styes and carbuncles. One of these actually burst

Left Hornsea 1938, an old photograph found in a Leeds flea market.
Right Me aged eleven, during a First XI cricket match at St. Bede's.

Our wedding day with, left, my mother and father, and right, Elspet's mother and her Uncle Jack. Elspet's father was in India and was unable to attend the wedding.

Left The family in the 1960s with Jonty being pushed by Jamie, Elspet, Louisa and myself. *Right* With Shelley, around the same time.

Jamie's wedding in November 1980. From left to right, Louisa, myself, Jamie, Elspet and Jonty.

Shelley sitting in her favourite armchair in Barnes.

Outside the Whitehall Theatre two days after the opening of *Chase Me Comrade!* with some of the children born to members of the Company from 1950-1964.

Reluctant Heroes; at the beginning of 1,610 performances.

DERMOT WALSH   BRIAN RIX   LARRY NOBLE   WALLY PATCH

Original cartoon by TOM TITT, from the "TATLER", September 28th 1950

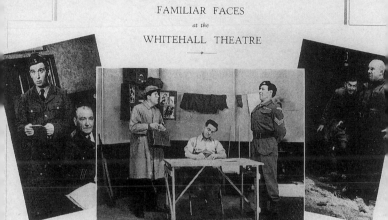

Left Basil Lord in *Worm's Eye View*. *Centre* Brian Rix, Larry Noble and John Slater in *Reluctant Heroes*. *Right* John Chapman and Wally Patch, also in *Reluctant Heroes*.

WHITEHALL THEATRE

(Corner of Trafalgar Square)   Box Office Phone
Licensed by the Lord Chamberlain to Mrs. A. Cooper   WHI. 6692

Evenings 7-30   Mat. Thursday 2-30   Saturdays 5-15 & 8-15

RIX THEATRICAL PRODUCTIONS
present

JOHN SLATER
BRIAN RIX
BASIL LORD

in

DRY ROT

A FARCE BY
JOHN CHAPMAN

with

CICELY PAGET-BOWMAN   WYNNE CLARK
DIANA CALDERWOOD   HAZEL DOUGLAS
CHARLES CAMERON   JOHN CHAPMAN
and
LARRY NOBLE

DIRECTED BY WALLACE DOUGLAS

SETTING BY RHODA GRAY

PRICES: Stalls 13/6, 8/6;   Dress Circle 12/-;   Upper Circle 5/6
All Seats Bookable (No Extra Charge)

THE NEW WHITEHALL LAUGHTER SHOW
OPENING TUESDAY, AUGUST

Left The publicity leaflet announcing the opening of *Dry Rot* in 1954. *Below* One thousand performances later, as seen by Hudson!

WHITEHALL THEATRE

HOME OF FARCE

BRIAN RIX RETIRES

FRANKLIN

"THE OTHER COMICS ARE STAYING ON!"

to "The Master" Best wishes — Stanley Franklin

Stanley Franklin commemorates my retirement from the theatre in 1977.

Left My second appearance as the subject of *This Is Your Life*. To the left is Ray Cooney and right, inimitable Eamonn Andrews. *Right* With Ray Cooney on Trafalgar Day, enjoying the anniversary festivities in the bank below our offices.

Standing on the balcony of the wonderful Victorian theatre at Normansfield, with John Earl, who was then with the GLC Historic Buildings Department and is now the Director of the Theatres Trust.

Left The theatre proscenium in greater detail. *Right* Addressing a packed audience at the Festival Hall as part of the Gateway Festival in April 1981.

The opening of the Rix Toy Library (now the Rix Centre) at Normansfield: 1979. From left to right, Lady Robson, Tony Turner OBE, Cathie Condry, Elspet, Leslie Crowther and me.

Dr Norman Langdon-Down, Elspet and Stella, Lady Brain, at Normansfield.

The 1980 Mencap Annual International Art Exhibition.

The Summer Fayre at Normansfield, 1988, with Charlotte, Jolyon, Jonathan Coy, Ben, Jack, Elspet, Shelley and Jamie Rix.

during Art (Imaginative Composition), but as his eyes were closed up anyway with his styes, the composition was extremely imaginative – not to say unintelligible – and he passed. During Geography he was suffering from a high temperature, diarrhoea and vomiting, so a letter from a kind invigilator to an equally kind examiner ensured a B pass, although Jonty had barely got beyond question one, whilst his English was mainly written as he was escorted to and fro from the examination hall by an additional invigilator, specially laid on for the purpose. You have to admire such perseverance, for Jonty even continued to try and open the batting for St Paul's and the Surrey Young Cricketers during that ghastly summer. Unfortunately, fellow schoolboys are not as sympathetic as examiners and invigilators, so his expected bonanza cricket season fell rather flat. A great pity, for being a cricket nut, I had hoped to see one of my young make an opening bat for a county at least, but it was not to be. However, I did have the pleasure of watching both Jamie and Jonty open for St Paul's over a period of five seasons and I've still kept a cutting from the *Sunday Telegraph* describing one particularly good innings by Jonty. Ah, happy carefree days . . .

Meanwhile, Jonty and Shelley apart, our other kids were becoming firmly involved in the theatre, Jamie at the University of Kent, Louisa at the Old Vic at Stoke-on-Trent, where the splendid Peter Cheeseman taught her a great deal. Elspet and I visited both their Christmas shows. Jamie had written and directed his which was, I believe, his own version of Bram Stoker's *Dracula*, and for all its faults a damn sight better than the two versions of the play which came over to the West End from Broadway the following year, and which no amount of blood-sucking could revive. Louisa was in a Christmas show in-the-round at Stoke, and I recall admiring the expertise which the actors displayed in that very difficult type of space. After the show, we left for a hotel out in the country, but thanks to a pea-souper of a fog we first ended up in a filthy farmyard, miles from anywhere. Eventually, a weary night porter welcomed three equally weary Rixes who stumbled into the hotel. No wonder they call it the Black Country. Well, murky anyway.

Mind you, the previous year when Louisa was appearing for Richard Eyre at the Playhouse, Nottingham, we nearly celebrated Christmas in a car park. We had gone up on Christmas Eve and had arrived two minutes late, so had parked in the forecourt of the Nottingham Roman Catholic Cathedral. We came out to find all was locked up and only the onset of Midnight Mass caused the gates to be opened, enabling us to sneak out, braving the singularly unchristian imprecations of the assembled congregation and an extremely irate cleric. Luckily, the Christmas spirit was waiting for us at home in large supply, and certainly our quality of wine was superior to any Communion variety.

Incidentally, 1976 had seen the beginning of an unhappy saga concerning Normansfield, which rumbled on for nearly three years, eventually involving us all, in some way or another. I think the easiest way is to quote from the official DHSS report which was eventually published in 1978 and was headed:

Committee of Inquiry into Normansfield Hospital

Late in the evening of May 4th, 1976, an informal meeting of certain members of the Confederation of Health Service Employees was held at Normansfield Hospital, Teddington, Middlesex. That night the hospital housed 202 mentally handicapped patients of varying ages, many of them suffering from multiple handicaps, some to the point of complete helplessness. Those present at the meeting were members of the nursing staff and they were angry that the health

104

authorities had apparently failed to take full notice of their grievances against the consultant psychiatrist in mental subnormality at the hospital, Dr Terence Lawlor. After some hours of discussion they decided to go on strike from seven o'clock next morning with a view to persuading the South-West Thames Regional Health Authority to suspend the doctor from duty.

Shortly after daybreak pickets were out at the hospital. Patients were attended by a skeleton nursing staff, helped by a few other staff and relatives. Nursing cover fell below danger level and the health and welfare of patients were endangered.

Later that day Dr Lawlor was suspended from duty and the nurses returned to the wards shortly after 3.30 p.m.

The Regional Health Authority on May 12th, 1976, appointed an independent committee, under the chairmanship of the late Mr Gerald Kidner, to inquire into the dispute and to report. Within a few days of the opening of this inquiry on November 8th, 1976, Dr Lawlor and his legal representatives withdrew from it (followed two days later by the medical member of the committee itself) and thereafter Dr Lawlor and others pressed for a public inquiry. Among those supporting the idea were the British Medical Association and the Hospital Consultants and Specialists Association.

Accordingly, on February 3rd, 1977, the Secretary of State for Health and Social Security, the Rt Hon David Ennals, appointed: Michael Sherrard QC; Thomas Fisher, SRN, RNMS; Dr Hector Fowlie, MB, ChB, FRCP, FRCPsych; the Hon John Scarlett, CBE, and Mrs Alys Woolley, to hold a public inquiry into the matter pursuant to Section 70 of the National

Health Service Act 1946 (now Section 84 of the National Health Service Act 1977).

Then followed the terms of reference, the findings and the recommendations. As you can imagine from that preamble, those findings made pretty unhappy reading. Here a few to be going on with:

7) Morale at the hospital was extremely low for many years and in general its peaks and troughs can be traced to the attitude and behaviour of Dr Terence Lawlor. He was the person mainly responsible for the crisis of confidence which in May 1976 led to the strike of the majority of the nursing staff.

8) Dr Lawlor made the very worst of an already poor situation. He was hypercritical of the nurses and he adopted and enforced an obsessively protective attitude towards patients, whose lives he needlessly and harmfully restricted. He was fettered by his fear of personal censure and of being held responsible for any and every untoward occurrence. His intolerant, abusive, and tyrannical regime drove away from the hospital other medical staff, paramedical and ancillary staff as well as talented teachers and others who tried to assist with the patients. Initiatives designed to improve the quality of life of the patients were stifled and opportunities for progress were lost.

10) The administration of the hospital was poor at every level. The administrator in post at Normansfield in the last two years with which we were concerned was well-meaning but unable to impose his intentions on those around him. He lacked initiative and drive.

11) When new health authorities took over Normansfield on the reorganization of the Health Service

in April 1974, it was already run down and experiencing difficulties. There was continuing failure to come to grips with the management problems of Normansfield and a persisting disinclination to thrash out the problems with Dr Lawlor or to seek to overcome his demoralizing attitude. There were fitful, sporadic manifestations of concern, but regrettably, these were often more ritualistic than realistic contributions to a resolution of the difficulties. All the members of the area management team must accept responsibility.

And that is only quoting four of the findings. There were many more — all equally depressing. The awful truth is that we, the Friends of Normansfield, had known there was something wrong since 1974, but every time we sought audience with the Area Health Authority we were listened to politely and then it was suggested that it was really none of our business. Eventually it became everyone's business — and the report recommended disposing of many, including Dr Lawlor, the AHA Chairman, the area administrator, the area nursing officer, the divisional nursing officer, the senior nursing officer at Normansfield, four of the five nursing officers involved and the unit administrator. The whole operation cost about £1.5 million for the inquiry and a total loss of confidence in the NHS mental handicap hospital system. A far cry from the days when the Langdon-Downs had run the place. Old John must have turned in his grave.

And all this could have been avoided if only they had listened to us, the Friends. At the AGM in November 1974, our Vice-Chairman, Harry Henshall, had said:

Some of you may doubt whether the Friends have the right to question the decision of the authorities concerned, perhaps up to Ministry level, for introducing

107

in Normansfield over recent years a system of administration which seems to have gradually taken away the warmth and understanding which hitherto existed between parents and hospital staff, and between the hospital and the Friends ... I think I would be hard put to it to account for the change which we are aware has taken place by merely totting up the complaints that have come to our ears. Our real concern is the widening distance and changing wavelength in communications between ourselves and the hospital. The basic blame for this situation, we are sure, has to be levelled against the administration.

And present, listening to those charges, was the Area Health Authority Chairman, Mr Harry Payne. He must have wished he'd taken immediate action when he read this in the Sherrard Report some three years later: "We cannot emphasize too strongly our view that members of a health authority, and especially the Chairman, accept, with the honour of their appointment, a personal commitment to ensure that decent conditions exist and that the highest possible standards are practised in their collective name."

And so it was that four years after Harry Henshall had fired warning shots across the Health Authority's bows, my annual report to the AGM of the Friends in 1978 began:

The findings of the Sherrard Report on the hospital are now there for all to see. Each of us will no doubt receive them in different ways but, in any event, I am sure you would wish to know your Executive Committee's reaction and recommendations to the AHA. Earlier attempts in this direction were not successful (the first being made by our Deputy Chairman, Harry Henshall, in his report to the AGM on November

23rd, 1974, and subsequent meetings with the representatives of the AHA in midsummer 1975 and January 1976), but this report has strengthened our resolve and, hopefully, our ability to influence the future.

A number of the criticisms we raised at those earlier meetings were fully endorsed in the Sherrard Report. The report specifically draws attention to our potential in the following words: "The League is a sensible body to whose perceptive views the AHA should, we believe, pay attention. It seems to us to have so much to offer the patients and the staff, and to be an asset to be cherished."

We have been cherished a lot more since then, I can tell you. And so have the residents, many of whom are now moving out into the community, with the active help of the Friends and, of course, other voluntary bodies, such as the MENCAP Homes Foundation, with Elspet as the Area Chairman. There are now Parents' Committees, which look at needs and problems on a very regular basis. There's no doubt the Normansfield authorities listen to us, and co-operate with us, far more willingly than ever they did in those bygone days – but, let's face it, it should never have come to such a pretty pass in the first place. Furthermore, as parents, we should have been heeded and certainly been stronger in making our voices heard by the authorities.

Oh, and Dr Lawlor? He eventually retired with his pension intact and is now engaged, I believe, in psychiatric matters in Australia.

One incident lightened the gloom a little in this sad story. As soon as the Sherrard Report was published I sought a meeting with the then Secretary of State, David Ennals, now Lord Ennals. That meeting took place in February 1979 and really wasn't a meeting at all. No sooner had I been ushered into the presence, than David poured his coffee straight down his trousers. Whether in fact he used this singular method to damp down any criticism of the NHS must remain a mystery, but he certainly dampened his strides; indeed, we spent most of out time together mopping up everything in sight, for the coffee went everywhere. Does the current Secretary of State ever wonder how that dreadful brown stain got on his carpet? (And now the office has been split in two, which is the lucky one? Health – Kenneth Clarke or Social Services – Tony Newton.) Perhaps a piece of office furniture has been placed judiciously over it? Or he has a new carpet. The old one must be pretty threadbare by now. Rather like the NHS itself, come to think of it.

I was also involved in a coffee incident myself around that time. I was making an after-dinner speech at the Farringford Hotel on the Isle of Wight and just preparing to stand up, as coffee was being served. Something distracted the waiter's attention when it came to my turn, and he solemnly poured boiling coffee straight into my crotch. Consternation all round, naturally, not least from me. Apart from implanting a ghastly stain on my new silk suit in a very awkward place, the steaming coffee also raised a vast blister on my nether regions, which was promptly stained blue as the dye ran out of my suit. Of course, the whole affair got my speech off to a very good laugh, but I don't advise would-be speakers to adopt this procedure. There are less painful ways of getting the audience on your side. I know, for I must have tried them all . . .

Obviously, the Sherrard Report dominated much of 1978 and I also found giving evidence quite a daunting experience. But not as daunting, or as tragic, as the other overwhelming incident of that year. Elspet's much-loved sister, Rhoda, died, leaving three young daughters, Carina, Jessica and Zoë, on the threshold of life, to cope as best they could, for Rhoda was a single parent, divorced from her husband John Georgiades some years before.

I say "much-loved" deliberately, for it would be difficult to communicate the affection with which Rhoda was held by all who knew her. It was only too evident at her funeral, for never have I seen such a sad congregation, as she was laid to rest with the sound of the pan pipes keening out over the lovely little churchyard at Achurch in Northamptonshire. Rhoda was only fourteen months younger than Elspet, so they were very close in every way, but it was Elspet who had gone into the theatre first, as an actress, whilst Rhoda had followed as a set designer. She had designed all the dozens of settings for my productions at the Whitehall and Garrick Theatres, including the television productions, but shortly before her death from cancer she had become a jeweller, making the most beautiful and distinctive creations. On the Sunday after her death, the *Observer* colour magazine devoted a piece to her work, and orders flooded in, never to be fulfilled . . .

Naturally, with Sherrard and Rhoda, not to mention running the theatres, there seemed little time for other distractions but, of course, there was. I was not only involved in the television programmes of *Let's Go*, but also in another first, as far as I was concerned, that of being a disc jockey on BBC Radio 2. Well, not a disc jockey exactly, for I wasn't putting the records on, or chattering away inanely day after day. My inane chatter was confined to Sundays for one and a half hours. At first the programmes went out at 1.30 to 3.00 p.m., but eventually we were moved to the morning spot between half past ten and midday. I loved the whole thing and was sad when it came to an end nearly two years later. I fear I blotted my copybook somewhat, for I insisted on giving all the theatres a plug whenever possible – both West End and regional – and also mentioning any worthwhile charity which drew my attention to any particular event. When the Appeals section of the BBC protested about this heinous practice to my producer, Ray Harvey, I replied that if it was good enough for *Test Match Special*, it was good enough for me. (Have you ever heard them on a Saturday morning? They plug every charity cricket match in sight. And quite right, too!) But all to no avail. When you start irritating the bosses at the Beeb you might just as well go quietly. I went quietly, playing my finale music, Stan Kenton's "Exit Stage Left", for the last time. But with great regret, nevertheless.

Other stirring events in 1978? Oh yes, a week in Corfu with the Lord's Taverners, to play two matches against the local Greek sides and to make a film about the trip, sponsored by Barclaycard and produced by Nicholas Parsons, which went out on a circuit later to help swell the funds for the charity. It was a marvellous escapade. All of us there with our wives – Roy Kinnear, John Alderton, John Price, John Cleese, Nicholas, me and others, plus the one and only Ken Barrington. Such a kind man. Such a loss to the cricketing world. He skippered one game (the match we won) and I skippered the next (the match we lost). It was a diplomatic loss, I assure you, but, in any event, it is no easy task to win in Corfu. I know, for I had been there three years earlier with Leslie and Jean Crowther, plus Elspet, of course, and Leslie and I had played in three matches on that occasion, losing the lot. The scoreboard has an uncanny knack of going backwards – or at least standing still – if you begin to approach a respectable score. It does not display the same bias on behalf of the local team. I'll never forget the mayoral reception which greeted the Taverners on the eve-of-match shindig. The Mayor insisted on addressing us in classical Greek, which left his poor interpreter floundering with no visible means of support. Eventually the Mayor stopped waiting for him and pressed on regardless, with not a single word being understood by anybody. The sight of John Cleese weeping with laughter in a corner had to be seen to be believed.

At the first match, we played in front of a crowd of around 7,000 (not bad for the size of ground — the old barrack square — I assure you) and we were led on by the local scout band in a parade which would have done credit to Monsieur Hulot, it was so disorganized. Such was the pomp and circumstance of our arrival, I'm sure the majority of the crowd thought we were the England XI, not a crowd of old has-beens, crocks, rogues and vagabonds. We never let on. And anyway, the haze of alcohol from the nearby cafés would have confused anyone. And did.

Two other overseas trips happened that year. One was a flying visit to New York to celebrate Jonty's eighteenth birthday. I'd better explain. After his A-levels, Jonathan had a year out, before going to Warwick University. He was determined to see the world and managed to get a part-time job with our New York representative, Rex Berry. Briefly, he had to try and sell space for *The Times*, regarding restaurants, shops, etc. Unfortunately, the job didn't last too long, for shortly after Jonty started, *The Times* went on a year's strike, and all itinerant workers were hurriedly laid off. So Jonty went to Israel to work in a kibbutz, but not before his coming-of-age was celebrated in the Big Apple.

Going to New York for a weekend is an expensive business and even though I had come to a business arrangement with British Airways, exchanging £25,000 worth of aircraft tickets for the equivalent amount of theatre tickets, I was loath to use any of this for a non-business occasion. Air India here in London were very helpful, however, and agreed to let Elspet and me fly Club Class, at stand-by price, as long as there was room. We flew out in style at a cost considerably less than taking the train to Manchester.

We had our party or, rather, Jonty's party, at the Backstage Restaurant — which was super (including a barber's shop quartet of camp waiters singing "Happy Birthday to You") and then prepared to return, via Air India, to London. Things were very different. Instead of the extreme politeness which had greeted us in London, we were suspected of trying to pull a fast one – for no one had ever heard of us – and we were herded into the rear of the plane with absolutely no ceremony whatsoever. We sat right at the back, next to the lavatories, which seemed to be in constant occupation throughout the entire flight. I was bursting by the time we landed at Heathrow, for I just never seemed to get to the head of the queue. How are the mighty fallen!

A trip to Palma, Majorca, at Kentucky Fried Chicken's expense, was a very different kettle of fish. First class all the way – and a cheque for the Friends of Normansfield of £17,000 as our reward for going, in return for one after-dinner speech. I wish I could earn money so easily for myself. Which leads me, quite naturally, to the time I did not make money at all – never mind easily.

It all started in the mid 1970s when my solicitor, Geoffrey Posner, told me that his brother-in-law (who was a reporter on one of the Nottingham papers) had said how difficult it was for first-time buyers of houses in that neck of the woods. So, with an architect friend, Malcolm Radley, I started to look round for suitable land. Eventually, we put together a saw-mill, an iron foundry, an allotment and a derelict house to make up a parcel of land on the London Road in Newark which would accommodate 146 first-time buyers' houses – and very desirable they were too, to be sold for around £9,000 each. I was very excited, for it was going to make us a small fortune, which would be very welcome as pensionable days came nearer. Well, welcome at any time. Suddenly, there was a snag. A compulsory purchase order landed through my letter-box informing me that the Nottinghamshire Constabulary wished to purchase the ground to erect a Divisional Police

Headquarters. Furthermore, any price they paid would *not* include bank interest. How did they think I'd bought the land in the first place? With mattress money? No, I'd made a small amount out of a property in Notting Hill and this had been added to by a generous Nat West Bank, so interest would have to be paid. Quite a lot, in fact, and Malcolm Radley and I would have to find it.

So we protested and argued and appealed. All to no avail. Eventually, I went to see a Miss Owens at the Home Office to put my case. Now I've no doubt Miss Owens is a kind lady to dumb animals, but she certainly had little warmth and affection to offer one particular dumb animal – me. Under the Police Act, I was informed, local constabularies had virtually unlimited powers to purchase, powers which were unassailable through the normal appeal process. Furthermore, there could be no question of compensation being paid to cover interest, the inference being that if I was greedy enough to borrow the money in the first place, I deserved everything that was coming to me. Miss Owen's office looked out over a graveyard. I felt like joining those long-gone occupants. Certainly my acidulous friend had finally buried any hopes I had of becoming even remotely rich – never mind seriously so.

There is a further twist to this tale. Some three or four years later, I was in Newark for MENCAP and happened to pass "my" site. The place was packed with first-time buyers' houses. Evidently the Home Office had been unable to raise the wind from a Thatcher Treasury and had offloaded the land to a bunch of builders. At a handsome profit, I have no doubt. With *all* interest paid. You would not be wrong in supposing that I was slightly miffed. Actually, bloody angry would be putting it too politely and I still have a feeling there was something underhand about it somewhere. Any investigative journalists want a story? For a fee, I might co-operate, with interest of course.

I seem to have mixed up the late 1970s somewhat in my rambling way, so will try and arrange a compass fix by settling on the remainder of 1979 – my last full year with Cooney-Marsh. The Sherrard Report had made me think again about my responsibilities to Shelley in particular, and the world of mental handicap in general. Had I allowed life to pass me by and only taken a passing interest en route? Oh yes, I had been Chairman of this and President of that – but had I really devoted enough of my time and energies to the problem? The answer became increasingly clear. No. And so I took my first stumbling steps towards the work I was to undertake from 1980.

Unfortunately, those steps were really in the wrong direction. I saw the post of the Director of the Joseph Rowntree Memorial Trust was being advertised. As I had been at Bootham with one of the family, I wrote to Richard Rowntree and made some enquiries. I received an extremely helpful reply, but it was patently clear that I was ill-equipped to consider myself (or be considered) for the job. An awful lot of housing seemed to be involved, and that was something I knew little about – as Newark had pointed out, all too clearly. So, regretfully, I withdrew from the fray. The post was eventually filled by an extremely competent man, Robin Guthrie, who has now moved to the Charity Commissioners as the Chief, and who also served with me on the Arts Council.

But taking that initial step, however faltering, had fired my imagination and led, in August, to my contemplative visit to Brixham and eventually, MENCAP. In the meantime, though, I still had my contract with Cooney-Marsh to fulfil, however much I might consider myself somewhat misemployed in theatre management.

My diary for 1979 indicates one or two other activities which might be of interest. In February I did an Open Door programme for BBC 2 which was called *World at Their Fingertips* and presented by the Radio Society of

Great Britain – of which I had been a long-time member, for I first became an amateur when I was thirteen (with the old Artificial Antenna licence) and had been G2DQU for more years than I cared to remember. Anyhow, the RSGB were anxious to counter the vision most people had of a "ham" being the incompetent fool portrayed by the inimitable Tony Hancock in his famous TV sketch, and they recruited me to front the programme. According to the *Radio Times*, "it [the programme] shows how amateur radio appeals to enthusiasts of all ages, performs valuable community services including emergency communications and involvement with the handicapped, and generates goodwill across international frontiers". Now you know. For my unpaid services to this programme I was made an Honorary Vice-President of the RSGB and treasure that still. The certificate hangs on my wall, among all my other souvenirs.

Louisa played her first lead in a television play for BBC 1, *Breakaway Girls*, Elspet appeared in *Fawlty Towers*, Jamie graduated from the University of Kent and joined the radical touring company Joint Stock as an assistant stage manager, Jonty went to Warwick University and Shelley stayed at Normansfield, where matters were improving rapidly under the aegis of a "Task Force", led by the redoubtable Joan Bicknell, who became the first ever Professor of the Psychiatry of Mental Handicap shortly afterwards, at St George's Hospital. Meanwhile, I Cooney-Marshed, but also appeared in a short film about people with a mental handicap, called *How to Survive in an Occupied Country*. The producer of this film was the remarkable Jimmy Wright, who was blinded in an air crash some years before, but in spite of this disability has produced many highly successful documentary films and was awarded the OBE a year or two ago for his efforts.

And then, a sad entry in the diary. The death of an old friend and fellow actor, Basil Lord. Basil had originally taken over from Ronnie Shiner in *Worm's Eye View*, but had then joined me to play Flash Harry in *Dry Rot*. He was very funny, as he was later in *One for the Pot* and *Chase Me, Comrade!* He was a splendid company man and in all the years I knew him, I never heard him say a bad word about anyone. In a profession not exactly unknown for bitchiness, this is an attitude greatly to be prized. At his memorial service at the actors' church in Covent Garden, St Paul's, I was able to tell this story:

One night in *One for the Pot* a potential car thief was chased by the police from Pall Mall, along Spring Gardens, through the Whitehall stage door, down on to the stage, across the stage, over the floats, through the stalls, up the stairs to the foyer and into a passing taxi, whence he escaped. Basil at this stage was holding my sister Sheila upside down over his shoulder, looking for a place to hide her. As this strange procession whizzed in front of his eyes, he turned to the bemused audience (who wondered it if was all part of the play), put his hand on Sheila's behind and said, "I feel a bit of an ass up here." Not surprisingly, my next line of "bottoms up", as I staggered out of a nearby cupboard, was greeted in stony silence. But I never begrudged him for nicking my laugh. He never did such a thing with malice aforethought.

Finally, looking through my diaries for the late 1970s, I kept running across the name E. Wise. For days I wondered why I was seeing Ernie Wise without Eric Morecombe – and then I remembered it was my shorthand for a company, part of the Cooney-Marsh set-up, called Entertainment Wise. This highly successful party booking organization had been started by an actress, once in *One for the Pot*, namely Jeanne Cook who, like me, had decided to concentrate on the business side of the theatre but, unlike me, was extremely happy and efficient at her work. She had been helped in the early days by old chums from the profession, principally Linda Cooney who had met and married Ray during the run of *One for the Pot* and who was (and is) a veritable jack-of-all-trades and can turn her hand to anything in order to support and help her husband. Further help had come from Rene Udwin, whose husband, Hymie, had run a most successful theatre, the Academy, in Johannesburg (playing many of Ray's farces) but who had decided to leave that beautiful, but stricken, country for the sake of his children. They were all putting their shoulders to the wheel to help Ray, but in spite of that, financial strains were beginning to show, for more and more of our theatres were being inhabited by managements who found it difficult to pay the full rent. That is, of course, if the theatres had any managements inhabiting them at all. It was all very worrying, especially for our accountant, Mike Collins, who was considered to be somewhat of a Jeremiah with his prognostications of doom.

But my main worry was still what to do in the future, as 1980 approached. So, on August 10th, Elspet and I went down to our little house in Brixham to try and make up my mind.

For five days we discussed this and that. Should I return to acting? Should I concentrate on directing? Should I retire, sell our London house, and live in the country? And anyway, what about Elspet and her work? And so on, and so on. By August 15th we still had not reached a conclusion and it was now time to return to London, back to a job I disliked, but which was rapidly coming to an end anyway, and back to a future indefinite. We were driving through Fore Street, Brixham, with Elspet at the wheel, and I suggested I popped out to buy the papers, the *Guardian* for Elspet and *The Times* for me. We started our journey and for some unknown reason I did a thing I had never done before – I turned to the appointments page. It was then that I saw this:

119

A successor to George Lee, OBE, the first Secretary-General of the National Society for Mentally Handicapped Children, who is shortly to retire, is now being sought with a view to commencement by spring 1980.

Applications are invited from persons considering themselves suitably experienced to be the Chief Executive Officer to this large national charity with 375 employees, which has twelve regional offices encompassing England, Wales and Northern Ireland, with 465 local societies and a network of training centres and residential homes.

This challenging and rewarding post calls for a high degree of personal commitment and an alert mind. Considerable administrative and organizing experience is essential, as is proven ability to write and speak in public.

I *did* consider myself suitably experienced, committed and alert. Elspet and I just looked at each other (a dangerous exercise for her – she was driving) and both of us realized I had to apply.

I knew George Lee pretty well, for it was he who had invited me to become the Chairman of the newly formed Special Functions Committee of the, then, National Society for Mentally Handicapped Children way back in 1961, an appointment I had accepted with pleasure. I used to chair the meetings between the Thursday matinée and evening performance of *One for the Pot*, clad in my dressing-gown, on the stage of the Whitehall Theatre. The rather staid and formal committee members must have thought it very strange, but accepted that "theatricals" were an odd bunch anyway and had to be humoured. Whatever they thought, we were a pretty successful committee and raised quite a lot of money in those hard-pressed days. We even ran yet another ball, very profitably, which made my involvement in that particular form of fund-raising some-what top-heavy. There was the Stars Organization for Spastics Ball, the Lord's Taverners Ball, the Normansfield Ball and now the National Society for Mentally Handi-capped Children Ball. You could really say that my life was, indeed, all balls and sometimes that's what it felt like.

So, George and I went back some time in our relation-ship. I had even stood up at a packed meeting at Central Hall to tell the assembled company that I was the father of a mentally handicapped daughter – specifically at George's request. He had wished me to do this, *pour encourager les autres*, and the result was amazing. Next day, practically every paper carried the headlines, "Brian Rix confesses . . .", "Brian Rix admits . . ." – hardly the words we would have chosen, but at least the problem was now coming out into the open, and for this, George must take much of the credit. And me, come to think of it, for coming out of the closet.

When we got home from Brixham that afternoon, I rang George at the office, said I had seen the advertisement and what did he think about the idea of my applying for the job? Was it the height of stupidity? George was emphatic in his response: (a) he thought it was a good idea and (b) it was the very opposite of stupid. The die was cast. I applied.

I must confess to a slight case of folie de grandeur, for I half expected the Society to welcome me with open arms. After all, hadn't I proved myself as Chairman of the Special Functions Committee all those years before, quite apart from the fact that I was the parent of a mentally handi-capped daughter and had been awarded the CBE for my services to the cause? The answer, to my amazement, was an emphatic "No".

I had followed all the rules of the game. Filled out my application form, been interviewed by the Management Committee, but my fellow-parents decided they did not wish to take a risk with a retired actor-manager, who might be a bit of a fly-by-night and anyway conducted committee meetings in full stage make-up and clad in a dressing-gown. The regretful letter from George, informing me of this, clattered through my letter-box in Barnes, and I was shattered.

So there I was, back to square one. My career as an actor forgotten, my career as a theatre manager about to end and an unpredictable future staring me in the face. But I've always been something of a fatalist. As my mother also used to say – it's a long road that has no turning and every cloud has a silver lining. I was hard pushed at the time to agree with my mother's boring old saws, but, in the event, she was right. Life did go on – somewhat haphazardly, I'll grant you – but my family and friends were as loving and lovely as ever, so things could have been worse. I think my mother used to quote that too. Or was it my nanny? The two are somewhat confused in my mind.

After my three-year contract with Cooney-Marsh expired, I stayed on as a consultant to help or hinder, as necessary, various projects which were in the pipeline. The main one of these, as we went into 1980, was the Scandinavian production of *Elvis* by a Swede, Finn Johannssen, but this production was planned to open in the UK before going north. It all ended in tears.

We had initially tried to set up the tour at the end of the West End run the previous June but it just didn't come together, so we regrouped and the tour began at the Winter Gardens, Bournemouth, on Boxing Day 1980. Then it was over to the Tivoli Theatre in Copenhagen, where *Elvis* received a riotous reception which boded well for the rest of the tour. I returned home, now in my consultancy role, well satisfied and believing all would be well. So much for my prescience. It never went well again.

The boot began to go in at Oslo. Takings plummeted

and all Finn Johannssen's deposit, left in London, had to be used to keep the artists paid. After that had gone, Finn was unable to raise the rest of the wind (he had been relying on box-office takings to keep him afloat) and I was suddenly woken one morning, in my comfortable bed in London, to be told that those in Oslo were not only bedless but likely to be confined to barracks, as it were, until the hotel bill was paid. Finn was nowhere to be found and the situation was pretty desperate. I knew this to be true, because Jo was there, battling to keep things going.

Cooney-Marsh telexed money out to the hotel, to release both cast and luggage from durance vile, and I made a quick flight to Oslo to instruct lawyers to act on our behalf to recover the money. We never did, and although *Elvis* still had a few good weeks left, particularly in Amsterdam and Denbosch, it seemed to be cursed since the departure of P. J. Proby and ended up losing its shirt for all concerned. It was even stranded on the other side of the world a year later in Sydney, Australia, and although I was now with MENCAP, I still responded to another SOS phone call from Jo Benjamin, and arranged for British Airways to transport five "whingeing Poms" back to the White Cliffs of Dover. But they'd every right to whinge on this occasion. It's no joke being abandoned by your Oz management and stranded 14,000 miles from home. Even worse than being ostracized in Oslo. And so we say farewell to *Elvis*, once so glorious, now in tatters and tears, rather like the show's inspiration, at the end of his career.

When the Scandinavian saga came to an end, and after Elspet and Louisa had appeared at the Theatre Royal, Stratford East, in Dion Boucicault's Victorian melodrama, *The Streets of London* ("an impressive mother and daughter duet from Elspet Gray and Louisa Rix", vide Michael Coveney, *Financial Times* – as they used to say), we both felt the need of a little relaxation. This time we flew out to

St Lucia, to enjoy yet again the delights of the West Indies. Actually, I was a little disappointed with this mini New Zealand, for although the gurgling geysers and sulphuric smells were not dissimilar, the hospitable attitude of the inhabitants was totally different. One was grudging, the other generous in the extreme. But as we had yet to go to New Zealand, we were not then aware of this difference. Merely that St Lucians had probably seen too many holidaymakers. But if your economy relies on such sybarites, surely you should greet them gladly? Well, that's my naïve belief, anyhow.

So, at the end of 1980, we winged our way home with many questions as to the future unanswered. They weren't unanswered long. Almost the first letter I opened on my return was from the Chairman of the National Society for Mentally Handicapped Children, Lord Renton, asking me to have lunch with him at the Carlton Club, two days later, on May 2nd. My heart turned over. My stomach developed butterflies. Was my journey to London, via Brixham, to have a happy conclusion after all? Was my mind about to be made up for me?

In the event, it was . . .

Intermission

We are now poised on the breathless brink of Act II. May I again offer you an entr'acte which brings forth a cricketing tale from the Long Room. I wrote it, originally, for the *Surrey County Cricket Club 1979 Year Book*. The only snag was it was unreadable for they printed it – if I may coin a phrase – arse about face. This is now the correct version, unless Fontana also get it wrong – and I suppose, in view of the title of this book, that's a possibility.

A Rose By Any Other Name

Although a true Yorkshireman who believes that Surrey's run of success in the County Championship just after the war was engendered by a great deal of luck, special preparation of the Oval wicket and a YORKSHIREMAN, Jim Laker, I have to admit (a) they did do well, and (b) I have now developed a soft spot for that brown cap and those rusty gasometers. Well, I would have to now, anyway, because my younger son Jonathan is a Surrey Young Cricketer – having been denied his Yorkshire birthright by a mother who frankly wouldn't travel further than the Brompton Road to further her offspring's chances. Well, I suppose you can't blame her. The poor soul is a Scot, born in Inverness, and people like that have no finer feelings really – let alone an understanding of a Yorkshireman's sensitivity. Why I didn't realize that when I married her, I shall never know. After all we were both appearing in rep up in Bridlington and as she had no problems about being married in a Yorkshire church (St

Nicholas, Hornsea, to be precise) at that time, I little realized that travel was her problem. From Bridlington to Hornsea is fourteen miles. She managed that all right. From our house in Roehampton to Brompton Road is four miles. She managed that too – but 200 miles back up the A1 – never! So there's our poor little lad denied that most important thing in a Yorkshireman's life, the chance to play for his county. Well, his dad's county anyway. I hate to say that, for the dear little chap doesn't seem to care a damn – which is very worrying. I have given this defection a great deal of thought, and can only blame one person – Alf Gover.

That's it! I can only blame him. To think I took my trusting blue-eyed sons, Jamie and Jonathan, to the East Hill nets and believed they could learn their cricket there without being tainted with unthinkable thoughts. After all, Jim Laker sometimes coached there – and if you meet such a brilliant Yorkshireman as Mr Laker and you know he's a defector who has suffered not one jot or tittle by his fall from grace, then you must be affected for the worse.

Of course, I'm not completely innocent in this catalogue of unfaithfulness. I, too, have fallen by the wayside, for I have to confess that I have actually scored 75 at the Oval. I can't remember the opposition – which is just as well – for they were probably not Surrey at full strength. Probably not even at half strength. In fact, probably not Surrey at all – but 75 is 75, even if scored against a team of ladies from the local Senior Citizens' Club. The thrill of seeing that scoreboard click up the runs has to be experienced to be believed. In fact, I was only out at 75 because I was gazing fondly at the scoreboard, already imagining the 100 coming up, instead of keeping an eye on the ball. I think the umpire should have given me not out, for, after all, I was distracted at the time of delivery – but no doubt the bowler might have had a few well chosen words to say about that.

I have also scored 1 not out at the Oval against very severe opposition – including the Bedser twins and the aforementioned Jim Laker. Eric Bedser got me off the mark. I made a fine flashing off drive, which trickled all of three yards on the leg side and enabled my partner to yell "Run, you silly bugger." This offensive remark galvanized me into life and brought me panting and sweating up to Eric's end. As it was quite clear I had collared his bowling unmercifully, he was swiftly taken off and replaced by his brother Alec. Meanwhile, the redoubtable Jim was having a go at me from the pavilion end. Honestly, I never saw the ball leave his hand. When I questioned him later, he told me he got many wickets from that end in the last half of the day – for he let the ball go a little earlier so it came out of the shadow cast by the pavilion. The dishonesty of it! Fancy cheating like that. No upright Yorkshireman would stoop to such tactics and I can only imagine that Mr Laker learnt those underhand ways from his Surrey colleagues. As my father used to say, "Never trust a bloody Southerner."

I have played, too, under the captaincy of John Edrich. I was inveigled earlier this year to turn out for him in a match at Epsom College. I was amazed at the total ineptitude of his leadership. He actually put us in to bat in the order in which we straggled to the ground. Unfortunately I was very late. I'd lost my car sticker so had to join the queue of cars waiting to get into the ground. If I'd not had the temerity to beg a policeman's help by explaining I was A PLAYER, I've no doubt I'd be queueing still. I only wish I'd kept my big mouth shut – for I arrived at the eleventh hour as the eleventh man – only to be told I was batting number eleven. Well, I mean – you could hear my disapproving intake of breath across Epsom Downs. Who was this young whippersnapper anyway? Sending me in as last man. Didn't he realize I had made 75 at the Oval? Didn't he realize I had once actually bowled out his uncle, the redoubtable Bill? Mind you, W. E. was well over fifty at the time, both in age and score, and was looking for a chance to give his wicket away – but his nephew wasn't to know that. No, no, no. Such denigration of my talent could not go unremarked. Unhappily, John was just leaving the pavilion to open the batting, so my protestations died on my lips – which was just as well – for Epsom College had just laid a new wicket which I think was on top of a gravel pit. The balls reared and bucked and leapt and cavorted like salmon in a pool. Young Edrich was ducking and diving as though he was meeting Lillee and Thomson at their worst. I sat back and relished my new lowly order in the batting. In fact, when John came in to tea and enquired if I wanted to bat (there were three of us still to go in) I had no hesitation at all in doing the unselfish thing and advising him to declare. This he did forthwith – which only goes to prove what a splendid skipper he really is – accepting advice from such a senior pro as me with such alacrity.

Well, there's my article for the *Surrey County Cricket Club Year Book 1979*. I realize my revelations of your players' duplicity, ineptitude and unsportsmanlike behaviour will come as a shock to many members. At least I shan't have to read it. Oh Lord, what am I talking about? I am a member. How low can you get? . . . Ah well, I suppose it is rather a long way to Leeds or Bradford or Hull or Scarborough or Harrogate to watch a real team playing. Come to think of it – as a Surrey member, I can always watch my northern friends in comfort from the pavilion when they honour the Oval turf. But I'll be wearing my Yorkshire County Cricket Club tie. So there . . .

Act III Beginners, please.

Act III

"A New Way To Pay Old Debts"

David Renton was nothing if not forthright but, as always, extremely courteous with it. He had supported my application to be Secretary-General of MENCAP (the acronym recently adopted by the National Society, which had also added Adults to the full title), but had received little enthusiasm from the remainder of the Management Committee. Another had been appointed the previous September and named Secretary-General Designate. But since then this A. N. Other had fallen foul of senior members of staff and, in effect, a palace revolution had taken place, the Management Committee had had second thoughts and Lord Renton had been deputed to ask me if I would consider allowing my application to go forward again. It would be accepted, he was certain.

Of course, my mind was already made up – but I asked for the customary forty-eight hours to take soundings around the family, and left the Carlton Club in high good humour. Even though six months had passed since my original thoughts on the matter, my enthusiasm for the task ahead was no less diminished and I was again heartened by Elspet's (and the family's) overwhelming support for my changing direction entirely – leaving the illusory glamour of the theatre and leading a major national charity into pastures new, over the next seven or eight years, with little or no glamour of any kind, as far as I could see, but an awful lot of hard work and, probably, hard words on occasions, too.

I communicated all this to the Chairman. We met at his flat in Lincoln's Inn, with the Chairman of Finance, Neville

Thompson, and a deal was struck. Not exactly lucrative, as far as I was concerned, but Elspet and I had worked all this out and as long as a few royalties kept coming in from the old productions – and Elspet continued working – it looked as though we could manage reasonably well from a financial point of view, although it would never match up to the golden days. But why dwell on the past? What about job satisfaction? It was what I wanted to do, more than anything else in the world, so as long as my pension contributions continued to be paid and my car was supplied, I was sure all would be well. In the event, it was – and over the years I worked with some success to increase the salaries at MENCAP, so by the time I left everyone was nearing respectability in the way of wages. Not as much as the public sector, I'll grant you, but not far short, and if you are working all hours of the day (plus the weekends as well) I believe you should be properly rewarded. Charity may well begin at home, but the charity worker shouldn't have to live in a hovel, just to prove it.

By May 8th everything seemed to be cut and dried. There was still the hurdle of the National Council to surmount, but at the meeting on May 17th all twenty-four members, plus the honorary officers, endorsed the action taken by Lord Renton and Neville Thompson. Not without debate though, even then. George Lee rang me in Brixham with the news. It seemed highly appropriate that the entire exercise, which had begun in that little Devon town, should come to a successful conclusion nine months later when we were once again there. If ever there had been a pregnant pause, this was it, but at least we had now reached a happy ending – which was, in fact, only the beginning.

The Royal Patron of the Society, Queen Elizabeth The Queen Mother sent a charming message, via Sir Martin Gilliatt, to Lord Renton:

Queen Elizabeth asks me to tell you how delighted she is to learn from your letter that Brian Rix is to be appointed as successor to George Lee ... This is a most imaginative appointment.

The Treasurer of the Society (and a past Chairman), Lord Segal, wrote in an equally kind tone:

I was very glad indeed to learn that you have consented, despite all that has happened, to take on the post of Secretary-General, and feel I must write to applaud your generous action, and to assure you of my fullest support.

Whilst the Chairman of the Society, Lord Renton, was perhaps kindest of all:

You have been wonderfully magnanimous in letting us approach you after what happened last autumn ... It is splendid of you to alter your way of life in order to devote the rest of your working years to our cause, and for my part I shall do everything I possibly can to ensure that you made the right decision.

With letters like that – who needs money?

The press, too, gave me some of my best ever notices. One or two of the magazines were practical, as well, raising quite large sums for MENCAP. For instance, Wendy Henry wrote a singularly sympathetic piece in the October 1980 edition of *Woman*, whilst the Editor, Jo Sandilands, started an accompanying Special Care Holiday Fund at the same time, which raised over £30,000 and allowed MENCAP to send away on holiday dozens of young people, who, otherwise, would never have been able to enjoy the experience. Perhaps the greatest benefit was to their parents, who were also able to take a break at the same time, a break which had generally been denied them for years. Incidentally, Wendy Henry went onwards and upwards as a journalist: she is now Editor of the *Sunday People*. If that is onwards and upwards, of course!

With a number of months to go before I started at MENCAP, I directed an old Whitehall farce, *Simple Spymen*, for the Oxford Playhouse. Michael Coveney in the *Financial Times* wrote:

> ... *Simple Spymen* (1958) by John Chapman is one of the very best of the genre and has been given an absolutely irresistible revival by Brian Rix as his contribution to the Oxford Festival and his farewell to the theatre ... Once the National Theatre has done its duty by Priestley, Rattigan and others teetering on the brink of theatrical respectability, I suggest they employ Mr Rix on a sabbatical to investigate the ignored riches of English farce between Travers and Ayckbourn. John Chapman should be at the top of the literary manager's reading list ...

A pleasant farewell notice indeed, but nearly ten years later only one non-Travers or Ayckbourn farce has been seen at the National – and that was certainly not by John Chapman, being written before he was born. *Tons of Money* was its name, a pretty indifferent piece that first saw the light of day at the Aldwych in 1922, three years before Ben Travers's first play, *Cuckoo in the Nest*, went on there. But maybe one day the National will recognize the considerable talent and opportunity which is extant in the world of English farce, although I'm not as optimistic as Michael Coveney.

In *Simple Spymen* were two old friends from the Whitehall days, Hazel Douglas and Derek Royle. Derek was described by Mr Coveney as being "simply one of the funniest men on the English stage" whilst Hazel gave him "tremendous support". They've never been at the National either, nor ever asked, as far as I know. But as Mr Coveney also said, "a tradition of critical snobbery has grown up around these plays, partly because they were so blatantly popular but chiefly because of our conviction that farce, unless written by a Frenchman, is an inferior theatrical species." Just as I commented earlier on, if you remember. It's pleasant to have such critical support. Also in the play, by the way, was the young man destined to become my son-in-law some months later, Jonathan Coy. He and Louisa had met at Chichester the previous Christmas in a very amusing production of *Charley's Aunt*, which was directed by the talented Patrick Lau, who is Chinese, born in Hong Kong and a somewhat unlikely director, you might think, for such a quintessentially English farce, but as Alfred Marks once commented about Patrick: "The snag with having a Chinese director is once you've had one, you want another twenty minutes later."

Then it was off to my ex-brother-in-law's house in Syros to begin the homework before going to MENCAP. John Georgiades (who had been married to Elspet's sister, Rhoda) and his wife Evie were delightful hosts and I was allowed to read, write and think without let or hindrance for nearly a month, whilst basking in that endless Greek sunshine. A few days back in London to see the Centenary Test between England and Australia at Lord's, then back to the sunshine on the Riviera with Tim and Anne Manderson acting as hosts, and more study, more writing and more thinking with Elspet victualling me as and when necessary. What an idyllic way to spend a summer, especially as all the work I was doing was preparing me for my most important role to date – Secretary-General of MENCAP.

It began on Monday, October 13th, 1980 with a meeting of all the Heads of Departments. They had been summoned by this memo, which I had written under the shade of a gnarled old olive tree, giving rise to the thought, perhaps, that gnarled old habits flourished at MENCAP which needed judicious pruning:

Heads of Department Meeting – 10.30 a.m. Monday, October 13th, 1980

It is my ambition to restructure the Management/ Secretariat of MENCAP into cohesive groupings so that unwieldly meetings such as this one, now pro-mulgated, become an occasional occurrence. How-ever, I would not care to do this without discussion, nor would I care to take up my new post without HODs giving me the benefit of their advice and help garnered from years of experience and expertise.

That being so, I would like to meet you all on my first day as Secretary-General, Monday, October 13th, 1980, and would want you to make every effort to attend. At the meeting I would ask you to state, briefly please, the nature of your department, its current briefs and activities, and its future ambitions and beliefs. Your own personal feelings, too, would be appreciated.

After this, we will open the meeting to a general discussion and I would then hope to offer my imme-diate plans for the future, or at least my feelings in general about MENCAP gleaned from recent visits to the regions and from my own personal experiences in the field. I trust we can keep the meeting crisp and concise and with luck we should be well on the way to concluding before joining the rest of the staff for a drink and a sandwich, which I am offering at lunchtime.

My belief that this first meeting was going to be unwieldly was reinforced when it became obvious that the small conference-room at MENCAP headquarters in Golden Lane, hard by the Barbican in the City, was patently too small to seat all those attending in any degree of comfort. Nearly two dozen people turned up, Directors of this, Heads of Departments of that – it was ridiculous. I had already prepared a plan of action – but as a new boy I wanted to carry everyone (or nearly everyone) with me and it would take a little time. Other meetings were arranged and gradually the rationalization of staff took place and groups were formed, with Group Directors having overall responsibility for the areas of work within their particular sphere of interest. These groups, too, were co-terminous (to use the ghastly bureaucratic jargon) with the four main committees of MENCAP, made up of voluntary members from the ruling body, the National Council. I will not weary you with all their top-heavy titles but their main concerns are education, welfare, housing and finance, with the latter controlling marketing and communications. When I joined, the word marketing was taboo, but gradually I persuaded the National Council that rather than indicating a contradiction in terms of our charitable status, it showed the world at large, and other charities in particular, that we had entered into the business of presenting positive images of people with a mental handicap, images which would increase the public's understanding of the problem and make them more willing to support us financially. Gateway (the leisure arm of MENCAP) eventually joined the group system, as did our legal department. When I retired, though, there were only seven Group Directors, which is a far cry from the long, long trail a'winding into the small conference-room on my first day in office that October Monday morn.

My memo to the Heads of Departments was considerably longer and more detailed than the quotation I have offered, and went on to include my early thoughts on MENCAP – again conceived beneath the shade of an old olive tree – but after I had done quite a lot of preliminary trotting about the countryside during the summer, trotting confined, by the way, to England, Wales and Northern Ireland. The Scots maintain a sturdy independence. A great pity, I think, but there we are. The best laid schemes o' mice an' men gang aft a-gley, and any schemes for union had ganged aft a-gley long before I joined. Such division, though, seemed to make a spot of nonsense of my opening quotation in the second half of my memo:

United thoughts and counsels, equal hope, and hazard in the glorious enterprise.

Having begun with Milton I ended with the first Earl of Beaconsfield (otherwise Benjamin Disraeli).

Between two such illustrious writers [I wrote] are indeed thoughts and counsels – mine and others – which may seem mere regurgitations to many of you but which, alas, are still grave areas of concern for most mothers and fathers – not forgetting their mentally handicapped children, as well . . .

During the past weeks I have been visiting regions, local societies, schools, Adult Training Centres, and hospitals as well as Mini-Olympics. I have also been on various locations with *Let's Go* in preparation for the new series and have seen the highly successful contract Gardeners' Group in Edinburgh, a Gateway camping holiday in High Wycombe, a hostel in Kentish Town – where I was also served an excellent meal – as well as many other activities, including the Diamond Riding Centre at Carshalton. On all these occasions I have talked with mentally handicapped people themselves, their parents, doctors, nurses, teachers, social workers and so on and so on. As a result, I feel more qualified than of yore to list the following as priorities or areas of concern and, of course, they are reinforced by my own observations and experiences as a parent. The list is not in any particular batting order for, in spite of all the magnificent work undertaken by the National Society over the past twenty-five years, parents still react, quite naturally, in the same way we all did when we first discovered we had a handicapped child, with dozens of confused questions seeking a sympathetic answer.

As I said, the list that followed was, indeed, higgledy-piggledy but included such burning issues as short-term care, employment, regions, local societies, marketing, sheltered workshops, Hospital Friends groups, Special Olympics, and the first mention of two ideas of mine which eventually came to pass – a charity consortium (which became the Independent Development Council for people with a mental handicap in 1981) and the MENCAP City Foundation (a grant-aiding body I envisaged being able to help any project connected with our work) which became effective in 1984. All this, and much more besides, were my first thoughts down on paper, ending with:

"Experience is the child of Thought, and Thought is the child of Action." So wrote Benjamin Disraeli. He could be right at that . . .

And, as it turned out, he was.

But it would be quite wrong for me to give the impression that my predecessor, George Lee, had let matters slip into chaos and confusion. All new leaders see areas where they believe they can change matters for the better. My successor was of this opinion, too. Such change is inevitable and should not be construed as criticism, for which it is generally mistaken. No, senior executives who have been in power for a long time often become myopic. Their many achievements, their differing activities, their loyalty to staff often obscure the fact that their once clear lines of demarcation and direction have become a tangled web. MENCAP was no exception. George had created a splendid organization out of Judy Fryd's original concept (Judy Fryd MBE being the founder of the Association of Parents of Backward Children way back in 1946), but after a quarter of a century he appeared to have lost a little of his enthusiasm. But who can blame him? After twenty-five years at the Whitehall and Garrick Theatres, I found myself coming through the same door again and again, with increasing rapidity and less imagination, as each succeeding year passed. So after Disraeli, may I quote Shakespeare yet again:

"And enterprises of great pith and moment – with this regard their currents turn awry, and lose the name of action." It happens to us all, in some degree, not just to Hamlet.

No more hackneyed phrases – for the time being anyway. Otherwise this will begin to sound like the *Oxford Dictionary of Quotations*.

Many of the senior staff George Lee had recruited over the years continued to serve under me. They were a splendid lot, and had toiled away for the cause, with little reward, for considerable lengths of time. One or two were fairly new – but the majority were eligible for their long-service medals. I would like to name them, if you will permit me.

First of all, George Lee himself, who genuinely dragged the Society into the realms of respectability, by sheer doggedness and determination. In addition, he was the co-founder of the International League of Societies for people with a mental handicap – and this body now embraces over one hundred countries. For this, he was awarded the OBE. Two others, who were also awarded the OBE, assisted him most ably. Ken Solly, the Deputy Secretary-General, and Alan Phillips, the Assistant Secretary-General (who became my deputy, for Ken had retired just before I joined), were incredible jacks-of-all-trades, who not only controlled the regional activities of the Society, but the administration, finance and Gateway, the leisure arm. Weekend after weekend, year after year, the three were stumping the country with no suggestion of overtime or time in lieu or any of the other emoluments which generally go with such activity, and their devotion to duty was not caused by any personal motivation, like mine. Three singular men, all of them Quakers.

Others who had served for many years were James Cummings, in charge of Education, brought into the Society originally by George, to run the Slough Project where those more severely handicapped were given consideration and education, possibly for the first time, by the Society itself and by society as a whole. James has now been succeeded by another dedicated man, an ex-head-teacher of a special school, Fred Heddell, who was responsible for writing all the study notes for the *Let's Go* television programmes and also the new series, *A Life of Our Own*. Then there was Harry Neal, who retired just after me (being awarded the OBE six months later), and who supervised the housing explosion for people with a mental handicap, which has taken place over the last few years as a result of the formation of MENCAP Homes Foundation. James Ross was responsible for Welfare, addressing himself wholeheartedly to the mind-boggling complexities of the Social Security system and fighting many long battles on behalf of our members. Together with Janet Campbell, he also controlled the Trustee Visitors' Service, which provides support for our offspring when we, as parents, are no longer around to cope. Rolf Hermelin was promoted by me to be head of our Parliamentary Affairs. That makes it sound like a large department; in fact it was Rolf and a secretary. In spite of such a tiny operation it was (and is) incredibly successful and since 1980 there have been more Acts affecting the lives of people with a mental handicap than all those enacted between 1944 and 1980. I cannot claim that Rolf was responsible for every bit of that legislation, but he was there, in both Houses of Parliament, offering advice and enthusiasm, in equal measure, to ensure that MPs and their Lordships were well aware of our cause and concern. Rolf, too, retired and did not live long to enjoy this. His place was taken, equally ably, by Mary Holland who, for an American, has a surprising knowledge of our parliamentary system. She'll kill me for writing that! Our newly created legal department was originally run by Gerald Sanctuary, but he was succeeded by Michael Whelton, also recently retired. Wherever Michael went in the country, he played to packed houses, for many, many parents are very anxious to know how they should word their wills and form their trusts, before it is too late. Marketing and Communications is in the hands of Alan Leighton, who joined the Society just before me, from television and radio in the Midlands, where he was the original agony uncle, as well as offering sound advice (well, he tells me it was sound) in the newspapers, too. Leisure, through the medium of Gateway, is controlled by John Oliver, under the chairmanship, until recently, of Ken Solly who, in turn, has been succeeded by the Mayor of Usk (ex-Mayor, by now), Roger Galletley. This organization is unique, having nearly 50,000 members in 700 clubs, with an army of over 20,000 volunteers making certain that everyone enjoys themselves, as well as learning new social and sporting skills which enable them to take their place in society more easily. Finally, Finance and Administration was run by Alan Phillips, when he was my deputy, but when he retired Clive Pelling was seconded to us by Barclays Bank, enabling our administration to become even less expensive, for the bank paid his salary. A pretty good way of helping to balance the books, I reckon. Would that there were more secondees.

Of course, many others were responsible for much, whilst I was Secretary-General, otherwise the small conference-room wouldn't have been full to overflowing on that first day. Edward Howe, Peter Pascoe, Marjorie Peacock, David Reid, Vicki Shennan, Tudor Davies, to name but six, plus our twelve Regional Directors (now reduced to seven Divisional Managers), the Principals of the Training Establishments, the Matrons of the Residential Homes and the myriad numbers of carers who have come on stream as Homes Foundation has blossomed, plus the staff generally, which has grown and grown since 1980 – and all offering care and support, as appropriate, for people with a mental handicap and their families.

And the families too, who provide the membership of this, the greatest parental body in the UK, even without Scotland. Around 550 local societies and Friends groups affiliate to MENCAP, giving it a membership estimated to be somewhere between 75,000 and 100,000, all struggling through local societies, Friends, Regional Councils, Divisional Executives and the National Council to bring about the millennium for those they love, led by our Royal Patron, Queen Elizabeth The Queen Mother, our President, Lord Allen, our Past President, Lord Renton, our Vice-Presidents, including the Archbishop of Canterbury, Lord Broxbourne, Judy Fryd, Pauline Fairbrother, Neville Thompson and now, since I stepped down as Secretary-General, me as the Chairman. We are a great lot – even if I do say it myself.

Above all, though, my main help came in those early days (and continued so to do) from a woman. Well, several women in fact. At Cooney-Marsh one woman in particular made life bearable – Jo Benjamin. At MENCAP it was Loretto Lambe. At Cooney-Marsh, two other women helped keep us on course – Jacki Harding and Sally

Vaughan. At MENCAP Marion Young, Nikki Gavin, Matty van Rooden and Mary Holland performed that duty. There were others, of course, but those I have mentioned really made it all possible. Let me explain.

Loretto Lambe was George Lee's best legacy to me. Without her, it's doubtful if I would have been able to find my way through the administrative labyrinth of the Society, nor to see ways round the log-jam of logistics affecting parents and staff. She knew everything, or at least gave that impression, for she's not Irish for nothing. Loretto was with me for four years, before moving to Manchester to run our newly formed Profound Retardation and Multiple Handicap (PRMH) Project. However, whilst I was Secretary-General, Loretto continued to serve the National Council and Management Committee, writing immaculate Minutes, as well as acting as Secretary to a number of other offshoot agencies which I started, such as the MENCAP City Foundation and the MENCAP Unit Trust. Furthermore, we liked each other – and that's not always possible when you inherit someone else's Personal Assistant.

Loretto was succeeded by Nikki Gavin, who more or less took over where her predecessor left off. A veritable mother hen, but far more glamorous, she protected me with fierce affection and loyalty from the day she arrived. I think I had better explain that I have a congenital inability to say "no", so Nikki would try and keep from me the fact that I had been asked to do this, that, or the other (unless it was really important), and invented all manner of reasons as to why I was unavailable. Once, however, things went really wrong. Unbeknown to Nikki, I had accepted over the telephone an invitation to address a group of doctors in a dining-room at Sandown Park Racecourse, Esher. Nikki had accepted an invitation for me to address a group of doctors in Harley Street. The entry in the diary simply read "meeting with doctors" – or something like that. Off I trolled to Esher – leaving the office early to make the journey – and the doctors there were somewhat surprised to see me, to say the least, for I had not confirmed my acceptance in writing. Nikki, however, *had* confirmed my acceptance to address the doctors in Harley Street, who were going mad at my non-appearance. By now the Sandown Park lot had happily settled for the fact that I had arrived and sat me down with a large gin and tonic, whilst they prepared a place at the top table. The Harley Street bunch, meanwhile, were cursing and swearing over the phone at poor Nikki, who could only believe that I had been run over by a bus, for I had left to speak at "a doctors' meeting" and should have been there by now. In fact I was, but some twenty miles away in the wrong dining-room at the wrong function. It was not sorted out until the morning, when a most sincere apology went to Harley Street and I was enjoined *never* to do such a thing again and certainly *never* to accept an invitation without consulting Nikki first. I meekly acquiesced and tried to do as I was told in future. I regret to say, I failed miserably.

Marion Young, like Loretto Lambe, came up with rations, so to speak. In other words, she was a part-time secretary to George Lee. Gradually, though, her job changed, and she is now responsible for negotiating the final details of the legacies left to MENCAP, as well as becoming involved with the legal department, helping out with wills and probate. It's amazing what you can do if you have a clear mind and a sympathetic disposition. Marion has both – and more.

Matty van Rooden became my Personal Secretary about two years before I left. As you might gather from her name, she is Dutch, but speaks and types English perfectly, although not when she arrived. She was always entering dates in my *dairy*. Until we bought her a word processor, I began to feel like a milk-maid.

Finally, Mary Holland. Mary joined MENCAP shortly after me, from the Spastics Society, where she had been organizing the "Save a Baby" campaign. The ultimate purpose of her appointment was to take over as our parliamentary representative when Rolf Hermelin retired, but in the meantime she worked with the Open University on the course, "Mental Handicap – Patterns for Living", as well as becoming the secretary of the newly formed Medical Advisory Panel. All these pop up in the story from time to time, in my tale of seven years as MENCAP's Secretary-General, such has been Mary's success in those three areas of work.

My first Members' Meeting on October 25th, 1980, took place less than a fortnight after that packed gathering at MENCAP HQ. This half-yearly shindig was packed, too, in the Lesser Free Trade Hall, Manchester (who was in the Greater?) and I gingerly put my toe in the water, which varied from tepid to boiling as the years went by, but on this occasion I was very much on show – the trials would come later, so everything passed off without incident. This is what I said, or part of it, to be more accurate. I opened by saying a tribute to my predecessor, George Lee, and went on:

I have, of course, only been in the actual hot seat for twelve days and I still find myself beset by – no, not bifurcation but trifurcation – if there is such a word!

In the first instance, when I stand upon a platform, I feel people are still expecting me to make them laugh. Actually, my first appearance on a Manchester stage was thirty-eight years ago, and as the play was *King Lear*, laughs then were very few and far between, as they will be today.

Secondly, as a father, I never cease to marvel at all the wonderful people who devote their lives and love and care to people with a mental handicap with none of the personal motivation which drives us.

And thirdly, as your new Secretary-General, it is my job to point out all the shortcomings in successive governments' attitudes towards those who are the most vulnerable in our population.

What have I found in my travels to underline this? That the three same fears which struck terror into Elspet's heart and mine, twenty-nine years ago when Shelley was born still apply today. What can we do? Who can we turn to? Then, later, what futures does our child have? And lastly, what will happen to our child when we are gone? Of course, MENCAP has done much to ease our problems – but the Society and local societies can do nothing until they know of parents and children in need of help and support. Only last week I met a father in senior management, whose daughter is fourteen months old, who had only the vaguest idea about MENCAP and who had changed jobs and geographical position in a desperate effort to move into a more supportive area. The help and advice he had received from his original doctor and social worker had been less than adequate – and this is a pattern repeated all too often in our welfare state. Parents are told about their child in the wrong manner by the wrong people and areas of family support services vary sharply from good – to adequate – to hopeless, depending on where you have the good fortune or the misfortune to live. Peripatetic teaching and instructions to parents as to how best to care, stimulate and teach their children in the early days are still virtually non-existent. Parents of the profoundly handicapped still imagine hospital is the only solution – but we know, with adequate local services, this is *not* so. Then, after education, what is the story? Sometimes no place is available in the Adult Training

Centre and your child is returned home to regress. Or ATCs with no special care units or further education facilities. And an ATC itself is not a means to an end. It is, often, the end itself. Not always, of course. There are Adult Training Centres, as in all things, good, bad and indifferent. But there is no watch-dog to maintain a strict monitoring of standards. And then, as age creeps on, often the fear that when you are no longer able to care for your offspring – hospital or some similar confinement may be the only solution.

All these problems we as a Society recognize and fight – and many more besides.

On Thursday I, and one or two colleagues, had an informal lunch with the Secretary of State for Health and Social Security, Patrick Jenkin, and the Under-Secretary of State for Health, Sir George Young. Both seem to me to be caring, thoughtful men and we can only hope within present financial restrictions they will be able to act upon all the areas we discussed.

So what had we discussed? In the first place, the 1971 White Paper "Better Services for the Mentally Handicapped" which, all agreed, had fallen well behind schedule. Furthermore, the attempt to co-ordinate Health and Social Security had not been successful because there was no single authority to provide services for mentally handicapped people and insufficient funds had been made available. Moreover, as long ago as 1957, the Royal Commission Report (which led to the Mental Health Act 1959) had recommended a shift in responsibility for mentally handicapped people from the hospitals to the community. I was able to tell the Ministers that twenty-three years later (remember, this meeting took place in 1980), this still had not been achieved – and even those people with a mental handicap who had been transferred to life in the community often faced totally inadequate support. I went on to trail the future development of the MENCAP Homes Foundation, asking for grant-aid for the early management requirements (we were given a few crumbs from the DHSS table) and ended by saying, "Above all, what we are looking for is action, arising from the 1971 White Paper, as to how to make existing services better. We have been patient long enough."

All this, I reported to the members. Seven years of hard slog went by before I retired – and still our patience was stretched to the limits. But we had had some successes along the way. I would like to take them one by one, year by year. Oh yes – and the failures as well . . . Here we go again.

1980 – or what's left of it

With only two months in which to operate before we all broke up for Christmas, there appeared to be little I could do except continue on my somewhat steep learning curve. I reckoned without the day-to-day pressures which build up in MENCAP so quickly, partly, I suspect, because parents, too, build up a head of steam over all the problems they encounter, and that steam needs a release valve which can act pretty smartly. The Secretary-General is that blow-hole.

On my very first afternoon in the office – after that gathering of the unexpectedly large numbers of senior staff, I read my first letter, which was nothing short of an ultimatum threatening UDI. The threat was from our North Wales members who no longer wished to be attached to their English colleagues in the North-West. Nor, for that matter, did they wish to be attached to their Welsh colleagues in the south either – for, as I soon discovered, the divide between the north and south of Wales is even greater than the one we experience in England. This was a problem which was to beset me for nearly two years. The reason the North Welsh were grouped with the North-West English was purely geographical. It was far easier to get from Cheshire to Clwyd than it was to get from Clwyd to Glamorgan, whilst Powys, Dyfed and Gwynedd bounced around uneasily on the periphery. Furthermore, the Welsh Office was soon to bring forth its Strategy for Mental Handicap in Wales, and this strategy would be looking for a coherent and cohesive cohort in the Principality. It was my job to effect that amalgamation. It involved a great deal of travelling, I can tell you, a great deal of diplomacy (buttering-up might describe the process more accurately) and any amount of bravery, for there is nothing more overwhelming than a Welshman when he's in full flood. But I survived. Everyone gradually saw the sense of a cohesive body and MENCAP YNG NGHYMRU (MENCAP in Wales) actually came into being in 1982. As you can imagine, MENCAP in Northern Ireland had to follow on soon after, but, not unnaturally, they stuck to English for their title.

English, written English, was very much to the fore when our elder son, Jamie, married Helen Middleton Murry on Saturday, November 8th, 1980. Helen and Jay had been together ever since university days, and now, as Jamie had a new job with BBC Radio, they decided to take the plunge and make the whole thing official. Helen's father is Colin Middleton Murry when he writes about *his* father, John Middleton Murry, or about John's first wife Katherine Mansfield, or about his own mother, Violet, John's second wife, but he is Richard Cowper when addressing himself to the science fiction scene. D. H. Lawrence, on learning of Colin's birth, declared "another John Middleton, ye gods!" but I suspect his two daughters, Helen and Jackie, had a far more loving upbringing than Colin ever encountered with his father. Anyway, we had a great party in Devon, where Helen's father and mother (Ruth) had a beautiful house in Diddisham, overlooking and owning quite an area of Dart Estuary mud. Fortunately that was one occasion when I didn't have to make a speech, which, in view of things to come, was quite a relief. Things to come, as far as Jamie and Helen were concerned, included our first grandson, Ben, followed two years later by his brother Jack. Super lads, both.

I had to make a speech, though, at the conference we held on December 10th, 1980, which had the provocative title "Better Services for the Mentally Handicapped – When?". Note, by the way, the mentally handicapped were still not people. The principal speaker was the very same Secretary of State for Health and Social Security, the Right Honourable Patrick Jenkin MP (now Lord Jenkin), I had praised at the Members' Meeting and I should mention that the original "Better Services" document had been published in 1971, so the "When?" referred to a nine-year delay in any action. Here's what I wrote to the Secretary of State when the conference was over:

> I would be less than honest if I did not express the deeply felt disappointment which was unanimously expressed by both parents and professionals, during and after your visit. This disappointment stemmed, possibly, from the numerous rumours which had emanated from the DHSS in various forms during the past weeks, but even if these straws in the wind had not been blowing around, I feel the delegates would still have expressed their unhappiness.
>
> Speakers in the afternoon session criticized the failure to give clear policy guidelines which would lead to improved services for mentally handicapped people, although there was a general welcome for the proposal of a Consultative Document to give greater flexibility for funding – but then the possibility of a lengthy delay in the preparation of this Document did not give rise to any optimism. It is obvious that

funding for "Better Services for the Mentally Handicapped" is the fundamental problem and we were dismayed to hear that the major step forward of transferring National Health Service assets to local authorities was still only a thought for the future. However, in the event of this progressive step taking place, we would still give voice to uncertainty, for you stated it was Government policy to allow local authorities complete freedom to organize their services. There is a general feeling that, even now, the quality of these services varies considerably from locality to locality. Nobody can deny that quite a number of authorities fail to reach even minimum standards. We believe that central Government has a duty to enforce stricter control and monitoring to ensure that services of the highest possible quality are provided for mentally handicapped people. If existing mandatory responsibilities are insufficient, then they should be strengthened.

We were pleased to hear of your conviction that all children should be removed from mental handicap hospitals as soon as possible. However, your "special offer" of £1 million over four years to match on a £1 for £1 basis voluntary funds raised specifically for local projects to help mentally handicapped children out of hospitals, was greeted with incredulity and heavily criticized.

Is the Government now saying that parents and friends must raise the money to provide residential homes for their children who cannot be returned to the family home? Is the £1 million incentive a disguised change of policy and a further erosion of the welfare state which hits hardest at the most vulnerable groups? What will this "special offer" provide over four years? What about the real issues and implications? Who will be responsible for the running costs, staffing and management of any of the local projects? Are parents expected to do it? Where is the justice in a system which says it is the local authorities' mandatory responsibility, but they are now apparently being blatantly encouraged to ignore this?

Even now, parents report there has been a serious deterioration in family support services in many areas and those present at the conference found little in your speech to alleviate their fears for the future.

We will send you a copy of the full transcript of the day's proceedings early in the New Year, but, because of the depth of feeling expressed, I felt it was necessary to inform you as soon as possible.

On a personal note I would like to thank you for your obvious interest and concern for the welfare of mentally handicapped people and believe that you would do far more if only times were different. Unfortunately, this generosity of spirit is not easy to share with parents of mentally handicapped people who are often in desperate need.

It would indeed be a sad reflection on society if in 1990 we are still asking the question, "Better Services for the Mentally Handicapped – When?"

I think you'll agree that the letter to the Secretary of State was couched in somewhat different terms to the description of my meeting with him which I gave to the members in October. It is amazing what two months can do when you are actually at the coal-face. All manner of attitudes change, particularly those affecting your social conscience – and I should know. After all, I was once a Bevin Boy.

But at last we had it in an official speech and then in writing. Hospitals were not suitable places for children with a mental handicap and at least 15,000 adults shouldn't be there either. But the £1 for £1 scheme was, as predicted, a disastrous idea. After centuries of neglect, why should it be left to the voluntary agencies to get the Government of the day off the hook, when it came to providing accommodation? For generations, hospitals had been the only alternative offered to parents when they wished to place their mentally handicapped children in care. Now to dole out a few measly pounds to try and right a fearful wrong was adding insult to grievous injury. It took the Department years to get rid of that microscopic million. No one could – or would – come up with schemes to match the criteria. But no one tried very hard, either.

My speech at that December conference – on the Government's consultative paper on the structure and management of the NHS (nothing changes) – was entitled "People First", but I had already latched on to the fact that I would be called upon to make many, many more perorations in the years ahead. On some occasions I was matching the output of leading politicians at the hustings, making as many as three and four speeches a day. Appearances on television and radio proliferated, too, as did press calls, of one nature or another. For instance, on November 17th, 1980, I was briefed to welcome an "assembled audience of academics" and at the same time enjoined to make an amusing speech to the press whilst launching the "Certificate in the Further Education and Training of Mentally Handicapped People". After this mutually exclusive brief, I then had to go on to make a speech entitled "The Work Ethic Questioned". Not bad for a non-academic ex-actor-manager who had been the chief executive of MENCAP for only five weeks. It certainly kept me on the hop. But it didn't make too many column inches, either, nor encourage laughs like I used to get back at the Whitehall. But then, you can't have everything as I was to find out, on the very first Monday in January 1981.

January 5th was the date, just after we'd settled into the office again following these interminable Christmas/New Year holidays, when I met the Trustees of Pirates Spring for lunch. I'd better explain that Pirates Spring had originally been purchased by the Society, way back in the 1960s, to provide a holiday home for people with a mental handicap, but now that those same people were going away, in ever-increasing numbers, to ordinary holiday places, the need for such an institution had become a thing of the past. So Pirates Spring had been turned into a home for children who had behavioural problems, on top of their mental handicap. All very laudable, but the house was too big, too dilapidated and too exposed to the southeast coast elements.

Thus, the Trustees had joined me for lunch (gala pie and salad) in my office to discuss what could be done and, perhaps most important of all, who would relieve us of this tiresome building. We were not too sanguine. It was nothing to do with the gala pie.

Actually, gala pie (or ham or cold chicken) and salad became my staple lunchtime diet during my seven years at MENCAP. All manner of folk trooped into my office over those years to enjoy a dry sherry, white wine or orange juice, plus the inevitable pie, meat and lettuce. Benefactors, Cabinet Ministers, Under-Secretaries of State, Charity Directors, Directors of Social Services, Chief Police Officers, the DHSS Mental Handicap Client Group, doctors, writers, editors, gossip columnists, friends, enemies et al – all enjoyed the frugal delights of my table and great were the rewards therein. Double Diamond may work wonders – gala pie does even better.

Two who lunched with me once were John Profumo and his wife, Valerie Hobson. Lest you think I am straying too far from Pirates Spring, you should know that Valerie

Hobson had opened the place, when it became our holiday home, in July 1963. I know, because I was there in my capacity, at that time, as Chairman of the Special Functions Committee. It was a singularly brave move on Valerie's part, because it was her first public appearance since the scandal which had engulfed her, and her family, the previous year. It was at that opening that I came to recognize the expression "hounded by the media", for that is what happened to Valerie Hobson – Mrs Profumo – on that day. She was extremely courageous and only prepared to expose herself to such indignities because of her mentally handicapped son. Indeed, she had been one of the earliest supporters of the Association of Parents of Backward Children, long before I "confessed" to my involvement in Central Hall.

But Pirates Spring had outlived its useful life, and we, as a Society, could be said to be housing young people and children in totally inappropriate accommodation. We decided to sell the place (God knows how we would find a buyer) and move the residents to ordinary housing in Folkestone. We succeeded. Exactly one year from that lunch, all the youngsters were enjoying the delights of spacious homes, in a very up-market road, and the residents of Folkestone (the neighbours, anyway) providing support and understanding beyond our wildest dreams. So much for the genteel, upper-class image of our watering places. Well, that's what I thought at the time. Teignmouth, in Devon, was to prove me wrong a year or two later.

But hope for disabled people was at hand, generally, in 1981. It was the International Year of Disabled People (IYDP) and for the first time, as far as I'm aware, those who were mentally handicapped were bracketed along with all others who were physically or sensorially disabled. At last we had come out of the ghetto and, as Secretary-General of MENCAP, I sat down at the same conference tables as the Directors of RADAR (Disabled), RNID (Deaf), RNIB (Blind), plus all the others, without feeling the least bit inferior. Not that I felt inferior, anyway, but you know what I mean.

A great deal of the credit for the rapport achieved in this country during IYDP must got to the President, Lord Snowdon, and the Chairman, the late Sir Christopher Aston. Kit Aston, who was knighted by the Queen during his year of office when his terminal illness, cancer, was disclosed, displayed an untiring devotion to the task in hand, even from his hospital bed. Indeed, just before he died, he announced the formation of the Snowdon Council to continue the work begun by all concerned during IYDP and also his positive plans for the future, including bringing together large charity organizations which, in the past, tended to work independently.

Alas, he died, and the Snowdon Council met once and floundered. Admittedly, we later foregathered at Buckingham Palace, under the chairmanship of the Prince of Wales, but nothing came of it. However, the Prince continued with his Advisory Group on Disability, whilst some of us concerned with the world of mental handicap (MENCAP, MIND, Barnardo's and the Spastics Society, plus many others) came together to form the Independent Development Council for people with a mental handicap (IDC) and this group continues to this day. I had the honour to be its first Chairman for five years – but now I am retired my successor serves on the Council. One day he'll be Chairman, too, if it continues. Fashions change.

Early in 1981, I met with the Secretary of State for Education, Mark Carlisle, along with some of my colleagues, including our Chairman, Lord Renton. We had gone to press on him a number of important clauses for the forthcoming Education Bill and, to our great delight, we were largely successful. I found the Secretary of State to be a thoughtful man, who listened closely to our arguments and, in the event, was swayed by our logic. His successor, Sir Keith Joseph, seemed an odd sort of cove when we went to meet him at a later date, whilst *his* successor, Kenneth Baker, exuded a politician's over-confidence which I, personally, found rather off-putting. I'm told he's the funniest man in the Cabinet. Certainly his Education Reform Bill, as it stands at the moment, is hardly a load of laughs. It could have "grave effects on children and young people with special educational needs". So said our President, Lord Allen, in the House of Lords in April 1988.

Mark Carlisle didn't survive too long at Education, but long enough to ensure the new Act determined that appropriate education and training would be given to mentally handicapped children from the moment of diagnosis, and that a duty would be placed on health authorities to provide parents with information about voluntary organizations likely to be of assistance, once the child's handicap had been recognized. A great advance on the negative stance which greeted me when I went to see Enoch Powell about the same matter, way back in 1963. Mr Powell was then Minister for Health and confronted me with a load of statistics which proved absolutely nothing. Certainly, I was hard put to discern any charity towards us in his make-up. If I may quote a certain John Boyle O'Reilly: "The organized charity, scrimped and iced, in the name of a cautious, statistical Christ."

That meeting with Mark Carlisle was in February. In March I had another encounter which was to prove of the greatest importance to those who are profundly and multiply handicapped. It was all rather odd. In the first place, I had travelled to Birmingham for a two-day stay, so the television cameras from Pebble Mill could follow me around, to do a half-hour profile of me at my new work. All manner of activities had been laid on, including – can you believe? – a boxing evening for MENCAP at the

Albany Hotel. I was to be filmed making a speech from the boxing ring – before the bouts – encouraging the punters to put their hands deep into their pockets for our cause. But just before I went on, someone from the BBC sidled up to me and asked how I could moralize upon mental handicap from a boxing ring, whose usual occupancy led to brain damage. Quite right, of course, and it made my task even harder. If you've ever tried to address an audience sitting on all four sides of you, you'll know how difficult that is. If you have also had the ground cut from under your feet ... and you are appearing on telly ... as well as trying to get laughs – all at the same time, you will know it is impossible. But I did my best.

I did my best, also, when an interview was staged for Pebble Mill with various parents. One mother, Mary McCormack, a journalist, asked me what MENCAP was doing for those who, like her child, were so grievously handicapped, having both a profound mental handicap and additional multiple impairments, including extreme physical disabilities. I had to be honest and confess that I suspected we were doing very little – never a good thing to have to admit in a television programme showing how wonderful you are supposed to be – and promised to look into it. On my return to London I did, and discovered that apart from a residential experiment in Slough some years before, we had more or less abandoned the problem. It had to be addressed anew and some three years later our Profound Retardation and Multiple Handicap Project got off the ground. Not without difficulty, for the money for the Project had to be raised from new sources and a skeleton staff had to be recruited. However, with perseverance, the whole thing came together and is now housed in Piper Hill School in Manchester, with my old PA Loretto Lambe as the Co-ordinator and Dr James Hogg, the Deputy Director of the Hester Adrian Research Centre (part of Manchester University), as the Consultant, plus a secretary, Della Pryke, who, apart from working so hard for the Project, also found time to decipher my indecipherable writing and type the manuscript for this book. Della has now moved on, so who will type my next?

My grateful thanks to them and others, mainly volunteers, for their dedicated work will, in time, transform the lives of those who so often are left, as adults, to drift into oblivion, cared for by their parents with little or no help from the state and with a desperate, loving devotion as their only resource. I pray our PRMH scheme will change all that.

As if to underline the difficulties encountered by all parents of mentally handicapped children the MENCAP Week Conference, held in June, was entitled "Right from the Start '81", to develop further the excellent report which had been published in 1975, under the same title, and written by Ms Bernie Spain and Dr Guy Wigley. The conference came about as a direct result of parental pressure, for there was considerable feeling that the age-old problems facing parents of newly born, or newly diagnosed, mentally handicapped children were (and are) still considerable. The opening address, by Professor Joan Bicknell – Chair of Psychiatry of Mental Handicap, St George's Hospital Medical School, University of London, to give Joan her full title – underlined this:

It was a common experience ten years ago for families to tell us that from the moment of diagnosis at birth or in childhood, very little was offered until the formalities of schooling were to be decided upon. Now when we see younger parents with the youngest generation of mentally handicapped children, we hear of a different complaint; they receive a mass of uncoordinated information from a whole variety of people, none of whom have adequate links with other workers involved with that family. Today the greatest

162

challenge for us to get the service "right" is to co-ordinate the many people involved.

Well, at least it seemed that, at long last, considerable interest was being taken in mental handicap and, truthfully, I think it is. But, as Joan stressed, interest does not necessarily lead to first-class support and succour:

Much work remains to be done on the various crisis points in the life of a mentally handicapped person; many of these, sadly, are inflicted by the services we create and by the way society responds to handicapped people. While the birth of the handicapped child is a major life event for everyone involved, so also may be the choice of school, in particular if it is the school the parents least want. School leaving may be a life event if the adult services are inadequate, so also may be dawning sexuality if there has been inadequate education on the management of sexual drive for both the mentally handicapped person and his or her caregivers.

Joan must have been gazing at the tea-leaves over that last point. It was to be my penultimate battle, before retiring from MENCAP in October 1987. The case, which caused such a furore, was over the sterilization of Jeanette, when a bunch of elderly men – the Law Lords – decided that her sexual drive could best be curtailed by tying off her Fallopian tubes rather than attempting to solve this life event by alternative means. But more of this anon.

Let us return to Professor Bicknell's final statement, which seems to underline, even more, the point I have just made:

Remember that mentally handicapped people are not sick but vulnerable, partly because of their own deficits, but also because of how society responds to them and attempts to care for them. Our services must have the philosophy that encourages skills, minimizes deficits of the handicapped person, but that does not perpetuate the "sickness' model of care.

Of course, many other wise words were spoken by a variety of contributors (including Mrs Linda Wonnacott, a parent from the Southend and District Society of MENCAP, who spoke most movingly about the early support which could be given by others who had borne a handicapped child), but Joan Bicknell seemed to sum it all up in her closing line:

For the whole life span, help must be at hand when needed, help that is not a "put down' but help that uplifts the family, including the handicapped member, who then find their own inner strengths to help themselves.

Hurrah for Joan Bicknell, first Professor of Mental Handicap and now, thankfully, one among . . . well, not many, but quite a few.

The dignity accorded to mentally handicapped people by Joan, and others, contrasted starkly with the lack as illustrated on television in an ATV (now Central) documentary by Nigel Evans, *Silent Minority*, which was transmitted in July. It purported to show life in a large mental handicap hospital, St Lawrence's at Caterham, and was quite horrifying. Unfortunately, it was soon alleged that a number of scenes had been, as it were, stage managed, so the impact of the documentary was somewhat diminished. One scene showed a young man tied to a post for hours on end, whilst another focused on a line of naked shivering men, crouched in their wheelchairs, waiting for the ablutions. It was ghastly, but also questionable as to whether the Great British Public would stay tuned to such a catalogue of unpalatable pictures. In the event, enough did, and the press took a great interest in the programme. There were parents' meetings, Friends' meetings, and a great deal of abuse was hurled back and forth. All of us who had offspring in any mental handicap hospital, no matter how good or bad, were made to feel inadequate and inhuman for allowing our children to be abused so appallingly in such places. There was no let-up for several weeks and then, as is so often the case, the whole thing went away and the press concentrated on another scandal. We were left feeling somewhat battered and questioning whether, in fact, *Silent Minority* had achieved its original purpose and made that same Great British Public rise up in their thousands to demand the closure of long-stay hospitals. Unfortunately, they seemed to be singularly disinterested and the long slog to make community care a compassionate reality continued.

The next two stories to hit the headlines were both about mental handicap in general and Down's syndrome in particular. The first concerned a newly born Down's baby, delivered in Hammersmith hospital, who was suffering from duodenal atresia (a blockage of the small intestine) and whose parents were refusing permission for the comparatively simple life-saving operation to be performed. The local Director of Social Services, David Plank, intervened, the child was made a ward of court, the operation was performed and the baby placed in care, eventually returning to her parents.

The second story concerned a well respected paediatrician, Dr Leonard Arthur, who, at the instigation of the pressure group LIFE, faced a charge of attempted murder of a Down's syndrome neonate. The case was heard at Leicester Crown Court, Dr Arthur was acquitted without a stain on his character, and returned to work. Unfortunately, he died soon afterwards from a brain tumour. From my point of view, as Secretary-General of MENCAP, both cases had many implications.

In the first place, I wrote this letter to the *Observer*.

The reference to Down's syndrome babies "even at their best being severely handicapped" and to the fact that Mr George Carman QC had stated they are "a time bomb of infection and defects" only serves to perpetuate the unbalanced views of Down's syndrome which dominated reports emanating from the recent trial of Dr Leonard Arthur. The degree of handicap among Down's children at birth varies enormously and this is not always apparent at the time. What is a fact is that thousands of families have successfully coped, very often with little support, in bringing up Down's syndrome children who are able to lead fulfilling and complete lives. Perhaps, if we all took opportunities to meet and talk to Down's syndrome people about our own feelings and attitudes, we would understand more clearly that they do, indeed, have a valuable and positive contribution to make in a caring society.

And, in the second place, I asked for a debate in our National Council and, subsequently, at our half-yearly Members' Meeting – and, as a result of these discussions, I was able to compose the following statement which was issued, by MENCAP, at the end of October 1981:

In recent times the advance of medical science has given parents of a mentally handicapped child a choice as to whether or not life-support systems are to be used or a life-giving operation is to be performed on that child. To help parents in reaching this agonizing decision every support and counselling must be offered by the medical, paramedical and social services. However, MENCAP sees it as vital that other experienced parents of mentally handicapped children are involved in this counselling process for only they know, at first hand, the joys and sorrows as well as the practical problems ahead. If, after all this consultation, the parents concerned still feel unable to give permission for a life-saving operation to be performed on their mentally handicapped child, then a procedure similar to that carried out in the recent "Hammersmith case" should apply, with the full responsibility for the child's future being assumed by the local authority concerned.

Clearly, any legal action of this nature must be backed by the best medical advice possible as to whether, in fact, the operation is medically possible and is likely to have a successful outcome. Also, parents faced with a decision concerning the quality of life for their child in the years ahead should be assured that all services provided for mentally handicapped children, adults and their families are of a uniformly high standard throughout the country and available right from the start. MENCAP notes, unhappily, that this is certainly not the case at the present time.

It is an unfortunate fact that many medical and paramedical staff are only vaguely aware of such services as do exist and, therefore, the training of *all* professions having contact with, or having responsibilities to, mentally handicapped children and their parents should include positive aspects of the potential development of all handicapped children, together with the total range of education and training facilities available. In addition, such professional training and experience should ensure that everybody responsible for the welfare of mothers and their children should be sensitive to the manner in which parents are informed that a child has been diagnosed as being mentally handicapped and that parents should be given guidance as to the services which are available to them and their mentally handicapped child, such guidance to include the parental input referred to above.

Further, MENCAP is conscious that many school children, who will become parents, are unaware of the possibilities of giving birth to a mentally handicapped child. With this in mind it is urged that those involved in education should create opportunities for discussion and teaching so that pupils understand, and are sympathetic to the problem.

MENCAP, the Royal Society for Mentally Handicapped Children and Adults, reiterates its objectives which are:

"To increase public awareness and understanding of the problems of mentally handicapped people so as to secure provision for them commensurate with their needs" and offers support for all mentally handicapped people, no matter how severe their handicap. Mentally handicapped people have rights equal to every other citizen in accordance with the principles of the United Nations Charter of Human Rights. In addition, the law of the land must pertain in all decisions regarding life and death.

Finally, MENCAP believes that ante-natal screening, including amniocentesis, should be made available to every mother-to-be who desires it. The termination of a pregnancy, after counselling and in accordance with the law, is a decision entirely for the parents concerned. In this respect, genetic counselling should be more readily available for parents-to-be who are at risk. Furthermore, research into the causes of mental handicap is of the utmost importance. Great stress should be placed on the *prevention* of the problem before this becomes an issue for some and a tragedy for others.

This view on amniocentesis, and the right of parents to decide the outcome after the diagnosis of a damaged foetus, was again upheld by MENCAP's National Council just after I retired and was debated, once more, because of the David Alton Private Member's Bill to reduce the abortion time-limit. People often ask me how I can reconcile the defence of the newly born baby in the Hammersmith case and the right to abort at an earlier stage, as in our statement. I reply that like so many other parents, we would not wish such a tragic disablement on any of our children, but once they are born, we will fight tooth and nail to ensure the best possible quality of life for them. I'm sorry if that seems a contradiction in terms, but there it is.

One final point. The case of Dr Arthur was all the more poignant, for he had married the great-granddaughter of the man who gave his name to Down's syndrome, Dr John Langdon-Down himself.

A far happier occasion, for all concerned, was the church service which was held at the beginning of Mental Handicap Week (now MENCAP Week) in St Martin-in-the-Fields, Trafalgar Square, towards the end of June. Apart from the vicar, Austen Williams, and the Crouch End Salvation Army Band, the entire service was conducted by people with a mental handicap from the London Region. It was both moving and inspiring and, in the words of Neville Thompson, soon to be MENCAP's Treasurer, "it recharged my batteries for the months ahead." A year or two later, the service moved to St Lawrence Jewry, next to Guildhall, in the City, when the occasion was conducted by the Reverend Basil Watson. When MENCAP achieved its fortieth anniversary in 1986, the BBC televised the event and I cannot believe there has ever been a more emotionally charged occasion shown on our screens in the middle of Sunday morning, other than the Cenotaph Remembrance Day Service.

I was not too keen to perform my next duty on that June Sunday afternoon in 1981. I had to make a speech from the base of Nelson's Column in Trafalgar Square. My predecessor had started this custom some years before, but now the novelty had worn off and the only people who came to listen were coachloads from the church service (who knew, at first hand, all the problems they were facing), a number of disinterested foreigners who resented being interrupted in their task of feeding the pigeons, a handful of skinheads who had come in the hope of trouble and a dozen or so drunks who lay around the plinth in various comatose positions, snoring loudly. It was anything but uplifting and my speech, too, fell into the same category. You see, you're supposed to make a political speech in Trafalgar Square – that's why you are permitted to use the place – but my political utterances had to be carefully culled for any political expression, with a large "P", which might offend against our charitable status. The result was a neutered mouse of a declaration – which was not worth anyone's time and trouble. I suffered this Trafalgar Square indignity for one more year only, and then settled for the church service as the most meaningful way of showing what people with a mental handicap could do, if they were only given half a chance, and spent many hours chasing up the BBC to make the eventual television broadcast in 1986 a reality.

I suppose you could say that our gatherings on the first Sunday in MENCAP Week were really social occasions which gained acceptance for our cause.

Indeed, many social occasions did – and do – so I think I might as well follow *The Times* and the *Daily Telegraph* and head this next section:

Court and Social
1981

– or if you prefer the more egalitarian *Independent:*

The Gazette
1981

CLARENCE HOUSE, March 24th: The Secretary-General of MENCAP, Mr Brian Rix, attended upon Sir Martin Gilliatt, the Private Secretary to Royal Patron, HM Queen Elizabeth The Queen Mother.

The meeting was to discuss a possible visit by Her Majesty later in the year to open our new national headquarters in Golden Lane. I found Sir Martin, by the way, to be an absolutely charming man, not dissimilar to his old school friend Brian Johnston of BBC fame, and also discovered he is an inveterate "angel", always backing West End productions. Regrettably I had no idea of this when I was at the Whitehall, which is the nearest theatre to Clarence House, so never had such an unlikely investor to add to my list of names. Never mind, Sir Martin has invested quite a lot of his time and energy for MENCAP in a different way, and for this we are very grateful.

ST PAUL'S CATHEDRAL, April 12th: The marriage took place yesterday in the Chapel of the Order of the British Empire, in the Crypt of St Paul's Cathedral, of Mr Jonathan James Edward Coy, younger son of Dr Peter Coy and Mrs Elizabeth Coy, to Louisa MacGregor Rix, younger daughter of Mr and Mrs Brian Rix. The bride was given in marriage by her father and Mr Christopher Coy was the best man.

A reception was held at the Warehouse Restaurant, St Katharine's Dock and the honeymoon was one night at Claridge's. Jonathan was on tour playing Dick Dudgeon in Shaw's *The Devil's Disciple*, whilst Louisa was appearing at the National Theatre as Margaret in *Much Ado About Nothing* and Charlotte in *Don Juan* – so parting was soon to be such sweet sorrow which, unfortunately, could not lead to Louisa following Juliet's words "that I shall say good-night till it be morrow". The tour went on for months and the newly married couple had to cope with the misery of parting for long periods. I speak from personal experience. Newcastle and Edinburgh are an awful long way from home – particularly if your home's in London. Anyway, their marriage survived, and they are now the proud parents of two super kids, Charlotte and Jolyon. There speaks a proud grandfather for you!

You may wonder why the wedding took place in the Crypt of St Paul's. The CBE I had received in 1977 allowed me the privilege of my children being married and grandchildren being christened there. As it turned out, Louisa was the only one to take advantage of the opportunity, but it was a great event, several months before an even greater one in the same building when the Prince and Princess of Wales were married. At their wedding, Sacrist and Minor Canon the Reverend Michael Moxon sang a solo, but at Louisa and Jonathan's he officiated as the Vicar performing the marriage ceremony.

If all this sounds a bit high-flown, I can assure you that everything became a little less inhibited when we moved to the Warehouse for the reception. There the volunteer working the video camera became so paralytic on champagne that he took several hundred feet of the floor, was completely out of focus for the speeches and concentrated the camera on his girlfriend, instead of the bride and groom, as they left the reception. A complete stranger who had gate-crashed the event from start to finish (each family thought she was a guest of the other side), took our hired limousine away at the end of the afternoon and Elspet and I, in all our finery, had to hail a cab to take us home. A somewhat anti-climactic end to a perfect day, especially as I had no money on me and had to rush into the house to grab my cheque-book to pay the driver. I felt an absolute berk. The father of the bride who had just married in St Paul's returning home in a tatty old black cab. I suppose I'd have felt an even bigger Charlie on a bus.

DINNER – DUBLIN, May 7th: The Secretary-General of MENCAP will attend a meeting, followed by dinner, in Dublin this evening to address parents in the Irish Republic who have mentally handicapped children.

Well, that was the plan, but the date happened to coincide with the funeral of the hunger striker, Bobby Sands, so things were changed somewhat. In the first place, I was met at the airport by security men who took me round the city's outskirts so as to avoid a demonstration in the centre. I was driven into an underground car park, up in a lift to the ground floor, and ushered into a room with about 350 awaiting to hear my words. As soon as my speech was over, instead of a leisurely dinner, I was hustled into the lift once more, down to the basement and around the Dublin periphery, back to the airport. No one was taking any risks with a well-known Englishman in Dublin that night, even though I had only come to talk to fellow parents about our mutual problem, mental handicap. I was back in London, all within the space of about five hours. The original plan was to drive me from Dublin to Belfast after that dinner, but no one was taking any chances in that direction. So it was Barnes, London, for a night's fitful sleep and then back to Heathrow for the flight to Belfast the next morning. You can imagine the security there, too, especially as that evening I was attending a fund-raising ball where an army band was playing, which put eveyone's teeth on edge. Not the playing, which was excellent, but the security risk of a load of bandsmen in a soft target area. All went well on that night, but it was tragically different for many bandsmen in Regent's Park only a few months later, when the IRA blew up the bandstand.

FUNDAMENTAL FROLICS. June 1st: A performance took place this evening at the Apollo Victoria in aid of the Royal Society for Mentally Handicapped Children and Adults' rural training centre in Somerset. Demand for places at Lufton is greatly in excess of those available and the money raised (£40,000) will be used to finance a project to provide further accommodation at Lufton so that more young people will benefit from the experience of living and training there. Those taking part included: Jon Anderson, Rowan Atkinson, Elvis Costello, 20th Century Coyote, Ian Dury, Chas and Dave, Neil Innes, Griff Rhys Jones, Chris Langham, Alan Price, Nico Ramsden, Alexei Sayle, Mel Smith, Pamela Stephenson and the SFX Band.

Quite a cast, I'm sure you will agree, largely organized by MENCAP's Jane Tewson (who went on to form Charity Projects), Jane Charlton and Nico Ramsden, musician son of Dennis and Christine Ramsden, who were such friends at the Whitehall and the Garrick many years before. I think I should mention that Mel Smith seemed to be around a lot of the time, too – in fact he directed the show with Nico – and to all those artists and organizers we owe a great zonking vote of thanks. A year or two later, Lufton was to receive another financial boost – this time from the Country Landowners' Association – but perhaps that's more understandable than a load of pop artists and comedians working their socks off in the extremely urban vicinity of Victoria. But to all – our gratitude.

> 100 GUINEA CLUB, Dinner, June 3rd: A dinner of the 100 Guinea Club was held last night at the Dorchester Hotel. Among those present were the founders, Mr Ronald Gerard, Mr Raphael Djanogly and Mr David Evans – with Captain Anthony Swainson, OBE, RN, the organizer. Also present were Mr and Mrs Brian Rix of the Friends of Normansfield. This function raised £18,000 to enable the Friends to reinstate riding for those people with a mental handicap resident at Normansfield. The Chairman of Friends thanked all who attended for their generosity – for each had paid 100 guineas for the privilege.

When Raphael and Ronald and Tony and others came to present the cheque to me some time later, at a lunch at MENCAP, the inevitable gala pie and ham was produced, but as three of my guests weren't too keen on pork, I hurriedly poured out a few more sherries and sent my secretaries scuttling out for more acceptable food from Ravellos, the local Italian restaurant. They duly obliged and rushed back with – wait for it – shellfish, in the shape of crabs' claws. By the time we staggered to the table – now sprouting chicken wings – I reckon we had got through enough fortified wine to make such sensitivity on my part an absolute nonsense. But I received the cheque, though, with gratitude; and riding goes on this day at Normansfield for all those who enjoy it.

INSTITUTE OF HEALTH SERVICE ADMINISTRA-TORS, Norwich, June 5th: A meeting of the above

Institute took place in Norwich yesterday. The principal speaker at the afternoon session was Brian Rix, Secretary-General of MENCAP.

And that, really, is all I can say about that. However, this visit was to have a profound effect on an idea which I had been nursing ever since I knew I was joining MENCAP as its chief executive. It had always seemed to me that MENCAP's resources were stretched to the utmost and that grant-aiding of interesting projects connected with mental handicap was quite beyond its capabilities. I had therefore devised the idea of the MENCAP City Foundation, believing that, as MENCAP was on the edge of the Square Mile, we should be able to interest a number of businessmen and businesses in our scheme. One idea I had was to form an Investment Trust (which other charities had done) to provide the initial finance. And that was the point I had reached when I boarded the train at Liverpool Street to make the journey to Norwich.

We departed at 11.30 a.m., and I installed myself in the restaurant car to await food. A few minutes later a BRPRO (a British Rail Public Relations Operative) went through the train, encouraging all and sundry to partake of a new, experimental £2 BR luncheon which, in reality, seemed to be a re-hash of breakfast, but at a quarter of the price. Stoically I ordered my mixed grill and sat back to await events. Suddenly a pretty young woman, accompanied by a City-suited gent with a loud English voice came roaring in to take advantage of the cut-price nosh. It soon became clear that my friend with the loud voice really didn't know his female companion, but had just attached himself to her using the eggs, bacon, liver, sausage, sauté potatoes, fried bread, tomatoes and mushrooms as a pretty thin excuse. Certainly thinner than we would be, after such a lunch. Anyway, when the smacking of lips and clattering of plates had died down, the train was approaching Ipswich and our attractive young lady decided to get off – after paying her £2, of course – leaving only City gent and BR (Brian Rix) aboard BR (British Rail) – well the restaurant car, anyway.

City gent, being a friendly cove and having recognized me, decided to join me for coffee, which was extra, by the way, and nearly as expensive as the lunch. It soon transpired he was a financial consultant and ran his own financial services company, most successfully, in Norwich. Cards were exchanged and I found I was speaking to Michael Wynne-Parker, whose very English voice has never become any quieter (maybe that's because he's a Governor of the English Speaking Union), but who is now a very good friend, not only to Elspet and me, but also MENCAP too. We soon turned to the subject of the MENCAP City Foundation and the idea of an Investment Trust. My newly found friend was somewhat dubious and felt there might be a more unusual way of raising funds. Had I thought about a Unit Trust? "Well, no," I said, "has anyone?" "Not as far as I know," was his reply and by the time we had reached Norwich, Michael had promised to set up a meeting at one of his many clubs in London with another friend, and an expert on the Unit Trust scheme, Edward Myatt – then the Chairman of Intel Ltd. As good as his promise, Michael arranged the meeting and we were off to a flying start.

The scheme we devised was for a Unit Trust to be formed in the ordinary way, with investors invited to keep any capital growth from their units, but to covenant their income to the MENCAP City Foundation, which was yet to be formed. Of course, this required permission from all and sundry, including the Department of Trade and Industry, as well as the Inland Revenue. We were lucky in our advisers though, particularly Charles Scanlan of solicitors Simmons and Simmons and Gordon Hearne of our Unit Trust Trustee, Coutts and Co. Eventually all was agreed and the Board of the MENCAP Unit Trust came together for the first time, under the chairmanship of Edward Myatt. My goodness, we were an ecumenical lot: David Hopkinson, Chairman of M & G Investment Managers Ltd; Mark Weinberg, Managing Director of Hambro Life; Michael Wynne-Parker (who had recovered from his lunch) of Wynne-Parker Financial Services; Clive Fenn-Smith, Managing Director of Barclays Unicorn Group Ltd; David Rothenberg, a partner in accountants Blick Rothenberg and Noble (and son of one of MENCAP's most generous benefactors, Helmut Rothenberg); Neville Thompson, Treasurer of MENCAP, and me. It was agreed that we had to raise money for the launch and I'm happy to record that this was made available through the generosity of Mark Weinberg (now Sir Mark of Allied Dunbar) and our bankers, Barclays. And so it came to pass that nearly two years after that fateful fatty train journey the, then, Chancellor of the Exchequer, Sir Geoffrey Howe, launched the MENCAP Unit Trust for us. There was only one snag. He launched it on the day the Argentines invaded the Falklands. The media had eyes for little else and we nearly sank as surely as the *Belgrano,* but, unlike that unhappy ship, we lived to fight another day.

The Unit Trust performed extremely well for the next four years under the expert guidance of John Allard of M & G. Investors did well but, unfortunately, were not too great in numbers. Edward Myatt and I went to see Hoppy – David Hopkinson CBE – just before his retirement, once more to seek his advice. The answer he proposed was startlingly simple. Expand. Bring in other charities so that the total fund will grow considerably. And that's exactly what we did and in June 1987 the United Charities Unit Trust, embracing Dr Barnardo's, the Country Landowners' Association, the English Speaking Union, Guide Dogs for the Blind, the Royal Society for the Protection of Birds and, of course, the MENCAP City

Foundation, was launched. We again chose a lousy opening date with astounding percipience. The 1987 general election was announced and instead of being relaunched by the Chancellor of the Exchequer, yet again (Nigel Lawson this time), we received his understudy, First Secretary to the Treasury, John MacGregor – who did his best in the circumstances. But of course the press were all up the road in Downing Street. Ah me! Again, we survived and now the fund is approaching very respectable figures, with all six charities benefiting individually, according to the amount that is covenanted to each by their own supporters.

So, as far as Michael Wynne-Parker and I are concerned, the cholesterol was worth it after all. We don't even begrudge the £2 we each had to fork out for the BR lunch. If we'd met at breakfast it would have cost four times as much.

SHERIFF'S LUNCHEON AT THE OLD BAILEY,
July 13th: A luncheon was held at the Old Bailey yesterday at which the Secretary-General of MENCAP joined Her Majesty's judges as guests of the Sheriffs of the City of London.

Actually, it turned out to be shepherd's pie and apple tart, just like being at school, but enjoyable all the same. I missed the tomato ketchup though. Apart from the pleasure of indulging in conversation with many of the best legal minds in the country (well, that's what I'm told) I was also able to start a dialogue with one of the Sheriffs, Anthony Jolliffe, who would become London's Lord Mayor the following year. Our conversation turned to the MENCAP City Foundation and before many weeks were out we had agreed that if he became Lord Mayor, as was likely, according to the usual run of things, he would certainly embrace the Foundation as the main recipient of his year's appeal. And so it came to pass. Thank you, Tony, Sir Anthony Jolliffe, for making the MENCAP City Foundation a reality. Many people with a mental handicap have reason to thank you too (not forgetting our original Governors, Lord Allen, Neville Thompson, Michael Wynne-Parker, Edward Myatt, Paul Newall, Helmut Rothenberg, the late Roger Paul, oh, and me), for you made our original capital base secure and now, with another charitable Trust, represented by Jock Nangle, plus the income from the Unit Trust, we are able to be pretty generous with our grants. It's amazing what a mixed grill and a shepherd's pie can lead to . . . apart from obesity. *O tempora, O mores!* O my gala pie!

THE WEDDING OF HRH THE PRINCE OF WALES TO LADY DIANA SPENCER, July 29th: Last evening The Queen, Prince Philip, Prince Charles and members of the Royal Family attended a fireworks display in Hyde Park. A signal was given for a chain of beacons to be lit from one end of the country to the other in celebration of the happy occasion. A loyal message was conveyed by the Secretary-General of MENCAP, Mr Brian Rix, via a television link-up from Windsor Great Park. Similar messages were conveyed from other parts of the country.

Well that says it all, doesn't it? Quite exciting though.

BUCKINGHAM PALACE, September 12th: Her Majesty Queen Elizabeth has graciously commanded that the Society be known as the Royal Society for Mentally Handicapped Children and Adults.

What a wonderful pat on the back for all our members in that International Year of Disabled People. One more recognition of the status of MENCAP – but also a marvel-lous tribute to those many thousands of parents and helpers who had struggled for so long to achieve the slightest glimmerings of recognition. And now here we were, a Royal Society. Absolutely splendid!

> ROYAL WEDDING FUND, September 21st: It was announced today that, as a result of the sale of the official Royal Wedding programmes and other means, approximately £1 million has been raised for distri-bution to worthy causes. The fund will be adminis-tered under the chairmanship of Lady Marre and her committee will include the Secretary-General of MENCAP, Mr Brian Rix.

I was lucky with that one. I immediately informed all our local societies of this new crock of gold and asked them to get their applications in a bit smartish. This they did, and I'm happy to record that nearly 50 per cent of that fund went to help mentally handicapped people. A pity the Prince can't marry more often. Perhaps he'd better move to the Middle East. Three more Wedding Funds, at least.

> ITV APPEAL FOR MENCAP, October 18th: An appeal by the Secretary-General of MENCAP on behalf of that charity was transmitted on all ITV channels yesterday evening. The programme was made by Yorkshire TV.

Yes, and what a saga that five-minute recording turned out to be. I first went up to Leeds in June to make the appeal – but was met by an irate producer who said there was no way we could go ahead on that day, for all the electricians were on strike. That was pretty standard practice at Yorkshire telly in those days. When I was on tour, I remember doing several *Calendar* programmes from there in Stygian gloom.

Anyway, I was offered lunch (*not* mixed grill or shepherd's pie) and then shoved on the next train back to London. The weeks went by. Several dates were set for the recording, but all had to be cancelled for lack of light. Then it became doubtful if the appeal could be made at all, so in desperation I suggested that I would be more than happy to do it in the open air, if that would help matters. It would, and a fresh date was set for my trip to Leeds. I arrived, to be driven over to a local MENCAP house and marched round to the garden. It was then that we ran into another major snag. There was no autocue. This is the machine used by all newsreaders, who follow the script which seems to be appearing out of the middle of the camera lens. As they say, it's all done by mirrors.

Autocues are often used by the presenters of magazine programmes, too, and always by the President of the United States and generally by Margaret Thatcher. The last two use those invisible screens which look like bits of plastic atop a microphone stand. But for me and my five-minute speech, which had to be exactly four minutes and twenty seconds long, not five minutes at all, there was nothing as the autocue is driven by electricity and thus an electrician is required to switch it on. But all the sparks were on strike, and I didn't know the words. Consternation!

Then I had a brain-wave and asked if there was a fresh roll of lavatory paper in the house. There was, and I proceeded to write the appeal, in capitals, on a large selection of sheets. Not without difficulty, I may add, because the particular house in question used the finest Andrex and my ballpoint kept puncturing it. Oh for the good old Jeyes or Bronco of yesteryear. But I persevered and eventually made the appeal, somewhat incongruously, with the sunlight dappling through my hair and the gnats flitting past, reading my script from a roll of loo paper which a bemused floor manager unrolled just below the lens until she was enveloped in yards of the legendary toilet tissue, rather like that Labrador puppy in the advertisements. How I kept going, I shall never know, but I did, and the appeal raised many thousands of pounds, which all goes to prove the gods were smiling on me that day. Actually, I should think they were falling about with laughter.

SECRETARY-GENERAL'S EVENING ENGAGEMENTS
WEEK COMMENCING OCTOBER 12TH, 1981:

October 12th	Dinner, Garrick Club, London
October 13th	Metropolitan Region, Informal Evening, London
October 14th	Poppy Ball, Intercontinental Hotel, London
October 15th	National Housing and Town Planning Conference, Harrogate
October 16th	Rotary International Conference, Bournemouth
October 17th	Metropolitan Flag Day Reception, London
October 18th	Friends of Normansfield Council, Kingston
October 19th	East and West Sussex MENCAP Groups, Crowborough

As you can see, my job seemed to turn a seven-day week into one of eight days.

DINNER, October 12th: Mr Helmut Rothenberg was the host at a dinner at the Garrick Club last evening for the Secretary-General of MENCAP and others, including Lord Pennock, Sir Derek Ezra, Sir Robert

Haslam, Sir Peter Reynolds, Sir Roy Sisson, Mr Peter Bowring, Mr Peter Grant and Mr Antony Pilkington, to interest them in the works of the Royal Society for Mentally Handicapped Children and Adults.

Quite apart from starting the Rothenberg Memorial Trust (for emergency finance) and the Rothenberg Fellowship (to train overseas students), Helmut went on to host a number of these dinners, which must have led to over a quarter of a million coming MENCAP's way. Not unnaturally, he is also a Governor of the MENCAP City Foundation. Would that there were more like him. He's a splendid friend.

And now you know why I put on a stone in weight whilst at MENCAP. Apart from mixed grill and shepherd's pie, I was constantly guzzling a variety of nosh, from the finest cuisine to the worst fast foods. Furthermore, the only exercise I ever managed was standing up to make a speech, or sitting down to listen to someone else's. But I wouldn't have missed it for the world. Well, the speeches – yes – but the job, no.

BBC CONTINUING EDUCATION RECEPTION, Broadcasting House, November 12th: A reception was given last night by the Continuing Education Department of the BBC, at which they thanked all those who had served them well in a variety of ways. Among those present was Mr Brian Rix, who has made a contribution as the presenter of *Let's Go*.

The reason I'm mentioning this is that I met a producer at that party, Stuart Evans, who asked me if I ever had any spare time to do the odd schools broadcast, if the part offered was interesting. I agreed that I could make time available, and so it was I ended up playing Falstaff in *Henry IV, Part I* and Josiah Bounderby in Charles Dickens's *Hard Times*. I loved it, because it gave me the opportunity to play the sort of role I never would be offered in the theatre. Unfortunately Stuart retired after *Hard Times*, which was hard luck on me, for the offers stopped. But I wish you'd heard my Falstaff. Extremely unlikely though. It was broadcast at midnight.

BUSINESS ENTERPRISE LUNCHEON, November 17th: The second such luncheon was held yesterday at the Savoy Hotel. In the chair was Sir Derek Ezra.

Each year this lunch is held. Originally it was under the auspices of the Institute of Directors, but is now supported by the CBI (Confederation of British Industry). It's a prestigious affair, with the award going to the most go-ahead company in the UK as judged by an expert panel, including the CBI itself, the *Sunday Telegraph* and the Henley Business College. However, at the lunch the money raised, which is considerable, goes to MENCAP. It was my job each year to make a short speech giving an up-date on MENCAP's activities, particularly as they applied to the world of business. My last luncheon in 1986 was perhaps the most bizarre. In the first place I was attending a breakfast meeting at the Labour Party Conference in Blackpool and had to fly down to make the Savoy on time. A kind benefactor, Les Hamilton, laid on a private plane to make this possible, so I could be at the lunch by a quarter to one and as I walked in, I realized that all eyes were on one man, Ernest Saunders, who had not long before concluded his spectacular Guinness/Distillers coup. Everybody wanted to meet him. But where were all those back-slappers a few weeks later when Mr Saunders faced criminal charges over the Guinness affair? Not crowding round him then, as I recall. They weren't crowding round us, either, even though my speech asked, quite movingly, for their help.

PARLIAMENT, THE HOUSE OF LORDS, December 1st: "Mental Health (Amendment) Bill". Reference was made by The Lord Bishop of Norwich to an article by the Secretary-General of MENCAP which appeared in yesterday's *Times*.

The Lord Bishop said:

No one who read that powerful "cri de coeur" by Mr Brian Rix in *The Times* of today can fail to be moved, not only by his own experience but, it seems to me, by the overwhelming and unremitting logic of his argument. It seems to me there is no earthly reason why a child or young person or older person suffering from mental handicap should be dealt with in any way in law that is different from a condition of blindness or deafness or the stunted growth of a limb. I accept totally what the Minister has said about the Government having an open mind on this matter, and I am sure that the Government will be prepared to give urgent reconsideration to this most vital part of the Bill.

So what was in this cri de coeur that, thankfully, had made such an impression? Well, here it is, although some parts you will recognize from earlier pages in this book:

WHY CALL MY DAUGHTER SICK WHEN SHE IS NOT?

The day parents are told they have a mentally handicapped child is hardly a high point in a family's history. Whatever the future, their feelings are of shock and grief, rejection and guilt, a desire to run away and pretend it has not happened.

Then the questioning begins. What can we do? Who can help? Who can we ask?

Southend and one or two other enlightened places provide a caring "task force" of parents, doctors, social workers and others who move into action the moment they are asked. But the majority must fend alone.

So it was with us when our eldest child, Shelley, was born thirty years ago. No support, no counselling, few friends. We were left to flounder for five years until circumstances made it possible to pull strings and ensure she was admitted to Normansfield – then the most desirable, *small*, long-stay mental hospital in the south of England.

But under the Act applicable in those days, Shelley could not simply be admitted – she had to *prove* she was mentally handicapped, even though at that time she could neither walk nor talk.

So it was County Hall and two London County Council doctors for Shelley. She had to be *certified*. My wife and I will remember that day with anger and humiliation to the day we die. Anger at the way Shelley was treated by one of the doctors certifying her – orders barked, aptitude tests thrust, disapproval apparent. Humiliation at the way we had to drag her through the bureaucratic processes demanded by the mental deficiency legislation, which had been in force, with modification, since 1913.

Then came a false dawn. The Mental Health Act 1959 was supposed to remove all that. It was primarily designed to provide hospital treatment for those who suffer from mental illnesses, such as schizophrenia, dementia, psychosis, manic depression, etc, by detaining them under compulsion for an unlimited period. In contrast to mental handicap, these are real illnesses requiring medical treatment – often resulting in a complete cure.

For reasons of expediency and laziness, mental handicap was incorporated in the same Act but, as mental handicap cannot be cured, medical treatment is often irrelevant and compulsory detention in hospital of no benefit. In fact it can worsen the condition, leading to serious psychological damage and physical deterioration. I know this because I am now Secretary-General of the Royal Society for Mentally Handicapped Children and Adults (MENCAP), a job that enables me to assuage – just a little – some of the guilt I felt all those years ago.

For years MENCAP has recommended the removal of mental handicap from the 1959 Act, arguing that research in many other countries has shown the only way to progress is to provide adequate education, social training and psychological support, individually geared to the needs of each mentally handicapped person. This can most effectively be carried out in the community, away from the restrictions of a hospital ward.

MENCAP also point out that no other handicapped person – whether blind, deaf or crippled – can by law be forcibly detained in hospital just because of the handicap. Why then should mental handicap be treated differently? It is both illogical and cruel to incarcerate someone in hospital simply because his or her intellectual development has been retarded.

Ever since the 1959 Act lumped mental illness and mental handicap together, many people, not unreasonably, have assumed that the two are synonymous. This confusion causes great distress and anguish to families with a mentally handicapped relative – frequently referred to by neighbours and others as "mad", "loony" or "nutty".

In its recent White Paper explaining the changes proposed in the Mental Health (Amendment) Bill, which has its second reading in the Lords today, the Government shares the concern over this confusion and for the needs of the two groups to be recognized. It is sad to record that most newspapers described mentally handicapped people as mentally ill, and vice versa. The only common denominator is the word "mental". If a mentally handicapped person was described as being "intellectually disabled" the disparity might become clearer.

The few mentally handicapped people who commit a serious crime should not be sent to prison or to a special hospital, like Broadmoor, but be committed to a section of one of the secure hospital units whose establishment was recommended by Lord Butler and his committee in 1974. There they would receive training and social support rather than psychiatric treatment. Other alternatives could be considered.

Closely connected with the issue of removal of mental handicap from the 1959 Act is guardianship. This provision also involves compulsion. Under the Act, a mentally handicapped person of any age, whose detention in hospital is regarded as unsuitable, can be placed under guardianship which would reduce his or her status to that of a child of fourteen. It can confer a string of powers on the guardian over the "patient" more akin to Dickensian times than the second half of the twentieth century.

It is true that the new Bill proposes some changes in the guardianship provisions. Perhaps at MENCAP's initiative, the powers of guardians are reduced. But it does not go far enough. I and my colleagues at MENCAP will seek the removal of the powers of compulsory hospital detention and guardianship placements. Instead we would like to see the introduction of an informal and non-compulsory guardianship system which could deal in a humane and dignified way with the very small minority of mentally handicapped people now compulsorily detained in long-stay institutions.

In February 1979, during a six-hour Commons debate, reviewing the 1959 Act, none of the many MPs taking part supported the (Labour) Government's view that mentally handicapped people should be detained under the Act. Most of the speakers, amongst them Dr Gerard Vaughan and Mrs Lynda Chalker, both now Ministers at the Department of Health and Social Security, pleaded for the removal of mental handicap from the scope of the Act. It will be interesting to see if they continue to support MENCAP throughout the passage of the Bill.

Mentally handicapped children became eligible for education only ten years ago. They have been waiting now for twenty-one years to be removed from a punitive and discriminating Act which can instantly reduce their rights to naught.

Twenty-first birthdays used to mark coming-of-age. Isn't it time the Government and the medical diehard reactionaries gave mentally handicapped people a birthday present and freed them from their constraints? Life hasn't bestowed many gifts on them up to now.

And do you know, that birthday present was forthcoming. Or, rather, a Christmas present, for just before New Year, Lord Renton and I, plus our parliamentary representative, Rolf Hermelin, were asked to visit the Under-Secretary of State at the DHSS, Lord Elton, to put forward further proposals. This we did – and although the wording in the eventual 1983 Mental Health Act was not quite what we had wanted, the intention was clear. In future, only those mentally handicapped people who suffered from abnormal aggressiveness or serious irresponsibility would be subject to compulsory detention. Furthermore, they would be described as "severely mentally impaired". The rest – many hundreds of thousands – would be freed from the yoke of the old Act and the old prejudices. It was a singular victory – and a fitting end to the International Year of Disabled People.

That, in the natural course of things, would be the way to end the story of 1981 – but there are still three social events to record:

CLARENCE HOUSE, December 10th: Her Majesty Queen Elizabeth The Queen Mother, Patron of the Royal Society for Mentally Handicapped Children and Adults, officially opened the Society's new national headquarters in Golden Lane, London EC1. Her Majesty met National Council members from every Region of the Society and had a friendly word for members and former members of staff.

So read the Annual Report, but from my point of view, perhaps more significantly, the Queen Mum opened our new workshop – in the next-door building to our HQ – where young people with a mental handicap were learning the art of dried flower arranging (which they did – and do – extremely well), and these widely differing arrangements are then sold in a variety of outlets. Furthermore, the young people are paid a reasonable wage and it is amazing to see how they have blossomed (if you'll pardon the pun) over the years. The whole operation has now expanded, to include MENCAP Business Supplies, and is a living example of how such young people can progress, if only they are given a chance. A lesson to us all.

UNIVERSITY NEWS, The University of Hull, December 11th: The Honorary Degree of Master of Arts was awarded to Mr Brian Rix in recognition of his work for people with a mental handicap. He was accompanied by his wife, Elspet.

As a matter of fact, I was quite lucky to have Elspet with me, for her year had been pretty busy too. She had started the TV series *Solo*, in which she played Felicity Kendal's mum. She went on to become a close relative of a number of the new comedy stars – on television or on stage that is – for she was Rowan Atkinson's mother in the first series of *Blackadder* and Griff Rhys Jones and Mel Smith's aunt when those two appeared, separately, in the West End revival of *Charley's Aunt*. A very successful family, I think you would agree.

But back to that MA Honoris Causa. There's a super photo of Elspet and me on my desk at home and, honestly, I look quite good in the old mortar board and gown. However, I went on over the years to receive quite a number of honorary degrees – and I look such a berk in the flat soft cap of a doctor, I have to keep those photos hidden from sight. Maybe Fontana will insist on reproducing one. If so, please don't laugh.

Oh, just one thing. If I give the impression I received these degrees in any flippant way, nothing could be further from the truth. I was greatly honoured by their bestowal and felt, too, that the world of mental handicap received a further leg-up – at least in academic eyes. Let me list the universities out of gratitude.

Hull	Hon MA	1981	Manchester	Hon LLD	1986
Open	Hon MA	1983	Nottingham	Hon DSc	1987
Essex	Hon D Univ	1984			

and Humberside College of Higher Education, Hon Fellowship 1984. To all – my thanks.

* * *

Finally, possibly the finest accolade of all, THE YORK-SHIRE PERSONALITY OF THE YEAR, 1981. Yes, I'm proud to say that was awarded to me. Against strong opposition, too. Freddie Trueman, Richard Whiteley, Michael Palin and Frankie Howerd were all in there with a chance, but the oldest amongst them got it. There's something to be said for longevity, after all. Oh yes, and the presenters of the award? The Barnsley Junior Chamber of Commerce. There I go, name-dropping again. I really will have to stop this Jennifer's Diary and go back to straight recording of events. Which leads me, quite naturally, to:

1982

The Times, Birthdays Today, January 27, 1982

As I say, enough of the frills and furbelows of the social whirl. From now on, in the story of my time at MENCAP,

I will try to stick to the straight and narrow. It won't be easy, and I'm sure you'll forgive me a small digression from time to time, for life would be very boring if there were no lighter moments, even in the world of mental handicap. Like the time I compèred a concert at the Commonwealth Institute in Kensington High Street, on the Saturday of Shelley's birthday.

All went well, until the end, when I wished Shelley a happy birthday, for she was in the audience, along with many others who, like her, were mentally handicapped. The small band on stage struck up the usual refrain, the entire audience responded, Shelley rose from her seat and rolled towards the stage (she has always had difficulty in walking), climbed up the steps, gave me a big hug, bowed in triumph to the audience and turned her attention to the steel band at the back of the stage, who had just finished playing. Flinging caution to the wind and her arms around the nearest steel band musician (who, along with the others happened to be huge, black, and a Borstal boy) she led him into a wild kind of jive. In seconds all the audience who could get on the stage, got on the stage – grabbed a Borstal boy apiece (if there was one spare) and joined in the celebratory dance. It was an incredible sight. Wild gyrations, flailing arms, raucous voices, all belonging to people who, in spite of all their handicaps, were having a great time. As for Shelley, she continued to dance as long as her poor old legs would let her, but what a birthday present it had turned out to be. What's more, it all goes to prove that the love of the stage runs in families. Shelley took her bow as to the manner born, as if she had just given the performance of her life. And I suppose for her, in front of so many people, she had.

At the beginning of January in 1982 I gave another of my famous gala pie lunches, this time for Young and Rubicam. Y & R, originally American, are now one of the biggest advertising agencies in the world with a very big operation here in the UK. It so happened that a number of agencies had volunteered their time and efforts for various causes, during the previous year, IYDP (International Year for Disabled People), and Young and Rubicam had lighted upon us. They did a splendid radio commercial about mental handicap and were so enthused with the response, and the award it won them, that they decided to adopt MENCAP as their special charity. As they have continued to do ever since. I think I can do no better than quote from our 1982 Annual Report when our then Chairman, Lord Allen of Abbeydale (Lord Renton had retired and was now our President) wrote:

> This relationship enabled us to maximize the effective-ness of our limited advertising budget through the agency's comprehensive knowledge of the market-place. Y & R were asked to create a campaign poster and negotiate advertising space for the Mental Handi-cap Week Campaign and later the Christmas Appeal Campaign. Including what would have been the pro-fessional charges of Y & R and poster sites made available without charge, we obtained advertising space and services worth approximately ten times our actual expenditure.

Not a bad exchange for a few slices of gala pie.

Also at the beginning of January, I wrote a letter to *The Times* commenting on Peggy Jay's (she of the Jay Report) call for a new term to describe mentally ill people:

In the Mind to Suffer
Sir, I fully support Peggy Jay's initiative (January 6th) to resolve the "residual confusion in the public mind between the mentally ill and the mentally handi-capped", and I am grateful for her kind comments about MENCAP's public impact. However, it seems

to me that even if her faith in your readers is rewarded and a new generic term for mentally ill people is coined, this will only scratch the surface of the problem.

The fact is that people who suffer from *any* mental disadvantage (whether it be a handicap from birth or a developing illness) are generally thought of, in this country, as "loonies", "mongies" or even worse. Until young people are adequately educated about the true facts concerning the mentally disadvantaged, and are reminded of the sobering fact that "there but for the grace of God go I", mentally handicapped and mentally ill people alike will continue to be treated with ridicule and derision.

No amount of terminological tinkering will change that. Pejorative words arise, willy-nilly, through constant misuse.

And will continue so to do, I fear, for many years to come.

As I have mentioned, David Renton retired as our Chairman in April 1982 and became our first-ever President, a fitting tribute to his many years as an active parent and worker on MENCAP's behalf. He had suggested as his successor a senior wrangler who had been the Permanent Under-Secretary at the Home Office, Lord Allen of Abbeydale, and his suggestion was welcomed by the National Council. Both barons gave us great service in the House of Lords during this duopoly, and I know I can look to them for just as much support now that I am the Chairman, with Philip Allen as the President. But remember, Abbeydale is in Yorkshire, so, with a President and a Chairman from the same county, we must be careful not to emulate our cricketing cousins and end up pulling the team apart. Only Tykes could have invented the Boycott boycott.

In February, Alan Leighton and I met in my office with Jack Barton, the producer of the now-defunct TV series,

Crossroads. We had already spoken to the, then, Controller of Programmes of Central Television, Charles Denton, about putting a character with mental handicap into a TV soap as part of the ordinary storyline, just like it might be in real life. Charles had agreed with this (for, like me, he had a personal involvement in the problem) and the meeting with Jack Barton was the result. Jack was not only co-operative, but enthusiastic, and an outline understanding was reached to make this idea a reality. And so it came to pass. Some eighteen months later Nina Weill, an enchanting little girl with blonde hair, pigtails and Down's syndrome, graced our screens for some twelve weeks as part of the everyday story of everyday folk in a Midlands motel. Some fourteen million viewers watched Nina two or three times a week and there is no doubt that during the time she was on their screens, they thought about mental handicap more than they had ever done before and, what is more, with sympathy and understanding. However, screen heroes only have a limited life and when Nina's appearances came to an end, we at MENCAP sympathized with Sheridan's line from *The Rivals:* "illiterate him, I say, quite from your memory". We did keep Nina's memory from being completely "illiterated" though, by producing a poignant poster, showing her in an extremely unaccustomed pose, that of solemnity. It was a heck of a job for Young and Rubicam to catch her at it, though. Most of the time she was the happiest of mortals.

That poster was intended to be part of a massive campaign to show the world at large some of the problems facing parents of a mentally handicapped child. *The Times* carried the story of the advertising campaign that never was. Let me quote it in full, for it tells it all:

DOWN'S GIRL CAMPAIGN IS DROPPED
by Richard Evans

A nationwide advertising campaign to back up a mentally handicapped girl's debut tomorrow night in a popular television series has been halted by the withdrawal of "promised" backing worth £100,000.

Nina Weill, aged six, from Fulham, London, who has Down's syndrome, will be seen by an estimated fourteen million viewers when she makes the first of a dozen appearances between now and Christmas in *Crossroads*.

The Royal Society for Mentally Handicapped Children and Adults (MENCAP), which sees the girl's appearance as a breakthrough in educating the public about mental handicap, planned the advertising campaign next month in every national daily newspaper and local radio.

The message would have been: "You can turn off Nina's problems. Her mother cannot."

The Director, Chairman and Treasurer of the Health Education Council (HEC), had told MENCAP officials that it would provide the £100,000 needed to finance such a campaign. But the HEC's full council narrowly rejected the plan.

Mr Brian Rix, Secretary-General of MENCAP, who worked for two years to get a mentally handicapped person written into a popular television series, said: "Millions of people will see the problems of mentally handicapped people and become sympathetic. The advertising campaign would have been a fantastic follow-up. Instead what is happening is a tragedy and extremely short-sighted."

Dr David Player, Director of the HEC, said: "When we looked at the resources in the council we unfortunately had to say no."

In the television series Nina plays a child who goes to live temporarily with two *Crossroads* regulars, Sharon and Diane, when her mother cannot cope.

Mrs Hanna Weill, aged thirty-two, Nina's mother, said: "I just find it absolutely remarkable. How can they do it, especially when the HEC has never given any money before to educate the public about the mentally handicapped?"

No wonder the Health Education Council was abolished.

The day after my first meeting with Jack Barton, I had lunch with another character from the old days – obstetrician Frank Denny, who had safely delivered the last three of our children, Louisa, Jamie and Jonty, but had now retired. I don't mean he'd retired because we had stopped producing kids – but, simply, that he had reached the appropriate age. However, that age is, as I'm sure you know, more *pour encourager les autres* to seek promotion, rather than because senility has settled in. Frank felt he still had much to offer and how could he help MENCAP? Never looking a gift horse in the mouth, particularly one so skilled as Frank, I suggested that the resurgence of the MENCAP Medical Advisory Panel might be of interest (it had long been an ambition of mine) and could he help? Frank could and would and did. We were off, soon to be joined by that well-known, diminutive paediatrician, Dr David Morris, Professor Gwyn Roberts (Professor of Mental Handicap at Nottingham University), Mrs Betty Norman (really a doctor, mother of a handicapped son and now a Vice-Chairman of MENCAP), Professor William Fraser (Editor of the *Journal of Mental Deficiency Research* and, now, Professor of Mental Handicap, University of Wales) and, for a short time, Professor Neville Butler (Professor of Child Health, Bristol University). Neville was a highly entertaining and brilliant man, but somehow our meetings always seemed to get obliterated from his diary, so he retired from our deliberations. A pity. We missed his enchanting eccentricity and had to make do with other variations: David Morris, alas – no longer with us, always cycled to our meetings and arrived with bike clips on his trousers and a rose in his buttonhole. Furthermore, David had often been described by me as the only paediatrician who sat on his patients' knees, which gives you an idea as to his height, whilst Bill Fraser wandered around for over a year with his glasses held on by two paper clips and a piece of string. You can see that Professor Butler was not alone in his whimsicality.

Nevertheless, this amorphous mass, making up our Medical Advisory Panel, was, and is, packed with intelligence and has produced some excellent work for the Society. They've also produced a lot of laughs. To illustrate this, they decided that a layman should lead their deliberations, so they would have to speak understandable English, and thus I was chosen to be their first Chairman, a position I coveted until I had to retire on becoming Chairman, rather than Secretary-General, of MENCAP. The Panel has been served throughout by Mary Holland, who is really our political representative, and they are a great bunch, displaying their knowledge and individuality to the full when we paid a week's visit to Washington some three years after the formation of the Panel. Elspet joined us on that occasion, which came about through the good offices of the Joseph P. Kennedy Junior Foundation. This was formed by the Kennedys to honour the eldest son of the family, who was killed most tragically, in the last war, whilst on a suicidal bombing mission to take out a German V2 rocket launching site in Normandy. Joe Kennedy was a highly experienced operational pilot who, with another officer, an expert in radio control projects, volunteered to take a "drone" Liberator bomber loaded with 22,000 pounds of high explosive into the air and stay with it until two "mother" planes had achieved complete radio control over the "drone". They were then to bale out over England and the "drone" was to continue the mission under the control of the "mother" planes and crash-dive on to the target. Something went wrong, the "drone" exploded, killing the two pilots instantly. To think that Joe's next two brothers, JFK and Robert, met equally violent deaths. Quite appalling. Added to that, one of their sisters, Rosemary, is mentally handicapped, and that is why the Foundation has two firm objectives: "To seek the prevention of mental retardation by identifying its causes and to improve the means by which society deals with its citizens who are already mentally retarded."

And that is why the MENCAP Medical Advisory Panel was in Washington. In particular to see the projects which had begun with the seed money provided by the Foundation including, of course, the famous Special Olympics. But we visited Congress and the Senate, met Senator Chaffee in his vast Senate office (those facilities make our MPs' accommodation and numbers of staff look ridiculous), for the Senator was trying to get a Bill through to help disabled individuals attain their maximum potential. I fear he has not succeeded. We also visited the Department of Health and Human Services, the White House on a VIP visit (but President Reagan was asleep – he'd just returned from his abortive meeting with Mr Gorbachev in Iceland), the Kennedy Institute of Ethics and many other interesting places.

We attended a couple of highly enjoyable social occasions, too; one at the home of Eunice Kennedy Shriver and the other at the British Embassy, where the Ambassador, Sir Oliver Wright, acted as our host. Anyone who was anyone in the world of mental handicap in the USA entrained and planed and helicoptered in from all over the States just to see our splendid Lutyens Embassy, but, you know, not a single person with a mental handicap was present. Does he take sugar?

Back to February 1982. Alan Leighton and I made arrangements with the Kent County Constabulary to produce a video, *Let's Get It Straight*, which presented the facts about mental handicap. I introduced the subject, whilst a number of young people told of their experiences, particularly those of being mocked by many in the world at large. The video was very well made, at no cost to us. Sony produced dozens of free tapes and the resulting work was seen by hundreds of people at meetings up and down the country. Furthermore, the video received an award from the International Television Association, whilst the accompanying leaflet also received an award, this time from the Plain English Campaign. A creative month, February, wouldn't you say?

March saw me speaking at a "rival" fund-raising event – that of the Special Olympics. As I have already mentioned, this was originally the creation of the Kennedy family, particularly the Shrivers, and is a splendid effort to provide athletics on a world-wide scale for people with a mental handicap, which has met with increasing success and now many countries take part. Although it is a separate body from MENCAP, nevertheless many of our "clients" are the same, particularly those who are members of the Gateway Federation (the 700-plus leisure clubs sponsored by MENCAP), and we are only too glad to help. Also supporting the cause on that March evening were Lord Renton, the Duke of Devonshire and Sir Eldon Griffiths MP – who is the Chairman of Special Olympics UK – so you can see that I wasn't exactly out on my own.

However, in the same month, I did make a speech on my own for Gateway itself, in Cardiff Castle. All the local big-wigs were there, including the Lord Mayor. Unfortunately, the zip on my flies had just failed as I was leaving the Angel Hotel to address the gathering, and a highly amused housekeeper had lent me several safety pins to do myself up, for I had no change of clothes. Now those of you who have ever tried to get in or out of trousers when the flys are done up will know it is an impossibility; thus all the repair work had to be undertaken with the trousers in situ and the resulting pinning-up made the front of my pants look like the foothills of the Brecon Beacons. Thus I found myself on the platform in Cardiff Castle with my papers spread carefully in front of me hiding my guilty secret, with legs crossed and awaiting, in some considerable embarrassment, the Lord Mayor to finish his speech of welcome. Then, I knew, I would have to stand up and my lumpy apparel would be revealed. But relief was at hand. I suddenly heard the Lord Mayor making that hoary old joke, expressing surprise that I was there beside him with my trousers on. I was able to jump up and inform the audience that it was only through the sterling support of three safety pins that this was so and things might well have been otherwise but for the housekeeper's efforts at the Angel. I was happy to assure them, though, that I did put in the safety pins myself. It's amazing how laughter can defuse the most awkward of situations. I should have guessed that being known for losing my trousers would stand me in good stead one day.

Around this time, too, MENCAP Homes Foundation got off the ground with three homes – ordinary houses in ordinary streets – established for people with a mental handicap to live there, with appropriate care, of course. This was the proverbial acorn. In 1987 we opened 103 homes in that year alone, an increase of one hundred houses per year in five years, and the acceleration goes on. Only two things hold us back (well, three – if you count money): staff, and volunteers to serve on the committees, but generally both of these can be found eventually. To think we could have been doing this for years, instead of believing long-stay hospitals were the only answer. But it was a handful of parents who dreamt up the concept – and that handful has now become a crowd and that crowd will eventually become a multitude.

May was the month in which our first grandchild, Ben, was born. The date was the 16th and he was delivered safely, after a long labour, to Helen and Jamie. A year later, to the day, his cousin Charlotte was born, to Louisa and Jonty Coy, whilst a year later still, Ben's brother, Jack, was due on the 16th, but messed things up by being a week late. After that, everything went to pot and Louisa and Jonty's son, Jolyon, was born after a further pause of eighteen months, in September. But I wonder what odds you could get on two grandchildren being born on the same date, a year apart, never mind three: 100 to 1 – or better?

June had me broadcasting in Test Match Special from Lord's, in *A View from the Boundary*, the Saturday lunchtime filler. On my appearance, though, rain had stopped play, so I rabbited on quite happily for nearly two hours, along with Brian Johnston, Fred Trueman and Don Mosey. Gosh, I envy them that job. Imagine watching all the Test Matches from a prime position, being fed and watered and, furthermore, being paid to do it. Some people have all the luck! The same month included, as usual, our MENCAP Week Conference which was entitled "16 . . . And Then What?" – which alluded, of course, to continuing education for mentally handicapped pupils.

The conference was addressed by the Rt Hon Sir Keith Joseph, Secretary of State, Department of Education and Science, and as usual on these occasions, he told us nothing new. However, he sportingly stayed behind for a short time, to answer questions, and one of those questions, well prepared – almost scripted you might say – came from me. I simply asked when the two major departments (the DHSS and the DES) concerned with young people with a mental handicap would begin to get their act together. Not in so many words, of course, but that was the gist of it. Sir Keith was perplexed. The question had nothing to do with his speech and he decided to cut his viva voce short and leave. Unfortunately, the conference was being held in Cinema 1 at the Barbican Centre in the City of London and those of you who have found how to get there will know it is extremely difficult to make your way into the building, never mind out of it. With me in hot pursuit (not firing questions at him, merely trying to escort him out) the Secretary of State attempted to solve the mystery of the Hampton Court Maze, which is the Barbican building. We ran up staircase after staircase, and then down again, until the mystery was solved and Sir Keith came upon his car, which had been dodging around like a yo-yo. All I can say is that the Minister was a damn sight fitter than I, for when he left I was completely puffed out, whilst Sir Keith seemed to be in complete control of his breathing. But not always in complete control of the education system alas — and the bridge between childhood and adulthood for mentally handicapped people is still made of balsa wood, liable to snap at any time.

In July, Chris Pym, from the Open University, visited our, then, Education Director, James Cummings, to talk about some co-operative effort and they came up to my office to further the discussion. I fear it was then that I hijacked their conversation and the idea of the Open University course for people interested in mental handicap was born. Of course, it took considerable time to come to fruition, particularly as it was a community course, not a degree one, and I had to raise a large sum of money (around £350,000) to pay for it. Actually it wasn't too difficult. The DHSS chipped in with a generous £100,000, Vivien Duffield opened up the purse strings of the Clore Foundation for an equally generous £50,000, whilst the MENCAP City Foundation filled in the final shortfall, when all other donations had been added. In November 1986 the OU course was launched, after much hard work by Professor Malcolm Johnson, Anne Brechin, Dorothy Atkinson, Linda Ward, Jan Walmsley and our own Mary Holland, as "Mental Handicap: Patterns for Living", the first course of its kind in the world for all those involved with children or adults with mental handicap: parents, care staff, volunteers and professionals. 8,000 took the course in its first year, and now there is a Part II for people with learning difficulties to study – *Working Together*. It is a unique contribution to help those who wish to take their rightful place in the community. Of course, the BBC televise the videos, as for all other OU courses, so that is another feather in the cap for the corporation – *Let's Go*, the OU, *People First* and now *A Life of Our Own*. Auntie has never been stuffy, as far as MENCAP is concerned.

In the same month of July another further education idea was conceived, this time with the University of Kent, where Jamie had studied. I was invited by the Vice-Chancellor, David Ingram, to see if we could enter into a joint venture for a BA in Mental Handicap. Money would again have to be raised, however, and, as things developed, I found myself more able to cope with OU financial requirements, rather than those of Kent. As a result, sails had to be trimmed but, even so, there is now an MA post-graduate course in Mental Handicap available at Kent, which all began six days after the OU course was first discussed. At neither of these July meetings was gala pie on offer, but if this was missing, we were certainly casting our bread on the waters.

Later in July came that terrible incident in Hyde Park when the cavalrymen were killed by an IRA bomb, together with a number of their horses. And let us not forget the seven members of the Royal Green Jackets' band who also died in the Regent's Park bomb at about the same time. It so happened on that day I was going to the Royal Garden Hotel, near Kensington Gardens, to collect a substantial cheque for MENCAP from *Woman's Weekly*, just after the bomb had exploded. Of course, I didn't know this and I was driving along Cromwell Road with no trouble at all when suddenly the traffic snarled to a halt. Later I realized it was because ambulances and rescue workers, needing to reach the scene, were on their way, but, at the time, only a radio newsflash gave me a clue. So

I abandoned my car in a side road and started to walk to the hotel. On the way, I ran into Lord Snowdon, who told me the grisly details, so it was in a somewhat subdued mood that I entered the hotel. To make matters worse, we could see all the activity near the bomb site from the hotel window, high up on a park-side floor, so what should have been a happy occasion turned out to be the very opposite. When you are as close as that, though, you realize the bestiality of such behaviour and wonder, even more, how people can sustain any quality of life in the Lebanon, the Occupied Territories and, from time to time, Belfast. What a piece of work is a man! So often ignoble in reason, if I may paraphrase the Bard.

A procession of a different kind from fleets of ambulances bent on their sad duty, was the Lord Mayor's Show on November 13th, 1982. Sir Anthony Jolliffe had taken as his theme, "Here's to the Best of Britain" and as his charity, MENCAP. His procession reflected both interests, with a large number of highly successful companies on view from their floats but, sandwiched in the middle, a float representing MENCAP "reflecting the wide range of leisure and recreational activities provided by Gateway for people with a mental handicap. MENCAP is honoured to have been chosen as the Lord Mayor's special charity." It was a great do, as was the Lord Mayor's Banquet at the Guildhall on the following Monday. Many of you will be familiar with the event through the medium of television, but actually being there adds another dimension. It's all very grand, with certain guests being presented to the new Lord Mayor and his Lady including, on this occasion, Elspet and me, with the onlookers applauding. Then into the Banquet, with the Great and the Good spread over a large area, dominated by the top table, with the new Lord Mayor, his predecessor and the Prime Minister all displayed for the diners to see, plus the watching viewers at home. Next, the speeches, the PM's view of the world at large, carriages and home to bed. Formal, yes, stiff and starchy, no. I sat next to Lord Goodman and had a high old time. But then, neither of us is at a loss for words for very long.

The Prime Minister refrained from making any jokes about the then Chancellor of the Exchequer, Sir Geoffrey Howe, even though he had managed to mislay his trousers on a train the previous week. As she had another well-known trouser-dropper in her audience, the thought might have crossed her mind, but somehow I doubt it. However, it certainly crossed Frank Johnson's mind in *The Times*:

> Sir Geoffrey has entered history as the Chancellor who lost his trousers. Pretty soon, people will believe that he lost them in the presence of Mrs Thatcher, or at a cocktail party for visiting heads of central banks, or in the chamber of the Commons itself. Eventually it will be said that he does it all the time, enlivening Cabinet meetings thereby. He will become the Brian Rix of monetarism. In the esteem of the British people his future is assured.

Once a trouser-dropper, always a trouser-dropper . . . I know! Bags I first, Sir Geoffrey?

November 1982 saw my first visit to a conference of the International League of Societies for Persons with Mental Handicap, held in the Conference Centre in Nairobi, Kenya, and it was great. Not the conference exactly, although that had its moments, but the whole atmosphere of mixing with other nationalities, in an African capital, and experiencing all the variations, the vagaries and the valedictions which such a conference engenders. For instance, we heard the final address by the retiring President, Professor Gunner Dybwad, and listened to the opening address by his successor, from England and Manchester University, Professor Peter Mittler, and we (my fellow delegates from MENCAP and I) were transfixed. There was one of our own side kicking own goals at a rate which would have outdone any panicking non-league club versus his home team, Manchester United. Peter seemed determined to pin MENCAP in their penalty area, by attacking our advertising (Young and Rubicam, please note) and our logo (Little Stephen), which was (and is) one of the most recognizable assets accruing to MENCAP. I and my fellow delegates sat amazed. I shall never understand why Peter did it, for the rest of his apparently unscripted speech was, as always, brilliant, wide-ranging and challenging. It seemed he had picked on our advertising to score Brownie points and those of us from MENCAP present were deeply disappointed and distinctly disillusioned. Here was one of the great gurus of mental handicap in the 60s and 70s holding us up as an example not to be followed. The rest of the gathering were fascinated to be told that one of the founding members of the ILSMH (Germany being the other) might have feet of clay.

My speech, in comparison, was boringly bland. I was to address the plenary session on the second morning and my speech was to be exactly forty-five minutes long. My speech *was* exactly forty-five minutes long but I reckoned without the Chairman of my session, who hailed from Argentina. As you may recall, the Falklands fracas was but a recent memory and my Argentinian Chairman's memory seemed longer than most. He was supposed to introduce me in a short presentation, but, instead, chose to gabble on for nearly half an hour. All the while I was desperately cutting and re-cutting my speech as the precious minutes ebbed away and eventually my forty-five minutes' peroration became a twenty-five-minute précis. But, even so, it commanded a degree of respect, accompanied by polite applause, although I cannot help feeling that the Malvinas had quite a lot to do with its circumscription. On the other hand its title, "The Situation of Families in Industrialized Countries", may have alerted my South American friend to the fact that my speech was unlikely to have the delegates rolling in the aisles. It didn't.

Then, with Elspet and a number of MENCAP delegates (for which we paid privately, I hasten to add) it was safari time and around the Equator we buzzed, crossing and re-crossing the great divide. Lions, leopards, elephants, croc-odiles – we saw them in profusion (ninety elephants in one night at Treetops) – but the most surprising moment of all was being asked to don a jacket and tie before going into dinner at the Kenya Safari Club, which had been started by film star William Holden. It takes me all my time to put on a jacket and tie in Barnes, so you can imagine my amazement at such a demand in the middle of Africa. In the event, the tie came from the receptionist and the jacket came from Elspet, who had borrowed it from journalist Romany Bain. I both looked – and felt – a real nana, for the jacket buttoned the wrong way and was quite clearly suited to the female figure. As I was not on female hormones, the resulting silhouette was rather odd, to say the least.

I was also extremely uncomfortable, as well as extremely hot, but the management seemed entirely satisfied by this absurd attire, as they had been in the Plaza Hotel in New York way back in 1963 when David Jacobs, who had recently been voted "Britain's Best Dressed Man of the Year", entered the restaurant – accompanied by his then wife Pat plus Elspet and me – clad in an extremely smart red jersey cardigan with matching tie and accessories. All his more formal attire had been packed for a flight to Jamaica. The head waiter took one look at David, literally saw red and held up a restraining hand. Voice quivering with indignation, he enquired if "Britain's Best Dressed Man" honestly thought he could sit down in the Plaza Grill dressed like that? "Britain's Best Dressed Man" thought he could but the waiter was adamant. Then David remembered that he had left his extremely smart velvet-collared black overcoat in the cloakroom. Would that be in order? The head waiter considered at length and agreed it would. So that's how "Britain's Best Dressed Man" for 1962 came to be sitting in the Plaza Grill, eating his Chicken Maryland, with his overcoat flapping round his ankles. All those years later, sitting in the middle of Africa, I know just how he felt. Ridiculous.

On our return to England we became involved in all manner of Christmas activities for the Lord Mayor's Appeal, but one was particularly embarrassing. It was the Annual Lord Mayor's Carol Service at St Lawrence Jewry, near Guildhall, conducted by Basil Watson, and I was asked to read the lesson. I always rather enjoyed such occasions as it gave me a chance to remember my theatrical roots and I readily accepted. On entering the church, I was shown the lectern and the text thereon, stuck in a large old-fasioned, leather-bound Bible. I noted that it had been typed out on a very old portable and that the ribbon was well past its sell-by date, for the words were virtually unreadable. However, if I concentrated I would be able to manage with not too much trouble. I had been reading then in the ordinary church lighting, but as soon as the service started (with the Lord Mayor in his grand and personal pew) all the lights were turned out and the entire ceremony was conducted by the light of a few candles at the altar and two other "follow candles" which were clutched on long holders by two church wardens. The time came for me to read the lesson. The two candle-bearers approached and led me, stumbling in the dark, to the lectern. I cleared my throat, looked at the text and realized that all the words, faint in the first place, had completely disappeared in the encircling gloom. Panic set in. There was now total silence as the recently carolling congregation awaited my opening words. All they heard were muttered imprecations and then witnessed the extraordinary sight of the reader (me) clutching hold of the extremely heavy King James's Bible containing the invisible writing, lifting it above his head to take advantage of the candles held aloft and reading for all the world like a weightlifter at the very top of the press or the clean and jerk. The only reason I had to be thankful was that the lack of light allowed my puce, perspiring face to be hidden from view – but, even so, I heard many a muffled titter, none more so than from the Lord Mayor himself. Ah well, it was Christmas. The time of goodwill towards men. And goodwill *from* men, too.

The Sales Force of Hambro Life (now Allied Dunbar) had decided to support MENCAP in 1982, from their sales commission. They helped others too, but to us they contributed no less than £150,000 to ensure that our Training Centre at Dilston Hall in Northumberland would remain ours, for our lease was up and the magnificent Hambro Life contribution enabled us to buy the freehold. What a fantastic Christmas present, especially with a cold New Year just around the corner, when our trainees might have been thrown out into the snow. But all was well and we entered 1983, snug as a bug.

1983

After two and a bit years in the saddle, life was falling into a fairly predictable pattern. There was a huge lull over the Christmas, New Year period, as if all the problems of mental handicap had gone away. Very few letters, even fewer phone calls and, of course, fund-raising at a standstill. Gradually, about the third week of January, life returned to 123 Golden Lane, as did the staff, many of whom took their holidays at that time. Committees, sub-committees, working parties met, and we began to get our usual stream of welfare and legal enquiries. I returned to the touring circuit, generally spending two or three nights a week away from home, exhorting the faithful and encouraging the faint hearts and then, almost invariably, there would be some story which hit the headlines and which needed an immediate response. 1983 was no exception and before the spring had turned into summer, we were deep in the Teignmouth mire.

For those of you who haven't visited the town, I'd better explain that it is a charming Victorian Devon watering place which seems, at first glance, to have fallen somewhat behind the times, failing to compete with the glamour and glare of Torbay. Regrettably, some of the residents of Teignmouth, particularly certain members of the Chamber of Commerce, had also fallen behind the times and they became bitterly opposed to the use of one of the best hotels, the Royal, by disabled people in general and those with a mental handicap in particular. It was awful. Of course, it's true that we at MENCAP do not encourage the mass take-over of any building for holiday purposes. That's why we had got rid of our holiday home, Pirates Spring, but the things that were being said about our members' sons and daughters defied description. For instance, a civic dignitary stated that mentally handicapped people were "eroding the sea front". I thought it was the sea that did that, not perfectly harmless humans. Another bright spark in the *Teignmouth News* suggested a rationing system:

> The handicapped could holiday in a hotel on the edge of Dartmoor where acres of ground will give them boundless pleasure and privacy. Once or twice a week they could hire a coach and come to Teignmouth to relax on the beach and splash at the sea's edge. The organizers could fetch them gallons of ice-cream and drinks. Come teatime, they could return to the tranquillity of the moor undisturbed, refreshed, and leaving others unperturbed.

Well, at least the writer only suggested gallons of ice-cream and drinks. With Hitler it was far worse. Gas chambers and death. But either method got them out of the way. The owner of the Royal, Paul Bourge, was threatened with the removal of his drinks' licence and it was even alleged that the Teignmouth District Council was considering an enforcement notice to stop Mr Bourge accepting handicapped people as guests. All this over a total intake of mentally handicapped people which made up about 22 per cent of the hotel's visitors.

I contacted the, then, directors of four other charities – Chris Heginbotham of MIND, Alison Wertheimer of Campaign, Tim Yeo of the Spastics Society and Rear-Admiral Willis of the Home Farm Trust. Together, we ventured down to Teignmouth and addressed a crowded public meeting. I can only describe the event as horrible. We were heckled and harassed and shouted down, particularly when I described Teignmouth as practising "an apartheid of disability". It was all recorded, of course, by the press and television and we received massive support for our task from them all, including a leader in the *Guardian* headed, TEIGNMOUTH'S GRITTED TEETH. It ended:

We now, quite rightly, encourage integration for the handicapped. Locking people away behind high walls, away from the able-bodied, is now seen to be unjust and immensely damaging. It is considered their right to enjoy holidays by the sea, not hidden away from view but as part of the wider society in which they have a place. This requires a degree of tolerance which the able-bodied once had but now appear, sadly, to have lost. Once, village idiots were accepted by the community. As society became industrialized, it started to lock them away. Now, we are trying to restore the earlier tolerance – and in many areas it is working. As Mr Rix commented, hundreds of modern

214

resorts accommodate the handicapped with no complaint. If the people of Teignmouth had their way, we would indeed be on a slippery slope – quotas for the handicapped today, restrictions for the elderly tomorrow. It seems a dotty, sick way to run a holiday town.

There was no pat solution to the problem, of course, but I put a suggestion to Hugh (now Sir Hugh) Rossi, the Minister for the Disabled, which he accepted. Simply, I could use certain limited Government funds to pay for a Liaison Leisure Officer, who, in turn, would seek out a band of volunteers to help all disabled people in the town and would act as a go-between, to smooth out the problems between traders and visitors. We were lucky in the appointment of Colin Down as the officer. He beavered away. People of goodwill came forward and the matter was, eventually, resolved. But it was pretty nasty whilst it lasted.

Other newspaper stories that year were more pleasant, as far as I was concerned. Angela Levin interviewed me at home for the *Mail on Sunday* and recorded me as saying: "When I was younger I could manage about a hundred jobs at the same time. Now it's dropped to about thirty, but I intend to carry on. I'll have masses of peace in thirty years' time when I'm stuffed in a box and burnt to a cinder." I seemed to be anticipating living till my ninety-first year. Well, I wouldn't complain at that.

The *Sunday Times* magazine did "A Life In The Day Of" by Angela Wilkes, and I must say I did sound to be a busy boy. On the other hand, the *Observer* magazine concentrated on the launch of *The MENCAP Famous Faces Collection*, which was how well-known people saw themselves and which was intended to raise quite a lot of money for the cause. All manner of distinguished personages contributed, including the Prince and Princess of

Wales, Sir Hugh Casson, Sir Robin Day, Ken Livingstone, Barry Humphries and many, many more. The commentary for the book was written by Benny Green and this is what he wrote about me, to accompany my self-portrait, which showed a pair of underpants encasing a splendid pair of legs, with particularly knobbly knees on view:

> Brian Rix offers a terrible example of what happens to doublet-wearers who dispense with braces. They are at last revealed as men who, as a result of sustaining severe surgical operations on both carti-lages, develop the defensive habit of striped under-pants. In "the good old days" of his Whitehall farces, Mr Rix showed his knees for a living. These days he shows his compassion also.

I hope you can understand that. I had to read it twice myself.

In 1983 we received additional helpful publicity yet again, through the good offices of Princess Di. This time it was in connection with the National Rubella Council which is composed of eleven charities who all have an interest in foetal damage caused by German Measles. The Princess is the Royal Patron and we were able to use HRH in a commercial "filler" for both BBC and ITV, when the campaign was launched. For some reason, which I do not understand, shots of the Princess moving and chatting to people could be used, but not her voice. Which seemed a pity – all viewers got was my voice-over speaking the commentary. But I didn't try any lip-sync, I can assure you. Oh yes, for those of you who aren't in the business that means synchronizing your voice to coincide with the lip movements of the person on screen. Somehow I don't think my baritone would have been an appropriate match for such a fair lady's soprano, even though I could have copied Bottom and spoken in a "monstrous little voice".

On the other hand, I was able to roar that it would "do any man's heart good to hear me" over the National Development Team, a small group of advisers, which examines and reports on mental handicap services and hospitals around the country and which is based at the DHSS at the Elephant and Castle. It all began on March 16th, when I met David Hencke for lunch at La Rocchetta, an Italian restaurant, which might well be thought to be a suitable background to hatch a little plot with distinct Sicilian overtones. Ever since I had joined MENCAP I had become increasingly irritated by the fact that the NDT (National Development Team) reports were largely kept secret by the health authorities commissioning them. The NDT was always asked to visit an area to comment on the local services available for people with a mental handicap and their comments were then hugged to the bosom of the authority concerned. Only occasionally would one be enlightened enough to go public. Furthermore, those outsiders who joined the Team (which had a core of three or four people) were made to sign the Official Secrets Act so that they could not disclose anything that had been noticed, even if it was pretty dire. These outsiders attached to the Team always included a parent of a handicapped person, and as Elspet was one of those serving from time to time, it seemed absolutely incomprehensible that she couldn't tell me anything about her visits unless, of course, she unwittingly talked in her sleep. I'm glad to say she did.

One final point. If a mental handicap hospital was reported to be guilty of some scandalous behaviour, the Secretary of State could, in theory, order in the NDT to make an immediate report. In practice this never happened, although God knows there were sufficient opportunities for the use of such ministerial powers. It was all very disappointing and disorganized. Hence the lunch.

Now David Hencke was at that time the Social Services

Correspondent (he's now moved on to be Lobby Correspondent) for the *Guardian* and had achieved a somewhat fearsome reputation at the DHSS for printing adverse reports on matters before they became public. In short, he was disliked intensely by those who worked in the Elephant House, as Alexander Fleming House at the Elephant and Castle is called, but was often a useful and friendly ally of MENCAP's. Now he was really about to prove himself.

I asked David, over our Lasagne Verdi and Verdicchio, if we could mount a campaign to have the NDT reports published and for the voluntary members of the Team to be able to avoid signing the Official Secrets Act, which might be all right for chemical warfare or nuclear warheads, but seemed ridiculous and draconian when applied to people with a mental handicap. David agreed, with glee, and proceeded to conduct an operation which would have put George Smiley to shame. Reports were whisked off desks before they had ever been read, smuggled to King's Cross or Euston or Paddington, photographed and returned without anyone being any the wiser. Senior members of staff proved to be only too anxious to talk, as did members of health authorities and David was able to compile a most damning set of documented evidence. It was investigative journalism at its best – for a cause which was both just and worthy – and the *Guardian*, too, must be congratulated on allowing so much space and editorial comment when the story eventually broke, over a four-day period. Here is the original article, published on July 20th:

Confidential reports reveal cruelty and neglect

SQUALOR IN THE MENTAL HOMES
KEPT SECRET
by David Hencke, Social Services Correspondent

Appalling and inadequate conditions for thousands of mentally handicapped people living in isolated hospitals have been uncovered by a national team of health experts over the last seven years.

Confidential reports covering fifty hospitals and thirty homes reveal widespread instances of over-crowding, understaffing, custodial attitudes to patients, fire risks and the denial of the basic human dignity of toilets with doors, adequate washing facilities or personal furniture for many patients.

In isolated cases the reports reveal evidence of unexplained cruelty and neglect and squalid ward conditions such as urine-soiled carpets and dirty beds.

The details are contained in eighteen reports – all but one confidential – prepared by the Development Team for the Mentally Handicapped, whose director, Dr Gerry Simon, a psychiatrist, is retiring this summer.

The reports have been leaked to the *Guardian* because of widespread concern that the team has not been effective in combating bad conditions in many hospitals and in advocating a new life in the community for thousands of patients who should be able to leave hospital without many problems.

The reports cover conditions in hospitals in Birmingham, Derbyshire, Hampshire, Hertfordshire, Lincolnshire, North Yorkshire, Nottinghamshire, Salford, Sheffield, Solihull, Surrey, the London Borough of Sutton, Warwickshire and West Sussex. Additional reports cover community developments in Devon and Cleveland. All but one have been kept secret after decisions by health authorities or the Deprtment of Health.

Members of the development team – including psychiatrists, psychologists, nursing officers and social services directors – had to sign the Official Secrets Act before they could visit the hospitals and are not allowed to divulge the content of the reports without risking prosecution.

The reports cover hospitals serving the constituencies of Mr Norman Fowler, the Social Services Secretary and Mr Kenneth Clarke, the Health Minister.

Examples cited in the reports include:

- A ward in Whixley Hospital, North Yorkshire, in 1980, where the team discovered a naked man left alone in a room who was covering the wall with faeces.

- A punishment block for defiant mentally ill and handicapped patients and a ward full of dirty beds with patients sleeping on filthy pillows in Farmfield Hospital, Surrey, in 1982.

- Fleet Hospital in Holbeach, Lincolnshire, was described in 1979 to be so dangerous as to be "a colossal fire risk".

- A part of Queen Elizabeth Hospital, Banstead, Surrey, in 1982, where single rooms for patients have been stocked up with furniture from the "scrap heap" according to the team.

- Evidence of unexplained injuries to a number of patients in 1980 at Balderton Hospital, Newark.

- Evidence of patients being exploited by working for £2.50 a week at Goddards Green Hospital in Hassocks, West Sussex, in 1982.

- Middlefield Hospital, Solihull, which in 1981 had been described as a liability rather than an asset because of bad conditions despite excellent nursing.

- Ransom Hospital, in Rainworth, Nottinghamshire, which was subsiding down mineworkings in 1980.

Many of the health authorities contacted by the *Guardian* said they had attempted to remedy some of these examples but none was able to say that it had been able to improve conditions for all the patients and their hospitals, even in cases where the team had reported seven years ago.

A typical reaction was from Mr David Leggett, district administrator for East Surrey, which covers Farmfield Hospital. He said: "It would be unfair to say that nothing has changed since this report but I would not be telling the truth if I said that every complaint has been remedied. Patients are still, for example, suffering bad toilet conditions, even though we have spent some money upgrading facilities."

In many cases nurses were congratulated by the team for trying to provide a decent service for the patients. In some cases the goodwill of nursing staff was said to be running out rapidly because of appalling conditions.

Last night, Mr Brian Rix, the Secretary-General of MENCAP, the Royal Society for Mentally Handicapped Children and Adults said: "It is ironic that only on Friday Mr Clarke said that mentally handicapped people were a priority service yet parents of mentally handicapped children are now faced with these reports in the *Guardian* showing otherwise. The time is long past that we should have to accept these intolerable conditions. We shall now be demanding action without delay. The Minister seems to speak with forked tongue. He has been spending his life suppressing reports on these hospitals yet claiming that the mentally handicapped are a priority."

Pretty hard-hitting stuff, I think you will agree and, regrettably, true. In fact, "the shameful secrets" occupied the whole of page eleven and were a scarifying indictment.

Such headlines as "staff attitudes twenty years behind the times ... overcrowded, bare, drab, barrack-like ... one bath for fifty-two people ... a colossal fire risk ... a modernized workhouse ... goodwill which cannot last ... unexplained injuries to patients ... should be closed" will give you some idea of the contents, covering ten hospitals in Derbyshire, five in Hampshire, one in Hertfordshire, six in Lincolnshire, four in North Yorkshire, one in Salford, five in Sheffield, one in Solihull, one in Sutton, eleven in Surrey, six in Warwickshire and Birmingham, five in West Sussex – fifty-six in all, spread right around England. David Hencke had done his work with deadly accuracy.

This was followed by an article of mine, which appeared in the *Guardian* the next day, which went as follows:

After yesterday's Guardian *revelations of persistent degrading conditions for the mentally handicapped Brian Rix of MENCAP appeals for action.*

OPENING HEARTS AND FILES

Since 1944, there have been twenty-four Acts and thirteen or more sets of regulations affecting the lives of people with mental handicap. Other important DHSS references include such high-flown titles as Better Services for the Mentally Handicapped (1971); Mental Handicap – Progress, Problems and Priorities (1980); Care in Action and Care in the Community – both issued in 1981. Yet this impressive panoply, erected by successive Governments and constantly referred to by those in authority, has fallen to dust when set against the melancholy, shameful and degrading list of conditions pertaining in many mental handicap hospitals and local authority areas, as chronicled in yesterday's *Guardian*.

Were those revelations the work of some irresponsible ghoul, intent on polluting the ear of a desipient journalist, seeking yet another shock-horror story for his yellow pages? Indeed, they were not. They came from reports compiled by the Development Team for the Mentally Handicapped – an eminently respectable group of professionals and parents working in that particular field.

The Development Team was formed in 1975, and later the then Secretary of State for Health and Social Security, David Ennals, stated the aim of the Team was "to offer advice to individual field authorities and others on the planning and development of their own services for the mentally handicapped in the light of local needs and opportunities and against a background of Government policy guidelines".

What this statement failed to mention, was that any *compulsory* powers of inspection had been removed from the Team, even though these had previously existed under the earlier Health Advisory Service. The Secretary of State also omitted the fact that the Development Team could only visit an area by invitation of the authority concerned. This was subsequently amended to allow the Secretary of State to direct a visit – but such powers have rarely, if ever, been used.

Further proving its toothlessness, the Team has to send its reports to the inviting authority and the distribution of these is left in the authority's tender, loving hands. Can you wonder that everything is subsequently shrouded in mystery – with all the consequent inaction, inefficiency and ineptitude which, yesterday, became tragically obvious? Indeed, the Team's first report in 1978 (they have published three general ones which we have been allowed to see) proudly proclaimed that "Reports are usually made available by authorities to all interested parties."

Aren't mentally handicapped people themselves

interested? Or their parents? Or those responsible for education, transport, housing and employment et al? The only way the majority of these became "interested parties' was by watching such television programmes as *The Silent Minority* or reading the horrific revelations "leaked" earlier this year about seven hospitals in Surrey and two in West Sussex.

The fact that so many reports have become readily available to the *Guardian* makes a mockery of this whole secrecy procedure. Even the members of the Team have to sign the Official Secrets Act before commencing work. You would think the DHSS guarded our most precious defence secrets and, God knows, enough of those have been leaked.

It is patently absurd that such draconian measures are necessary to protect the delicate sensibilities of the authorities concerned. Has not the world at large the right to learn the dismal facts about those who have been born so tragically disabled? After all, Hampshire published, in full, the Team's report on the Wessex Regional Health Authority way back in 1978. The regional health authority didn't fall apart and lived to provide better services, with considerable co-operation from the voluntary sector.

It is not as if the Government is against such a proposal in other areas. Reports of HM Inspectorate to the Department of Education and Science are now all published, a move which has been widely welcomed. More recently, Norman Fowler, Secretary of State for Health and Social Security, announced that the new Social Services Inspectorate would normally regard its reports of formal inspections as documents of public access. So, what makes our mental handicap services so different? After all, they are conducted in the electorate's name.

In the world of mental handicap, it always seems

that a scandal is required to move things along. That is indeed a sorry state of affairs – but if the reports which became known yesterday enable the Development Team to develop and really help to establish "better services for the mentally handicapped" promised in 1971, I am sure that all of us – Ministers, civil servants, local and health authorities, nurses, teachers and voluntary bodies – will be delighted. As for people with mental handicap and their families – they will be ecstatic and very, very surprised.

Of course, the proverbial hit the fan in no uncertain way. I was hauled in by Sir Robin Day to the *World At One* to talk to the Minister most concerned, Kenneth Clarke. To be fair, I don't think Kenneth had any real idea of what had been going on and genuinely didn't know that people like Elspet had to sign the Official Secrets Act. He promised to look into matters immediately – and did. In our 1983 Annual Report, I was able to write: "Reports made by the National Development Team were originally supplied to the inviting authority, for distribution at their discretion but, thanks to the campaign mounted by MENCAP and the *Guardian*, this has now been altered to enable the Team to publish its own reports. Other improvements in the Team's terms of reference are likely to be announced in 1984."

We never heard another thing about the Official Secrets Act. I suppose the decision not to make a volunteer sign was kept secret. It would have to be, wouldn't it?

So our battle with the Establishment bore fruit, as did a number of other events in 1983. For example, Chef and Brewer backed our first Pro-Am Golf Tournament, called the Bruce Forsyth Classic, which made a considerable amount of money in that first year. Unfortunately, the brewery decided, subsequently, to go elsewhere and the Classic became a thing of the past – as so many classics do. It's odd, though, that about the same time the Stars

Organization for Spastics was organizing the Bob Hope Classic, with my old friend Dickie Henderson working his socks off to make it a success. However, that, too, foundered when it was found that the amount raised or sponsored barely covered the running expenses and the charity received very little.

On the other hand, there is one golf classic – that named after Sir Harry Secombe – which has gone on for years and years and always increases its take for the lucky recipients, the Lord's Taverners. Now the Lord's Taverners started life in 1950 when a bunch of theatricals, headed by Martin Boddey, John Mills (before his knighthood), Michael Shepley, Stephen Mitchell, John Snagge, as well as some others, decided that as they spent a great deal of time watching cricket in front of the Tavern at Lord's it would be a good idea to club together to do something, in return, for cricket. And that's where the money went, at first, to youth cricket, as well as to the National Playing Fields Association, when the Duke of Edinburgh became the Patron and twelfth man. Mind you, there wasn't much money either, but it was a start. Gradually, the group expanded, to include prominent businessmen as well as famous actors and cricketers, but the numbers have always been kept down to around 750, although there are many more Friends in the regions. Originally, the money was raised by charity cricket matches and, eventually, a ball. Then the Harry Secombe Classic was added, followed by rugger and numerous social events. Such was the income, that a Foundation Committee was formed (on which I serve) and the funds distributed by us in the ratio of 45 per cent to youth cricket and 55 per cent to help disabled young people, both in leisure pursuits and general day-to-day problems of living. In 1987–88 we reached our first million pounds for the year and celebrated by awarding five other charities £5,000 each for unusually helpful work in the field of leisure, with an additional £500 for five handicapped individuals whose personal achievement was outstanding. This in one year alone, plus forty-two coaches for disabled people (known as New Horizons) and the balance of £829,469 being distributed in grant aid for all those we can help. Not bad for a bunch of rogues and vagabonds who only went along for the beer and remained to provide champagne. And I mustn't forget to pay tribute to the Director of the Lord's Taverners, Tony Swainson (you've met him before with the 100 Guinea Club) who, in spite of a naval briskness and brusqueness (some might say bloody rudeness) gets things done in an incredible way. It's a pleasure to work with him. Well, sometimes . . . and I should know, I was President of the Taverners in 1970 and now I've reached the sear and yellow they've made me an Umpire, in other words one of the Trustees. It's an honour of which I am very proud.

Two events clashed in the spring of 1983 which caused a certain amount of shilly-shallying. The London Marathon was booked at the Festival Hall on Sunday, April 17th, whilst the Gateway Festival (a biennial event) was booked on Saturday 16th. However, the Marathon organizers, headed by Chris Brasher, wanted to use part of the building on that Saturday for the registration of the runners. Long phone calls ensued between us and I can't remember exactly what was agreed – except that both Festival and Marathon proceeded exactly as planned but MENCAP seemed to receive around £60,000 in sponsorship. Not a bad deal, obviously. I only wish I could remember what it was. Incidentally, earlier I mentioned that the annual church service at the beginning of MENCAP Week is a battery charger for the year ahead. Well, so is the Gateway Festival. Dozens of young people with a mental handicap, plus their voluntary helpers, come from all parts of Britain to perform on the Festival Hall stage. A capacity audience, many of them, also, mentally handicapped, packs the auditorium – twice, for there are two shows – and a great entertainment ensues. Not only *is* it entertaining, but it is often extremely moving as well. I wouldn't miss it for the world.

Two conferences in that year, too, which didn't clash, but were of extreme interest to all parents who were experiencing the birth of a handicapped child or the problems of adulthood facing their growing offspring. The first was in MENCAP Week and the title self-explanatory – "Mental Handicap: Need it Happen – and When it Does?" The second was the opening salvo from the recently formed Independent Development Council for people with Mental Handicap (IDC), made up, as I mentioned, of distinguished individuals from the world of handicap. The conference, and the accompanying booklet, *Elements of a Comprehensive Local Service for People with Mental Handicap,* doesn't sound exactly charged with dynamism, but I can assure you it was and the booklet was a bestseller, well, in mental handicap terms anyway. Over the years I was Chairman, IDC went on to publish three other valuable books: *Next Steps*, which looked at progress, problems and priorities in the development of services, *Living Like Other People*, and *Pursuing Quality*. These publications were of the greatest possible help to all concerned and were an extremely useful addition to the Stamina documents, which MENCAP has been producing for years. Stamina is an acronym for minimum standards and these papers, with such titles as *Local Action for Services*, *Services for People with a Mental Handicap Over 16*, *Residential Care*, *Elderly People with a Mental Handicap*, *Hospitals*, etc, etc, have been the yardstick against which parents, local authorities and carers can measure how well, or otherwise, they are doing. They are checklists of the highest possible value and the brain-child of MENCAP's founder, Judy Fryd. IDC came later – much later – but it, too, is very valuable.

Towards the end of 1983 I had to speak at a dinner being held by the Association of County Councils in the Exam Schools at Oxford. Now if ever any of you have sat your Responsions there (the entrance exam) as I had done, you will know that it is a vast L-shaped room, totally unsuited to after-dinner speaking, especially when over 700 people are spread around in a space which could house the Graf Zeppelin. It so happened I was expected to make a serious speech but it was soon clear that a little laughter was needed to cheer the place up. At the afternoon session certain left-wing county councils had demonstrated noisily during a speech by Kenneth Clarke, then Minister of Health, before walking out en masse. They'd all walked back in for dinner, mind you, but as the Minister was still there as the guest of honour, you can see that you could cut the atmosphere with a knife. I didn't enjoy my dinner. I never do, anyway, before a speech, but on this occasion I toyed with my food (I believe that's the expression) even more than usual. How was I going to break the barrier of gloom which sat like a damp cloud over all?

Inspiration came as I stood up to speak. Realizing that I could never be seen or heard at floor level, I climbed into the invigilator's pulpit and there saw the printed rules for examinations, which had to be followed by the invigilator in charge. Luckily many of them referred to the problems caused by students' bodily functions assuming desperate proportions during an exam, and this not only coincided with my own peristaltic action at the time, but allowed me to get a first laugh by reading out the more scatological references to the assembled county councillors, Directors of Social Services, politicians, charity workers and David Blunkett's guide dog. The rest was easy. Putting my serious notes on one side, I launched into my long-practised list of theatrical stories which went down like a bomb. Having grabbed the audience's attention and goodwill, I was then able to ease in my original speech but played absolutely safe by ending on one final "woofer".

Never have I been so pleased to have a reserve of jokes at the ready. With that, and my reputation for descending trousers, I need never fear an angry mob again. Unless they don't care for farce, that is, or have heard all the jokes before. As I've been telling them for the best part of twenty years, I suppose that's a distinct possibility.

1984

If you believe in horoscopes, you could say that 1984 presented MENCAP with many unusual opportunities to make money. Well, that's what astrologer Russell Grant told me anyway one early morning on *Breakfast Time* telly. If, like me, you don't believe in the power of heavenly bodies to rule our destiny, you would be surprised to learn that the opportunities did occur and we at MENCAP seized them with both hands. To hell with incredulity. When I joined MENCAP our turnover was in the region of £5 million a year. When I left seven years later it was around £22 million. Now it has climbed to £40 million. You can see that we couldn't be too choosy as to whether the planets were in the right place or not.

The first opportunity occurred at the beginning of January when Bernard Braden and I began a series of interviews (half each) which benefited MENCAP and, at the same time, committed to posterity the careers of a number of well-known actors and actresses, accompanied by film clips of their work on screen. Again, using astrological portents, this was a happy conjunction of the stars with MENCAP in the ascendant. Well, I think that's the sort of mumbo-jumbo that is uttered. Not being Nancy Reagan, I wouldn't know.

I'd better explain how it came about. A company called Storytime had been formed when my old mate Johnnie

Slater was alive, to exploit those television tales which he told so well, and which won him awards in the good old days of one BBC channel only. His widow, Betty, had taken his place on the Board, along with Renée Wilson (one of the fearsome female film executives), her son Peter, Bernard Braden and TV entrepreneur, Richard Price.

Now it so happened I dreamt up the idea of a TV series of interviews called *Theatre Knights (and Dames)* and persuaded Storytime that it was an interesting idea. Furthermore, I also believed that those interviewees might be prepared to pay most of their fees for the first transmission to MENCAP, for a suitable credit on the screen, of course. I was right about that, but wrong in the number of theatrical knights we could interview. Lord Olivier couldn't for he was under contract already for his life story and Sir John Gielgud and Sir Alec Guinness had other reasons for not taking part, as did Dames Wendy Hiller and Peggy Ashcroft. We were left with an impressive bunch nevertheless – Lord Miles, Sir John Mills, Dame Anna Neagle and Dame Flora Robson, with Sir Michael Hordern expressing interest – but hardly enough names for a long-running series.

We changed the title to *An Invitation to Remember* and we were off. Since then, of course, we have been able to interview Sir Michael in the second series, Sir Anthony Quayle and me, with Sir Harry Secombe and Sir Richard Attenborough evading us as yet. Even if you add Dame Judi Dench you still have under a dozen Ks and Ds available, and these kind of programmes are generally sold in blocks of thirteen. That's why we changed the title, increased the potential, and we've had some splendid people in front of the camera as a result. The original series was directed by Vivian Kemble but now Mike Mansfield has taken over, and the interviewer these days is the indestructible Brian Johnston. Mind you, he's no stranger to investitures himself with an OBE and an MC, whilst there are an awful lot of CBEs and OBEs sprinkled about the other interviewees as well. To date they are Robert Morley, Michael Denison, Dulcie Gray, Donald Sinden, Gordon Jackson, Trevor Howard, Phyllis Calvert, Richard Todd, Leslie Phillips, Glenda Jackson, Christopher Lee, Sylvia Syms and soon her near-namesake, Sheila Sim – better known nowadays, I suppose, as Lady Attenborough. Not bad, eh? And on the very day I wrote this story I received yet another cheque for MENCAP from Storytime to the tune of £14,500, being the second payment for our little interview series which will still earn quite a lot over many years and will certainly be used as obituary material when those of us taking part find out who really runs the firmament . . .

What other prognostications came to pass, proving there were unusual opportunities to make money that year? Well, the Keep Fit Association for one. In the previous year, we had been promised twelve months' fund-raising by that body of women (forgive the sly allusion) and they hoped to manage about £40,000. In the event I went along to their annual event in June at the Albert Hall, when leotard-clad women display their suppleness and agility (with suitable musical accompaniment, of course) to a packed house of other women who have decided discretion is the better part of valour and do not perform. At the interval I was presented with the cheque: £107,000! That's an awful lot of coffee mornings and jumble sales. All of us at MENCAP were very grateful and suitably impressed. I even enjoyed the Albert Hall demonstration, particularly the women, who, after such incredible generosity, suddenly looked like Marilyn Monroe. Mind you, one or two did anyway. Equally, one or two looked like Bessie Braddock, but beauty is in the eye of the beholder. They were transformed. I was transfixed. "Tempt not the stars, young man, thou canst not play with the severity of fate" – and if that was good enough for John Ford, it's good enough for me.

Then came another unusual opportunity to make money for MENCAP. The Readathon. Actually, we were the first charity to take part in this exercise, sponsored by Books for Students Ltd. After the first year – which was by way of being an experiment – the sponsors decided that other charities should be involved and we would just have to take our turn. We were a bit miffed, to say the least. We felt we should have been given a second year to consolidate our work, for we had to help sort out all the teething troubles, but, in spite of numerous hurt and surprised telephone calls from me, we lost. We are still waiting for it to be our turn again. After all, it made £136,000 even in its first year. You can't chuck away that sort of money without a struggle, and it is fund-raising by very simple means. Children obtain sponsors, who support their improved reading skills and the money goes to the named charity. A great idea. It helps kids to read and mums and dads and aunts and uncles to cough up and be proud to do it. Oh and grandparents too, of course. I can't wait for it to be my turn with our lot. Especially if it is for MENCAP.

Another unusual event, which has now become a major plank in MENCAP appeals, was also sponsored for the first time in 1984. This was parachuting, and all who jumped netted us over £80,000 in that opening season. I don't know how (or why) people do it, but they do, and we are all very happy about their efforts and the money which is raised. There have been over 12,000 jumpers since that first year. All have some basic training as part of the deal and injuries have been of a relatively minor nature and confined to less than 0.05 per cent of everyone who has leapt out of an aircraft. But as far as I'm concerned, rather like the ladies *not* taking part at the Albert Hall, discretion is the better part of valour. I would rather don tights and a leotard any day. Come to think of it, I have done, when I impersonated a Russian ballet dancer in *Chase Me, Comrade!* at the Whitehall. Jumping into a sea of laughter is a damn sight easier than jumping on to Mother Earth, as I proved when a Birmingham policeman, Superintendent Martin Burton, invited me to make a speech at a luncheon in that city. He promised me a lot of money, but wanted a project to make it easier. At that time we were looking for a specially equipped bus to go with our PRMH (Profound Retardation and Multiple Handicap) project in Manchester, costing about £18,000. Our friendly copper agreed and the lunch was fixed. On the due date I sallied forth to Brum to be greeted by an extremely noisy audience, consisting mainly of bookmakers and publicans and their wives. You could see why they came along though. Superintendent Burton is very large and persuasive. When the lunch was over (about dinnertime – it went on for five hours) I received a cheque for £23,000. Not bad for a speech which was really the same one I had made in the Oxford Examination Schools, to keep the ravening hordes away from Kenneth Clarke. And not bad for one Birmingham copper with a load of generous friends. But I bet none of them believe in what the stars foretell. Only the punters go in for that sort of moonshine.

Another coach which came my way in 1984 was not connected with MENCAP but with the Friends of Normansfield. As that's for people with a mental handicap too, you can't blame Russell Grant for being slightly offbeam. It was being presented by the Lord's Taverners at the Stoop Memorial Ground, next door to Twickenham, when the Harlequins Sevens were taking place and the recipient was me, as the Chairman of the Friends. Representing the Taverners was none other than Denis Thatcher who, not wishing to use an official driver on a Sunday, had entrained and taxied to the ground at lunchtime. When the jollifications were over, Mr Thatcher, in need of transport, posed a question which must be recorded: "Anyone going near Number 10?" he asked. He was almost killed in the rush to take him there, in response to one of the best throwaway lines I've ever heard – only "the Palace" would have been better. Or perhaps that would have been confused with the theatre by those eighteen-stone loose forwards.

Funnily enough, I was able to play that gag on the Prime Minister herself a few months later when Elspet opened in *On Your Toes* at that very London theatre. I was at a reception at Number 10 but had to seek an early leave-taking because of the curtain-up time on press nights at seven o'clock. "Excuse me, Prime Minister," I said, "I must apologize for leaving so early, but I have to be at the Palace." And with that, I was off to Cambridge Circus, where the Palace is located, not the grander one at the end of the Mall.

There, the powers of our friendly Nostradamus, Russell Grant, came to an end. With no more windfalls that year, it was nose to the grindstone, to make ends meet, but even so we ended the year with a healthy paper surplus – which, I hasten to add, is not really a surplus at all for it is already committed to some project or other in advance. But grateful thanks to you all – Storytime, Keep Fit Ladies, Literate School Kids, Parachutists, Second Cityites, Lord's Taverners – plus the myriad supporters of MENCAP who made it all possible. Oh, and Russell Grant too – Old Moore himself – for predicting the future so accurately. Even if it was guesswork, there's an element of ESP around somewhere.

After that financial excitement, the rest of 1984 must seem drab by comparison, although never as drab as that predicted by George Orwell. He really got it wrong. But then he'd never met Russell Grant.

Luckily, there was an unexpected touch of glamour for me when Elspet went off to film in the last series of *Tenko* in Singapore. Her visit was for five weeks – but I managed to get a week off in the middle, and flew there to join her. She wasn't filming every day, so we had a marvellous time. I had two suits made when I was out there. Lovely material, friendly tailor, but when I got home they simply wouldn't fit anywhere. It must have been all the food we ate in Newton Circus. That, or the Indian meal we scoffed on my last night. We returned to the hotel and were standing by the reception desk, when I suddenly felt something running up the inside of my trousers towards a rather sensitive area. Terrified that it was a tarantula or some similar lethal miscreant, I did what I had been paid well to do over 12,000 times – dropped my trousers. The shrill shrieks of laughter which greeted this unexpected act – from *Tenko* cast members to young receptionists – quickly turned to shrieks of alarm as the biggest cockroach you have ever seen leapt off my underpants and went hurtling across the highly polished marble floor, skidding in all directions. Some wag remarked that it was now clear why cockroaches were so named – although encroach might have been more accurate. But it was a damn close-run thing, I can tell you.

Back in London, two lunches which are worth recording. One with the, then, new Director of the Spastics Society, Vice-Admiral Sir John Cox KCB, to give him his full title, when we discussed even closer co-operation between our two societies on the political front – with a small "p", you'll notice. This came to fruition when two other founder members of the Independent Development Council, Barnardo's (Director, Roger Singleton) and MIND (Director, Chris Heginbotham) joined our little group and together we formed the Community Care Campaigners. Our task was to visit the conferences of the various political parties and have breakfast meetings with all of those who were interested in community care, particularly Ministers or their Shadows. It worked remarkably well. We were a jolly little bunch and, with our advisers, we made a considerable impression on those we needed to influence most but, regrettably, no sooner had we worked on a Minister than he seemed to be moved to another department or was, quite frankly, sacked. Such names as Sir Gerard Vaughan, Sir Hugh Rossi, Sir George Young, Baroness Trumpington, Kenneth Clarke, John Major and, even, Norman Fowler all spring to mind, whilst those in the House of Lords kept changing like autumn colours, sometimes falling off the tree. All very difficult. I wonder if it's part of a deliberate policy? Never let the rulers get too friendly with the natives.

My last visit, as part of the group, was to a fringe meeting at the Conservative Party Conference in Blackpool after their election victory in 1987. I was chairing the occasion with Emma Nicholson (a newly elected Conservative MP) as the principal speaker and Sir John Cox as the winder-up. It was amazingly successful. We were in the Circle Bar of the Winter Gardens and the place was packed to overflowing but next door, poor old British Caledonian, trying to resist a take-over by British Airways, attracted only a handful. All rather encouraging, for it seemed to show that the rank and file of the Conservative Party is more interested in its social conscience than in big business. But I have no proof, mind you, just delight that we were able to attract such a large crowd who genuinely seemed concerned and involved, mainly at county council level.

After that it was back to London and my retirement. John Cox, a super guy, by the way, also retired shortly after me, after some strange goings-on at the Spastics Society, so the Community Care Campaigners had lost half their team at one go. But they are battling on, I believe, so good luck to them in their future endeavours.

The second luncheon I would like to mention is one with young Robert Lawrence. I'm sure many of you will remember Robert, for he is the Scots Guards' Officer who lost nearly half his brain at Tumbledown in the Falklands conflict, was awarded the MC, and the subject of much controversy when his book (written with his father, John) was published and also when the BBC produced a splendid drama on the subject for television written by Charles Wood and directed by Richard Eyre, who is now the Artistic Director of the Royal National.

Wing Commander John Lawrence has recently retired from being one of the Assistant Secretaries at the MCC and, over the years, I have got to know him well (and his wife Jean), particularly at Test Match time, for he was in charge of the Green Enclosure of "Q" Stand where all the relatives of those taking part in the Test are invited to go. As you will recall, women (other than cleaners and the Queen) are not allowed into the pavilion at Lord's so whenever Elspet comes with me to a Test, John has always been extremely helpful and allowed us to sit at the back of the stand, provided there is a spot of room. That, and a large gin or two before lunch, makes for very pleasurable watching. John and Jean Lawrence also live very near to us in Barnes, so that's how I know the story about Robert, his amazing recovery against all the odds, and his desire to get into the world of films. Hence the lunch with me, to see if I could help.

In walked this courageous young man, swinging his wonky left leg and left arm firmly dug into his jacket pocket. If you hadn't known of his terrible injuries you might have thought he had twisted an ankle playing tennis, such is the control he has obtained over his pretty useless left-hand side. Incredible. Anyway, we chatted away and it was soon clear that there was no way I could help directly, for now the army had no further use for him he was determined to get into the world of entertainment, and once that young man's mind is made up, it stays that way. Rather similar, I imagine, to the dogged determination – some might say bloody-mindedness – displayed by Sir Douglas Bader when he was also so tragically disabled as a young man.

From MENCAP's point of view, I could see Robert as being of inestimable value on the appeals front, but that was not to be. However, I was able to introduce him to Ray Cooney and Robert worked as a general dogsbody in the Theatre of Comedy with Thelma Holt for some months before managing to break into films, the first of which, *Tumbledown*, was greeted with such acclaim by the vast majority of viewers and with such loathing by a few blimps. They saw it as a party political attack, rather than as an attack on war itself and the way many of those who fight so bravely for their country are forgotten once the battle's lost and won. Anyone who doubts that should pay a visit to the Royal Star and Garter at the top of Richmond Hill. We should remind ourselves occasionally how much so many owe to so few.

So, I failed to take advantage of Robert's unique personality. On the other hand, one man's loss etc, and there is no doubt that Robert will achieve a position in the world of films if there is any justice around. And, you know, there is, as far as actors and directors and producers are concerned. I'm sure you'll hear of him again, now all that controversy has died down. As I reminded John at the time, today's newspaper wraps up tomorrow's fish and chips. I should know, I've had many a six penn'orth enfolding my bad notices. The snag is, you remember them.

Finally, in 1984 one very interesting piece of legislation received the Royal Assent, the Police and Criminal Evidence Act. We had worked on this for some time, as it had been put on one side due to the 1983 general election, meeting quite frequently with the Association of Chief Police Officers who were only too keen to help.

We had entered into the debates, particularly in the House of Lords through David Renton, Philip Allen and others, and we had seen considerable changes made in the way people with a mental handicap had to be interviewed. Gone were the old Judges' Rules and in their place were the Codes of Practice, which set out in great detail how mentally handicapped people were to be treated, questioned and identified, particularly the need for an uninvolved third party to be present. All a great step forward, but I often wonder how closely the Codes of Practice are followed when it comes to a great drunken punch-up on a Saturday night. I imagine this can still be the loneliest night of the week – not just for Frank Sinatra – but for many a simple soul who finds himself swept up into those police vans. We still haven't finally solved the problem and whilst hooliganism and football violence abound, I doubt if we ever will.

1985

I think I should begin with the scandal that never was. Put baldly, I left Elspet in London and went off with Honor Blackman to India. That, no doubt, is how one or two of our more lurid Sunday penny-dreadfuls might have led with the story, if there'd been one. But there wasn't. I'll tell you what really happened.

In March I had to go to India, as Chairman of the MENCAP Medical Advisory Panel, to attend a medical/scientific conference. Don't panic; as a non-medical person I was accompanied by some of my kosher medical colleagues and many others from the world of medicine involved in mental handicap, including our old friend Dr Hugh Jolly – shortly to die, poor man, from cancer of the spine. I believe that, altogether, 1,700 medics and paramedics attended with, as usual, the odd man out – me. But I loved it.

Anyway, when the conference – which was held in Delhi – was over, Elspet and I had planned to visit all her old stamping grounds in the subcontinent where she had been brought up as a child and, later, as a young woman. It was to be our holiday of holidays. We are still trying to arrange it.

Just before we left for India, Elspet received a phone call from a great friend of ours, Honor Blackman, saying she was leaving the cast of *On Your Toes* at the Palace Theatre in March and wondering if she could join us on our trip. She and Elspet could do Agra and Jaipur whilst I slogged away at the conference and then we could all go together to visit Elspet's old haunts in the north. It seemed a splendid idea and everything was agreed.

We reckoned without the tide in the affairs of women which led, on this occasion, to Elspet being offered the part of Peggy Porterfield, the very part Honor was leaving, at the time we should have been going to India. All of us thought it a bit of a joke, for Elspet was hardly renowned for her singing voice. But her Scottish grit came to the fore, and before you could say Harry Lauder she was singing away with the best of them. I know, because son Jamie, daughter-in-law Helen and I all attended that first night and we sat amazed and entranced as Elspet carolled away in "Too Good for the Average Man", with John Bentley, and positively glided through "The Heart Is Quicker Than the Eye", with Tim Flavin. As far as we were concerned, it was a transformation and Elspet continued to surprise us all until the end of the run some six months later.

But that left Honor and me in somewhat of a fix. Clearly, there would be little point in us looking at Elspet's past, without Elspet, and anyway we would probably now wish to return to England somewhat quicker than in our original plan. So Honor booked up with one of Cox and King's tours, "A Taste of India", or something like that, whilst I had a taste of Delhi at the Maurya Sheraton Hotel, which gave me absolutely no idea of what the country was like, for it was straight from the hotel to the conference centre and then back again. However, I did manage to sneak off and see such famous local sights as Lutyen's New Delhi, Qutabminar, Humayun's Tomb, Lahore Gate and Rajghat – which is Gandhi's Memorial. All very impressive but in my travels I caught sight of Old Delhi and many of its impoverished inhabitants. Pretty grim, I must report, but really no worse than parts of Cairo which Elspet and I had seen over the New Year, when we went up the Nile (or was it down the Nile?) with John and Betty Chapman (a marvellous trip) and ended our stay with two nights in Cairo. I'll never forget being driven out of a prosperous street, turning a corner and straight into a mountainous rubbish dump, with people actually living in caves burrowed out of the filth. Once you've seen poverty on that scale it's unlikely you'll come across anything worse in another city, and frankly, I didn't. But that doesn't make it any better, wherever you may be.

When the conference was over, I was able to fly to Agra and see the famous Taj Mahal but try as I could, I wasn't able to get to Jaipur. Indian Airlines (the internal airline) had just become computerized that very week and when I tried to book, sitting in their Delhi non-air-conditioned offices for nearly three hours, I was told there were twenty-seven people ahead of me on every flight's waiting-list. Those same twenty-seven stayed jammed in the computer for several days, I believe. I suppose the flight went to Jaipur half empty but, regrettably, I wasn't on it.

I was on the flight to Goa though, at the end of the conference week and had a simply splendid five days doing absolutely nothing except eating, swimming and sun-bathing. Honor was able to manoeuvre her package tour in a Goanese direction and she, too, had a splendid time. Perhaps the oddest moment came when I was sitting down to lunch, reading Frederick Forsyth's *The Fourth Protocol* and dwelling on the passage that mentions the Profumo scandal. I looked up and there, crossing my eyeline, was Jack Profumo himself. I hastily hid the book and greeted him, for he had just arrived for a short visit with Valerie, and was clearly startled to see me joined by Honor a few moments later. Explanations were forthcoming – they always sounded a bit lame – and we enjoyed each other's company for the rest of my stay. I say "my stay", for Honor remained on at the hotel after I'd left, the Profumos went somewhere else and I returned to work at MENCAP, still disappointed that Elspet and I had not been able to enjoy our original grand tour, but delighted that she was enjoying such a success in *On Your Toes*.

As for Jack Profumo, I later told him about the *Fourth Protocol*, when I first saw him on the terrace, and suggested it must be pretty grim to go on reading about yourself so long after the original story had broken. He nodded, a little sadly I thought. In spite of all his marvellous work at Toynbee Hall, his CBE and his apparent rehabilitation with the Establishment, it may always prove impossible for Jack to wrap up his fish and chips in yesterday's newspaper. That's one scandal the media seem to regurgitate at the slightest excuse. And I seem to be doing the same myself. Oh dear. Certainly *not* the scandal that never was.

Meanwhile, back at MENCAP I was busy putting divisionalization into place. Up to now, we had twelve regions, but a working party had decided that seven divisions in the UK would mean fewer chiefs, who could concentrate on administrative problems, and more Indians who could attend to all the many tasks they had to undertake in their attempts to help those with a mental handicap and their families. It was a pretty big change and not always easy to accomplish – for there's nowt so insular as counties when it comes to the crunch. However, by dint of a great deal of travel and speaking to all concerned, parents and staff alike, I and my Group Directors were able to make out a reasonable case for the change and gradually it took place. Even now, though, divisionalization is still working the bugs out of its system and it may be another year or two before practice matches up to theory.

Practice and theory came together, though, with great success when the, then, independent supermarket chain – Hillards – decided to celebrate their seventy-fifth anniversary by supporting MENCAP, and a magnificent sum of £175,000 was raised. It was then that the difficulty of local societies relating to the Royal Society was highlighted. There has always been a problem over fund-raising. Local societies or Hospital Friends' groups feel, not unnaturally, that they should be left to trawl their own particular territory without any interference from Head Office. Head Office, on the other hand, feel, equally naturally, that if the appeal is nationwide, then they should be allowed to dip into local pockets too, especially if they have done all the donkey work to get the appeal going in the first place. We had done just this with Hillards, fighting off four other major charities for our solus position but, in spite of this, there were a number of occasions when a local society felt that the money raised by a local supermarket should stay with them. Eventually a compromise was reached and, when requested by local Hillards staff, a percentage stayed in the locality, whilst the rest came winging down to Golden Lane. As Francis Bacon so wisely wrote: "Money is like muck, no good except it be spread."

1985 saw the birth of our youngest grandson (to date), Jolyon – to Louisa and Jonathan Coy. He arrived when the Community Care Campaigners were breakfasting with Dr David Owen and the, then, SDP in Torquay. The hotel could provide, and it was a very jolly occasion, with champagne accompanying the bacon and eggs and orange juice to wet the baby's head. It wasn't long, though, before the fizz went out of our newest political party but not, thank goodness, out of Jolyon. For that one happy birth,

244

though, there were two sad deaths. A stalwart MENCAP supporter, Treasurer and Chairman for many years, Lord Segal, died. For no personal reason, but just because he was a good, caring man, Sam Segal had given great service to our cause and we missed his kind and wise counsel. On the other hand, Elspet and I will always miss the laughter and goodwill from a close friend, Dickie Henderson, who died from the dread cancer. When Gwyneth, his wife, went to see him in the Cromwell Hospital just after they had told him the worst he was looking pretty glum, but he called for a bottle of champagne and when Gwyneth asked him why he was celebrating, Dickie brought forth a classic one-liner: "Why not?" he said. "At least it isn't AIDS." Eight weeks later he was dead.

I suppose, though, the most publicized problem facing MENCAP in 1985, spilling over to 1986, was "in vitro" fertilization, which eventually cost us one of our Patrons, Cardinal Basil Hume. It all began, originally, when the Warnock Report on Human Fertilization and Embryology was published in 1984 and then others began to get in on the act – especially Mr Enoch Powell who brought forth, with a little aid from LIFE and SPUC, his Unborn Children (Protection) Bill. The Warnock Committee favoured the licensing of experiments on human embryos up to fourteen days old, under strict control as to the purposes and conditions attaching to the experimentation. Old Enoch, spurred on by his, mainly, Catholic supporters, thought otherwise. His Bill would have prevented a human embryo being created, kept or used for any purpose other than enabling a child to be born to a particular woman and would have made it a criminal offence to be in possession of an embryo except with the authority of the Secretary of State for Health and Social Security, given expressly for that purpose and no other.

As well as heated debate in the House of Commons, there was much heated debate elsewhere, no more so than in the columns of *The Times*. First, a passionate article by Enoch Powell, then an equally impassioned response from Lady Warnock. After that, shoals of correspondence, including this letter from the MENCAP Medical Advisory Panel and the distinguished Editorial Board of the *Journal of Mental Deficiency Research*:

FROM MR BRIAN RIX AND OTHERS

Sir, We, the undersigned members of the editorial board of the *Journal of Mental Deficiency Research* and the MENCAP Medical Advisory Panel, fully support Lady Warnock's condemnation of Enoch Powell's Unborn Children (Protection) Bill (feature, May 30th) and agree that it would be "absolutely wrong" for it to become law.

Genetic diseases account for a substantial number of all human diseases. Chromosomal abnormalities are found in five to six births per 1,000. Genetic disease and congenital malformations occur in approximately 2 to 5 per cent of all live births and are the cause of 40 to 50 per cent of deaths in childhood.

Mental handicap is the most common disability in Britain, affecting perhaps as many as half a million people. There is no cure for mental handicap; it is a lifelong disability. Faced with an incurable condition, primary prevention is the ideal goal.

We know, personally and professionally, not only the tragedy of children dying of incurable diseases, but the tragedy of lives limited by handicap. Modern medicine is on the brink of preventing conditions that lead to damaged lives or certain death, but this knowledge will be futile unless further research to develop healthy embryos is undertaken.

This Bill is a giant leap backwards and, if passed, will deny future generations their most fundamental

Left The launch of the Bruce Forsyth Golf Classic in 1982.
Right Presenting *Let's Go* on television.

Filming with the Metropolitan Police Dog Training Establishment
for *Let's Go*.

Queen Elizabeth The Queen Mother opening the Golden Lane Headquarters of Mencap in December 1981.

Prince Philip at a combined Charities Exhibition, held at the BP City Headquarters in 1984.

After receiving my honorary degree from the Open University, I received honours of a less formal kind.

Louisa's wedding, 12th April 1981. Standing behind are Matthew Francis, Moray Watson, William Franklyn, Leslie Crowther, me, Elspet, Peter Bowles and John Georgiades. In front are Dickie Henderson, Jonathan Coy and Louisa with her bridesmaid Caroline Becker.

Left Cleaning the pool in Barnes. Well, about to anyway. *Right* And relaxing in the pool with Elspet, 1988 (or, rather, posing for *The Times*).

Launching the Mencap Famous Faces Collection with the then Sir Harold Wilson and Lord Allen of Abbeydale, then Chairman and now the president of Mencap. Yorkshiremen all!

Left With Glenys Kinnock at the launch of the Community Carers Campaign, 1987.

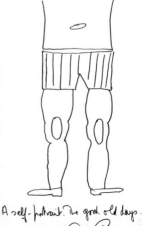

A self-portrait. The good old days...

My official portrait as
Secretary-General of
Mencap, 1981.

After the Investiture ceremony at Buckingham Palace with Louisa,
Elspet and Jamie.

In my dressing-room just before *Dry Rot*, 1988. The old make-up box was given to me by my parents in 1942.

On stage at the Lyric Theatre, Shaftesbury Avenue, in the revival of *Dry Rot*, 1988. As you can see, nothing changes!

Left Our grandchildren, Jack Rix, Charlotte and Jolyon Coy, and Ben Rix to the right. Easter, 1988. *Right* Walking in the gardens at Stourhead, Wiltshire, with Elspet and Jolyon.

Some of the family after lunch in the garden at Barnes, summer 1988.

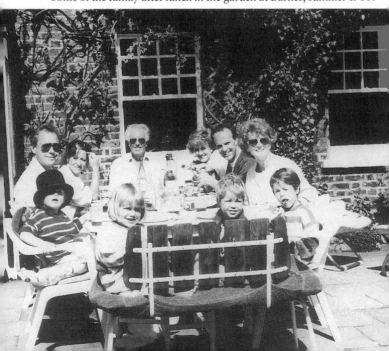

right – a healthy and whole life. The simplistic moral absolutism of some, must not be allowed to override the wellbeing of all.

Yours faithfully,

Brian Rix (Chairman, MENCAP Medical Advisory Panel),

William Fraser (Editor, *Journal of Mental Deficiency Research*),

Michael Baraitser, Brian Kirman, Alexander Shapiro, Jan Stern, Oliver Pratt, R.C. MacGillivray, David A. Primrose, Kenneth S. Holt, David Morris, Brian Stratford, Frank Denny, Elisabeth Norman.

The MENCAP National Council, too, debated the matter at great length, under the chairmanship of Lord Allen, and eventually issued this statement:

The Royal Society for Mentally Handicapped Children and Adults supports research related to the prevention of handicap at the pre-embryo stage, within the limits of the recommendations of the Report of the Warnock Committee Inquiry into Human Fertilization and Embryology.

The aims of such research should be to provide information on genetic disorders which would lead to the prevention of handicap; and to provide facilities which would offer an opportunity to women at risk to have a choice.

The Society supports the Warnock recommendation that all research projects be approved by a statutory licensing body and carried out under the supervision of a named licence holder who would be strictly controlled.

The Society, through observer status, will keep in

touch with those activities of the organization PRO-GRESS* that relate to research to prevent handicap.

The stage was set for a massive confrontation on this highly emotive issue. But it fizzled out when Enoch Powell's Bill failed to get a Second Reading – only to raise its head again for Kenneth Hargreaves's almost identical Bill in 1986 and when the Warnock White Paper came up for consideration at the beginning of 1988, at the same time as the David Alton Bill was being debated. Once more *The Times* offered me the hospitality of their columns, even though I was no longer Secretary-General of MENCAP, and I responded with this:

PARENTS – THEIR GRIEFS AND FEARS
by Brian Rix

When our mentally handicapped daughter was born some thirty-seven years ago, we parents were a beleaguered race. The standard advice given was still "put 'em away and forget 'em". That is, of course, if you were reasonably well-off and could afford a private home; if you were less well-endowed, the offer was certification and the mental hospital. Thus, the majority of parents had no alternative other than to choose care at home. This care, generally, was given lovingly and willingly but, nevertheless, placed an almost intolerable strain upon the family – for any additional help from the state was minimal. It is not surprising, therefore, that parents banded together, as the Association of Parents of Backward Children (now the Royal Society for Mentally Handicapped Children

---

* PROGRESS aims to increase knowledge about research into the earliest stages of human conception through a wider exchange of discussion between the public and scientists. Many eminent and caring people are involved.

and Adults), and things began to change – but slowly, as you can imagine. It's difficult to undo the injustice, prejudice and indifference of centuries.

However, during the last ten years more positive legislation has been enacted, affecting people with a mental handicap and their families, than in any previous decade in history. The majority of these Acts have attempted to help the day-to-day living of such families but the other vital problem – prevention – has not been addressed to any great extent by our legislators. That is, until now. And yet it is the prevention of mental handicap which all parents most earnestly desire – but with the knowledge in their possession are the majority of our Members of Parliament the best qualified to address the issue? I have my doubts.

On Thursday January 21st, consideration will begin on the Warnock White Paper, "Human Fertilization and Embryology – A Framework for Legislation". This offers an opportunity to prevent congenital disorders and MPs will be presented with two choices on embryo research: the first would ban such research altogether and the second would permit research on pre-embryos, under a statutory licensing authority, up to fourteen days after fertilization. Now if as a parent you are known to have a genetic defect, you may wish to take advantage of the latter opportunity, should such in vitro fertilization be available, thus attempting to produce a normal, healthy baby. Unfortunately, there is strong opposition to such an understandable view led, of course, by LIFE and SPUC (the Society for the Protection of the Unborn Child) – both of whom, as pressure groups, seem to exert a peculiar influence over our parliamentarians, when it comes to the free vote.

The same two groups are at it again over David

Alton's Abortion Bill, which goes for its Second Reading on the following day, Friday, January 22nd. Grisly and heart-rending stories have been trotted out to drive many a sensible MP into the lobby which could sentence future parents to an agony of indecision, guilt and, possibly, law-breaking. What will happen to women who choose to undergo amniocentesis to discover if the foetus is abnormal, should Mr Alton's Bill be enacted in its present form? Quite simply, they will no longer have this option, for amniocentesis is carried out about the sixteenth week of pregnancy – but the results are not known until the twentieth week. At present, if the foetus is found to be defective, the parents can choose to terminate the pregnancy; however, if the time limit for such a gestation period is reduced to eighteen weeks (or, in reality, seventeen weeks as propounded by Professor Stuart Campbell, *Times* letters, Jan 9th), then this choice will no longer be possible, leaving an unacceptable crime as the only escape for the distressed parents.

But mentally handicapped children will continue to be born and there will be many parents who care and grieve for them, often until their own health and strength give out – and this could be for sixty years or more. "If only" is the cry heard from many a mother and father, contemplating an unthinkable future. "If only" is my cri de coeur today. If only our legislators could wait for further advice and listen to the views of many of their constituents, who know the problem of mental handicap at first hand.

Next month, MENCAP's Medical Advisory Panel and the Forum of Mental Retardation of the Royal Society of Medicine are holding a conference to examine the legal, medical and ethical issues confronting parents and people with a mental handicap. Some of those parents and their offspring, along with law-yers, doctors and other professionals, will debate those matters currently before the House of Commons and also, those concerning marriage, child-bearing, sterilization and, indeed, survival. The guidelines produced by the conference will be debated in the months to come by all the interested parties and a set of firm proposals should be forthcoming before the end of the year, which could enable our legislators to respond, practically, positively and with integrity to the problems that confront us today.

Two years ago, *The Times* published an article of mine addressed to the Chancellor of the Exchequer, headed "Give Charity Basic Relief". I think the sub-editor, if around today, might entitle this article "Give Parents Basic Relief" – relief from all those who heap additional stress on shoulders already bowed down with unbearable burdens. Francis Bacon was right – "the joys of parents are secret, and so are their griefs and fears." It's time our griefs and fears were made known and counted above all else in any forthcoming Acts of Parliament.

The David Alton Bill, too, ran out of time but there is no doubt we shall continue to hear of this, or similar Bills, for some time to come – as we shall about Warnock. At least, though, I think MENCAP's attitude is pretty clear.

But back to Basil Hume. As you can imagine he was aware of our stance from an early date and wrote a most courteous letter to me in June 1985 as follows:

I find myself in a rather embarrassing position. You will recall that I wrote an article in *The Times* concerning the Powell Bill. On the day that this was read by some people a letter was received from MENCAP advocating the opposite to what I was arguing. As my name appears among your Patrons the contradiction was apparent to some.

I have a very high regard for MENCAP and its cause is one with which I would very much like to be associated, but I really would like to have a comment from your good self concerning my predicament.

With kindest regards and best wishes.

Yours devotedly,

Basil Hume

Archbishop of Westminster

The letter to which the Cardinal was referring was, of course, the one published in *The Times* from our Medical Advisory Panel on June 4th. I replied:

Thank you for your letter of June 24th and I can fully understand your embarrassment in regard to *The Times* and the Powell Bill.

I must make it quite clear that our letter was not from MENCAP itself, but from the MENCAP Medical Advisory Panel as well as the Editorial Board of the *Journal of Mental Deficiency Research*. Both Panel and Board members are medical practitioners held in the highest regard, but they act in an advisory capacity to MENCAP and in no way represent, necessarily, the National Council's views. That is why I was careful to sign the letter as "Chairman, MENCAP Advisory Panel" – thus disassociating myself from the office I hold as Secretary-General.

It so happened that both the Advisory Panel and Editorial Board were meeting on the same day and, because of the controversy over the Powell Bill, the matter was discussed at some length – even though it was not on the agenda. There was a unanimous decision, on behalf of both bodies, to enter into the debate and the result was the letter to *The Times*.

To add to the sum total of the information I am able to give you I would like to enclose our response to the Government Inquiry into Human Fertilization and Embryology dated April 1st, 1983. You will see that paragraph 28 contains a quite straightforward statement. "We oppose the use of developing human embryos in vitro for experimental purposes, *without stringent safeguards.*" I think this will be our ongoing stance, and it was interesting to note that the BMA took a similar view yesterday, when the subject was discussed at their conference.

Your position as Patron of MENCAP is highly valued and I would hate any difference of opinion between us to endanger that relationship. Rest assured MENCAP itself has, as yet, made no public statement in regard to the Powell Bill. There is no doubt, however, that many parents feel as I do, that the elimination of genetic tragedies – such as our children suffer – would meet with enthusiastic and heartfelt approval.

And, of course, as you have seen, such approval was indeed forthcoming from the National Council. It was inevitable that the Cardinal would have to resign. This he did, but not before the story had been leaked to the *Guardian*:

The Secretary-General of MENCAP, Brian Rix, should thank Christopher Whitehouse, a militant moral majority campaigner, for a letter he will receive this morning from Cardinal Basil Hume, Archbishop of Westminster. The letter says that Hume can no longer be a patron of the Society and his name must be removed from the stationery. MENCAP is lobbying MPs to vote against the Unborn Children (Protection) Bill and favours the Warnock Committee's proposals to allow limited research on embryos to detect handicap, whereas the Catholic Church is unequivocally against Warnock. Whitehouse, who works for the husband-and-wife team of right-wing Tory MPs, Nicholas and Ann Winterton, made it his business to pester the Cardinal about MENCAP and has now got a result. "I'm impressed with your mole structure but I'll be talking to the Serjeant-at-Arms about access to my private correspondence," he said yesterday.

Not a very happy way to learn of a Patron's resignation. Indeed, the Cardinal's letter of resignation arrived *after* the *Guardian* had been published. I commented on this, somewhat bitterly, in my reply:

. . . may I express my disquiet to see that your letter was "leaked" to the *Guardian* yesterday, referred to this morning – and to read of the overt pressure which has been brought to bear on you by Christopher Whitehouse, the so-called "militant moral majority campaigner". It seems unfortunate, to say the least, that this pressure could be construed to have affected your decision – and this can only be deplored . . .

And on that rather unhappy note, we had entered into . . .

1986

Once again, *The Times* offered me the Op Ed space (opposite the editorial, for those not versed in journalistic jargon) to fly a kite which MENCAP and other charities had been trying to get airborne for several months. We had all met at MENCAP and decided to try and persuade the Chancellor to give us a hand with charitable giving, even if he couldn't see his way to relieving us, totally, of the VAT burden. We therefore agreed upon another tack. You will recognize the headline, for I have already referred to it in another *Times*' article: "Parents – their griefs and fears" which addressed the problems of Warnock and Alton. This earlier article was published on my sixty-second birthday, January 27th, 1986, and coincided with *The Times*' first publication at Wapping. Quite an eventful date. Well, from my point of view, anyway:

GIVE CHARITY BASIC RELIEF
by Brian Rix

Thought transference is sometimes worth a little thought. I remember, in my early years at the White-hall Theatre, three farces about witches arriving in the space of a few days; all from different parts of the country, all written by entirely unrelated authors, and all of them terrible. Something about witches had been floating around in the ether, other than broom-sticks, and three people had picked up the vibes.

New and possibly exciting thoughts about relief from basic-rate tax for contributors to charity have been floating around the upper regions for the past few months. If these thoughts were to land – on Nigel Lawson's desk perhaps – those voluntary agencies who rely heavily on donations to be able to continue and expand their work would have cause for celebration.

I would hazard a guess that the Treasury might benefit as well. The costs of tax reform might be considerable. But even if reform were expensive, governments rely more and more on the voluntary sector to provide services – and with sufficient funds available, many charities would be only too happy to oblige.

Three of us have been working in unrelated ways

to try to bring this tax reform about. Three to my knowledge, that is; when you're dealing with the paranormal anything is possible. The National Council for Voluntary Organizations has been receiving messages from their ouija board; we at MENCAP have convened a working party representing twenty leading charities to turn the tax tarot cards; now our work has apparently been anticipated by several Ministers who are exuding economic ectoplasm as though the voluntary sector were acting as the medium.

We are all suggesting the same thing. Individuals and businesses who make contributions to charitable organizations would all be allowed to set these off against taxable income, without following the covenant route.

There is nothing new in the idea. It has been the practice in America for years; in West Germany, too, as well as Australia. We here have the covenant system – which was thoughtfully reduced to a four-year commitment by the previous Chancellor, Sir Geoffrey Howe, as far as charities are concerned. The only snag is that, by and large, the four-year covenant has simply not caught on. It seems too complicated, it seems to require tax counsel to sort it out and, anyway, isn't it for those whose incomes reach into the stratosphere? Not true, of course, but that is how most covenants are viewed by the vast majority of charitable donors.

Tax relief is something else. It is as simple to understand as any of the allowances which we currently claim against our tax. Wives (or husbands), mothers-in-law (if dependents), children, mortgages, personal pensions – just add charitable donations to the list – and your relief (probably against basic-rate tax only) will be granted – to a certain level of your income, of course, and on production of certified tax receipts.

We are all convinced, individuals, businesses, charities and now, it seems, Ministers, that such a financial provision will benefit all of us – ranging from the great voluntary bodies to the arts establishments and the vicar's tea-party in aid of the new organ bellows. All it needs is the Chancellor to recognize the benefits bestowed and it could be part of this year's Budget.

In spite of the image of charity workers as woolly-minded idealists we are, by and large, pragmatists. It is clear that we cannot realistically expect any government to pick up the total bill for providing the quality of care, of services, of training, of living which we know to be necessary. We are already playing a major part in this exercise. But we could do so much more. We believe that if people were allowed to set off donations against tax, many would be just that much keener to give to worthy causes.

In far-off days, women who gave birth to mentally handicapped babies were often condemned as witches. Not the jolly ones sent to me at the Whitehall, but poor unfortunate creatures who suffered the tortures of the damned for a simple genetic twist of fate. Even now, many view the causes of mental handicap with a sixteenth-century eye – but thankfully we no longer echo Luther, who demanded that a mentally handicapped boy be thrown in the river because he was "evil".

No, we have dragged ourselves, with some difficulty, into the twentieth century. Isn't it time we brought our charitable tax law up to date as well?

Such is the power of *The Times* (so we like to believe) that the Chancellor did, in fact, offer new tax incentives, for those making donations to charities, in his March

Budget: payroll giving relief for t'workers and 3 per cent dividend allowances for t'gaffers. (Employees can now donate £240 per annum to charity with full tax relief on the amount given. Employers – or rather companies – can donate up to 3 per cent of their dividends to charity, also with full tax relief.) All very satisfactory. I like to think that Lord Whitelaw may have had something to do with it too. He was subjected to the magic ingredients of gala pie at one of my office lunches and listened most sympathetically to my pleas for additional tax relief. I'm sure a quiet word from him must have worked greater wonders on Nigel Lawson than an article by me in *The Times*, even if it was opposite the editorial. I'm not proud – just grateful.

The Budget concessions were made, of course, in March. The next month, MENCAP celebrated its fortieth anniversary and much occurred during the following twelve months which showed how increasingly active and effective the Society had become since its humble beginnings in 1946. I've made reference to those early days on a number of occasions in this book, as well as mentioning our founder, Mrs Judy Fryd MBE. I would now like to recount the main points of the story of our genesis in her own words, which she wrote for *Parents' Voice* (the magazine she had edited), in celebration of those forty years.

"It only seems like yesterday." How often we say these words when recalling some event in our distant past. Yet whenever I am introduced to a parent of a newly born or newly diagnosed mentally handicapped child at a meeting, I remember that every day at least ten babies are born whose parents are starting at the beginning, as we did long ago. That is why, in this year when we celebrate forty years of endeavour, there is no end in sight to the task we set ourselves.

In the immediate post-war years when MENCAP was founded, there was little help available for our children other than admission to a long-stay hospital for the "mentally deficient". What little existed in the way of day services had been pioneered between the wars by voluntary bodies like the Central Association for Mental Welfare, run by Miss (later Dame) Evelyn Fox, and clubs for mentally ill and mentally handicapped people started by Elfrida Rathbone in Islington.

In 1944, having become frustrated by lack of help for my eldest daughter Felicity, I began to collect information with a view to starting an Association of Parents with Backward Children. I wrote to Medical Health Officers throughout the country asking how many "backward children" they knew of, how they became aware of them, and what services they provided. Some replied, "Don't you know there's a war on? I can't answer all these questions!"

In 1946 something happened to precipitate action. I was put in touch with a small residential school for backward children in Surrey. After visiting the school with Felicity, arrangements were made for her to be admitted for a month on trial. We took her down there, with the long list of clothing requirements, and returned home happy that she was at last to have a chance. The next morning, we received in our mail a telegram, sent off at 9.00 p.m. the previous evening: FELICITY NOT SUITABLE MUST BE REMOVED AT ONCE.

Our feelings can be imagined. I wrote a letter to the *Nursery World* magazine suggesting that parents of backward children, some of whom were corresponding in the paper, should band together to press for the facilities we needed. From the replies we agreed a subscription (3s 6d per annum) and formulated a programme of demands: more and better special schools and occupation centres; more frequent and helpful visits to parents, and research into causes and treatment of mental handicap.

There were at that time no schools for severely subnormal children, only for the mildly retarded. Local health authorities were empowered but not compelled to provide occupation centres. We began to press for proper schools, with properly trained teachers, under the auspices of the education authorities. People thought we were mad.

Our newsletter got a brief mention in a national newspaper. I received masses of letters from all over the country, telling heart-breaking stories of newly diagnosed (or undiagnosed) "mongol" (Down's syndrome) babies, hyperactive children or totally inert unresponsive youngsters requiring heavy lifting – and older men and women who had never been to school or occupation centres and for whom no grants or allowances had ever been received. Backward children were deprived of many things through being excluded from school – no ration of free milk, no family allowances. These were things which we successfully lobbied Government Ministers to have put right.

The correspondence built up, through letters and articles published in various journals. Soon I was able to put parents in touch with others living nearby and local branches started forming. In January 1949 we held our first meeting, to which all members were invited, at the Fountain Hospital, London. A branch was formed covering the South-Eastern area, along with the first Friends group of relatives of residents in a hospital for mentally handicapped children.

A year later, we held a second meeting at the Fountain Hospital at which we adopted a Constitution and elected a National Council. The Association of Parents of Backward Children (APBC) news-letter became *Parents' Voice* – I got this name from the newsletter of the New Jersey, USA, Association for Retarded Children. The Society grew and expanded its role to include setting up "pilot schemes", beginning in 1952 with the short-stay home near Liverpool. Later we built two hostels (one each for men and girls) and an industrial workshop at Slough, Bucks.

In 1960 we were fortunate in securing as Patron, Her Majesty Queen Elizabeth The Queen Mother, who graciously agreed to perform the opening ceremony at Slough and to take tea with members of the National Council.

I cannot pay tribute enough to these and other loyal and devoted parents and supporters, now numbering around 75,000, who over the years have kept the Society going at all levels, as well as to our conscientious and hard-working staff, past and present. Our first General-Secretary, Mrs Jo McLaren White, was employed in the 1950s part-time at £4 per week! She did much to help put us on the map, and her successors, George Lee and Brian Rix, have continued to foster the growth and influence of the Society as a well-known and respected charity. But there is still much to do before we can achieve the aim of one of our former National Chairmen, the late Frederick Ellis – to "work ourselves out of a job".

I think that story shows what a remarkable woman is our Judy – and also gives a clear picture of the desolate background against which we had to struggle to make our way. Now an indomitable old lady, Judy still battles on at every opportunity to improve the lives of people with a mental handicap, and has a very sharp tongue when thwarted. I know; I've felt the lash of it from time to time.

So what did we do to celebrate the fortieth anniversary? (By the way, you must have noticed how forty years now seems to have taken the place of fifty. Could it be because we fear our longevity is not what we anticipated?) We published *Day Services – Today and Tomorrow: MENCAP's vision of daytime services for people with a mental handicap into the 21st century*. This was the work of an extremely hard-working party, under the chairmanship of yet another parent, and a Vice-Chairman of MENCAP, Vic Stealey. The publication, together with an accompanying Stamina* document on Care in the Community, was the subject of our MENCAP Week Conference, opened by Baroness Jean Trumpington. We then took the whole shooting match on tour (minus Jean T.) at conferences up and down the country in an effort to spread the word. I think we succeeded, too, for the meetings were extremely well attended and the interest created seemed to be considerable. In addition we were able to show our new BBC television programme, *People Like Us* which was the pilot for the series which eventually became *A Life of Our Own*.

Then we published the report of the Ad Hoc Leisure Committee to MENCAP which made many clear and cogent recommendations covering leisure, sport and physical recreation, arts and entertainment, holidays, youth and leisure clubs for people with a mental handicap. The Report was largely written by the Chairman, Sir Alec Atkinson, and was an immensely useful document. Sir Alec had at one time been Second Permanent Under-Secretary at the DHSS, responsible for the production of SERPS (State Earnings Related Pension Scheme) which caused such a rumpus around the time of our leisure report. Our Chairman was on safer ground with us.

On the arts front, though, Sir Alec was Vice-Chairman of the Attenborough Report on Arts and Disabled People,

---

* Stamina are papers published by MENCAP, indicating the minimum standards required for mental handicap services in all fields of operation.

and again had a great deal to do with the writing, for Dickie was mainly away in New York filming *A Chorus Line*. Alec was, therefore, well qualified to be the Chairman of our ad hoc lot and, in the event, was quite excellent and the report was very well received.

In co-operation with the Office of Health Economics, we produced another extremely valuable booklet, *Mental Handicap – Partnership in the Community?*, largely written by a husband-and-wife team, Jean and David Taylor. It reviewed the development and co-ordination of NHS and local authority, residential, social and educational support for mentally handicapped individuals, and was very helpful although, perforce, technical.

Then there was our Open University course, which was launched in the November of our anniversary year; our participation in yet another International League Conference in Rio de Janeiro (which I hated – such a violent city) and our first Profound Retardation and Multiple Handicap Conference at Manchester University, which I chaired, even though stone deaf.

I had contracted an ongoing ear infection about eighteen months before in Egypt and had never really shaken it off. All that flying around the world only made matters worse and after my return from Rio, I was proper poorly, as we are reputed to say in Yorkshire. So much so, that it was quite impossible for me to fly to Manchester and Elspet had to take the Shuttle and deliver my speech at the opening of the PRMH Conference. I followed more sedately by train. When it came to listening to speeches, Mary Holland scribbled down what was being said, as she also did with the questions coming from the floor. It was a hopeless situation and I realized for the first time how little understanding we have for deaf people in similar circumstances. Eventually, after a further massive course of antibiotics, I recovered my hearing, only to be left with the dread tinnitus in my left ear – just like a constantly boiling kettle. Anyone want a cup of tea? I'd love to get it *off* the boil.

There was another flight to be undertaken that year, though, to Sorrento, to make a speech at the Road Haulage Association Conference Dinner. You may well wonder what that has to do with mental handicap. Very little, as far as I can see, but the members of the Association were extremely generous and several thousands of pounds came MENCAP's way. It had all been arranged by our, then, Head of Appeals, Fergus Logan, whose father-in-law, Major-General Freddie Plaskett, was the Director-General of the RHA. I was in good company, though, as far as speakers were concerned, for one was Peter Bottomley, Minister for Transport, and the other Sir Pat Lowry, who is such an emollient as the Chairman of the conciliation service, ACAS. He should attend our MENCAP National Council from time to time. We could do with a drop of oil, now and then. There's none so heated as a bunch of parents of mentally handicapped offspring. Quite right, too. Without that spontaneous combustion, we would still be in the dark ages.

As far as Parliament was concerned, in our fortieth anniversary year, there was only one Bill – eventually an Act – which was of importance. I believe, though, that it was the most important Act to receive Royal Assent since the Education Act of 1970 allowed our kids to receive some kind of schooling. It all began in the tea-room at the House of Commons and then, less than twenty-four hours later, in my office at MENCAP, and came to fruition, appropriately enough, in our celebratory year.

Tom Clarke, CBE, MP, is the Labour Member of Parliament for Monklands West. Once its Provost (for which he received his CBE) he drew first place in the Private Members' Ballot in November 1985. His immediate thought was to devise a Bill which would help the very people for whom we were struggling, those who were profoundly and multiply handicapped. I believe he had personal reasons for being so interested. Anyway, he phoned my office and invited me to tea, along with our parliamentary representative-to-be, Mary Holland, for Rolf Hermelin was elsewhere.

Off we went, and over tea and chocolate biscuits we decided that to attempt a Bill for a comparatively small number of people, grievously handicapped though they may be, would be a waste of a golden opportunity. Tom asked me what we most desired. I said, "Appropriate day services, opportunities for employment, leisure and integration – for people with a mental handicap, whether profoundly or otherwise affected." Tom agreed. Next morning, in my office, the three of us, joined by Rolf Hermelin, sat down to try and hammer out a Bill. I left with the Medical Advisory Panel for our trip to Washington, believing it was in the bag. I returned to find that all the disablement organizations had jumped on the bandwagon and Tom's Bill was now top-heavy, encompassing every disability that existed, with mental handicap – yet again – taking its turn at the bottom of the queue.

I'm glad to say, though, that the Bill, as eventually enacted, was of greater relevance to young people with a mental handicap, leaving school or hospital, than to anyone else: it meant that stated plans and services would have to be provided for their future. The clauses covering carers and representatives probably had more general relevance, but our lot could only look on the Tom Clarke Act – the Disabled Persons (Services, Consultation and Representation) Act 1986 – as the greatest step forward since the beginning of the 1970s. To its continuing shame, the Government has taken full advantage of the restrictions pertaining to a Private Member's Bill – that it must have no financial implications – and has only slowly and unwillingly allowed each section of the Act to receive the necessary support. The Association of County Councils and Directors of Social Services have been just about as unwilling. A comparatively small sum of money is the reason for this inertia. Did I hear mention of the welfare state?

On the social front we also had a good year. After all, you're not forty every day of the week, and in July we had a splendid reception at St James's Palace, in the presence of our Royal Patron, Her Majesty Queen Elizabeth, The Queen Mum, who was twice forty and then some. She was absolutely marvellous. It was the hottest day of the year, being well into the eighties, but she walked around four large rooms, holding over 700 people, and seemed to find time to chat to at least 350 of them. Amazing. The Chairman, Lord Allen, and I were stretched to the utmost – keeping up with her and trying to remember who everyone was. Never easy at any time. Almost impossible in such a press. Especially if you're short-sighted like I am, and can't read people's labels.

Perhaps the most impressive sights of all though, if you could focus, were Gary Gruby presenting the Queen Mother with a painting of Balmoral which he had recently done, along with the beautiful bouquet of dried flowers she also received from another member of our Golden Lane workshop, which the Queen Mother had opened five years before. When she first met Gary in 1981, he was largely incapable of communication, but now he is the star of our workshop and has gone on to even greater things in the business world. So much for those who were once deemed ineducable.

I also made another of my speeches, this time at Sudbury in Suffolk at the Mayor's Banquet. Actually, it was a jolly occasion and, although I was almost late for the event, having been held up in Friday night traffic out of London, I enjoyed myself. Then I returned to my hotel, just on the outskirts of Sudbury, which offered me splendid accommodation even though the hotel was comparatively new. I had a drink with the owner and retired to bed. No sooner had I hit the sack, than the fire alarm went off. It was my first experience of such an event, so, without hesitation, I joined the crowd rushing to the front door and blessed safety. Well, actually, there was no crowd – only me. However, the proprietor and his wife were there and, eventually, the fire brigade. Searches were made everywhere, the all clear was given and I retired to bed – for the second time. I had asked for a call at eight o'clock, plus *The Times* and tea, and was confident that all would be forthcoming. *Wrong*! At 8.15 I was tetchily wondering what in God's name had happened and, hearing only silence, decided to investigate. Nothing. Absolutely nothing. Nobody, no living creature was in the hotel but me. All had left with the fire brigade. There was my *Times*, stuck in the half-open door. There was the mail for all the non-existent visitors and staff. But no visitors and no staff. It was just like the *Marie Celeste*. It so happened I had to meet an old friend from my childhood, recently retired Reverend Peter Hollis, Vicar of Sudbury, for coffee at around 9.45 a.m. But where was the coffee? Where was the milk? I went on an exploration and found all in the deserted kitchen. At 9.30 a cleaner arrived. At 9.40 my friend. At 10.10, the chef. "Oh God," he said, "I forgot all about you."

And what else on the personal front? Well, in May I received a letter – completely out of the blue – from Luke Rittner, the Secretary-General of the Arts Council, asking me whether or not I would wish to become Chairman of the Arts Council Drama Panel and, inter alia, a member of the Arts Council itself. I demurred, discussed and did not decline. I refer you to the Epilogue. It's all part of my fall from grace. The Relapse. In the meantime, this appeared in *The Times* Diary:

Don't laugh, but former farceur Brian Rix has been asked to become Chairman of the Arts Council's Drama Panel. The Secretary-General of MENCAP, famous for dropping his trousers on stage, could soon be in charge of £25 million of theatre grants – quite a jump from wowing audiences with shows like *Let Sleeping Wives Lie* and *Reluctant Heroes*. Far from decrying the likely appointment as "suburbanite", Panel members who resigned last year over grant cuts welcomed the news. One, playwright Olwen Wymark, told me, "It would be tremendous. Brian is a vigorous campaigner – he has done a great job at MENCAP – and I'm sure he would be prepared to fight for cash." Although no mention of Rix was made at last Wednesday's meeting of the Arts Council, I understand that the approach to fill the vacancy, arising from the resignation in November of RSC actor Tony Church, has been made by the Arts Council Secretary-General, Luke Rittner.

On the morning of May 8th, 1986, I was sitting downstairs in my dressing-gown – Elspet fast asleep upstairs – and eating my fruit and muesli while reading *The Times*. Suddenly, a ring on the bell. Cursing, as Elspet had had a late night and wanted to sleep on, I rushed to the door to see our friendly Irish postman with a grin from ear to ear – and thrusting a tatty brown paper envelope in my direction. "I t'ink you'll be wantin' to see dis," he said, and left.

Dis seemed to contain a returned postal package so, without undue haste, I opened it. There lay a white foolscap envelope with On Her Majesty's Service gummed over the flap and a label indicating that it had been "officially sealed in the POST OFFICE", and an upside-down crown on the rear. Looking down, I saw that the address, through the transparent window, was our previous one at Roedean Crescent (which we had left ten years before) and, furthermore, had the wrong postal code – for we had been SW15 and this was one out, SW14. Some joker at the post office had scribbled +1 and SW15 alongside. To the right of the address was a mass of hieroglyphics – "gone away", "undelivered for reason stated", "RETURN TO SENDER" and there, on the envelope, was printed the very sender herself, "PRIME MINISTER".

Thank God some post operative had had the sense to ignore "personal", obeyed "urgent", slit open the envelope and sent it hotfoot, via our lovely Irishman, to our house at Barnes Common. It stated, in words similar to my CBE, that the "Prime Minister has asked me to inform you, in strict confidence" etc, etc, "that Her Majesty may be graciously pleased to approve that the honour of knighthood be conferred upon you". Furthermore, "I should be grateful if you would let me know by completing the enclosed form and sending it to me by return of post."

Return of post? Ye Gods – the letter had been sent on May 1st – it was now the 8th. Had I been stripped of my K in the meantime? Filling in the form even faster than for my CBE – plus a footnote about the wrong address and delay – I sprinted to the post-box in my dressing-gown and caught the first delivery. Back home and grinning broadly, I made tea for Elspet and, grinning even more broadly, I took her the cup that cheers, along with the *Guardian*, to her bedside – waking her none too gently. When she had recovered, I thrust my IN CONFIDENCE letter in her face. She read it. "Oh God," she said, "does this mean I'm going to be a Lady?" And, of course, it did.

On November 25th, 1986, I attended the investiture, along with Elspet, Jamie and Louisa – who had missed the previous occasion – and all the family came to a super lunch at L'Escargot in Greek Street. It was another of those late, late finishes. This time, thank goodness, the hire car had not been hijacked by a gate-crasher and we did not have to hail a taxi to get home. I bet I snored that night, dreaming perhaps of the great honour bestowed upon me, our Society, our members and, above all, our children – born so grievously disadvantaged – but now with a Secretary-General whose knighthood showed a recognition of their needs, their aspirations and their place in this corner of the world.

"Some say that the age of chivalry is past, that the spirit of romance is dead. The age of chivalry is never past, so long as there is a wrong left unredressed on this earth."

So wrote Charles Kingsley over a hundred years ago. The words still apply today and I'm glad that the Imperial Society of Knights Bachelor has recently recognized this with the SUNFUND, the special unmet needs fund, as part of the Society's new charitable status. Along with Sir David Napley and Sir Robert Crichton-Brown, I serve on the Charity Sub-committee. I am happy to report that the first fund-raising endeavour for those special needs remembered MENCAP and those people with a mental handicap for whom there is many a wrong left unredressed. Maybe we're still a long way from "working ourselves out of a job", as our first Chairman hoped would happen, but we're getting there. One day – the millennium. But I doubt if I'll be around to see it.

1987

As I had known for some time, 1987 could well be my last year as MENCAP's Secretary-General, but I was uncertain exactly when or how my retirement might take place. Our Chairman, Lord Allen, had made it plain that he wished to retire, preferably in 1987, but that he might be prepared to soldier on for one more year, if there was a good chance that I would be nominated to take his place in 1988. That would mean my going early, however, for under charitable status it is quite impossible for a member of staff, in receipt of a salary, to occupy an honorary office. Furthermore, any incoming Secretary-General would want to have his predecessor clear of the building for several months before he (meaning me) returned as the Chairman. A further complication was the fact that the Chairman of MENCAP has to be nominated and then voted into office by the local society nominee members, so there was absolutely no certainty that the honour would automatically go my way. Nevertheless, there were sufficient Honorary Officers around indicating they would like me to succeed Philip Allen, so eventually the matter was discussed (in my absence) by the Management Committee, who agreed to recommend my nomination to the National Council, provided I retired six months before I could return as Chairman. I'm happy to say that this was endorsed, nem. con., by the National Council, and I was able to leave at the end of October 1987, to await the vote which – eventually – confirmed my appointment as Chairman the following April. Lord Renton then retired as President, Lord Allen took his place and I stepped into my fellow Yorkshire-man's shoes. With relief and a certain sense of pride, I must confess, for nothing is certain in this life but, on the other hand, I had set my heart on being Chairman, not only because it was a great honour but also because it would allow me to carry on with a say in the Society's affairs, long after my official retiring age of sixty-five. Let's face it, there's life in the old dog yet. At least, I hope there is.

In spite of my anticipated sailing into the sunset, 1987 turned out to be the most eventful year in my term as Secretary-General. And it wasn't even a year. Ten months to be precise, but they were ten turbulent months, to say the least. First, I had to visit Australia and New Zealand, as a result of suggestions made at International League meetings, to see for myself how voluntary bodies in those two countries managed their affairs, for people with a mental handicap. As the visit was arranged to take place over four weeks in January and February, it was no great hardship, especially as I was accompanied by Elspet, as well as Jean and Leslie Crowther, who came along for the ride. At least that was the theory but, in spite of their holiday and cricket-watching arrangements, Leslie and Jean worked tirelessly with us, visiting homes, schools, training centres at the drop of a hat. Elspet, too, worked her socks off.

And there was plenty of opportunity, for the arrangements made in Adelaide, by Frank Davidson, in Sydney by Jim McLoughlin, Dr Lyn Gow and Roger Barson, and in Melbourne by Ian Parsons and John Rimmer, were pretty exacting and, also, entertaining. However, all had the good grace to allow Elspet and me the odd days off, particularly those which coincided with England winning the one-day matches against Australia and the West Indies. We saw four of these, including a day/night match in Sydney, but Leslie and Jean, having no official tie to our visit, were even luckier, seeing the actual final, whilst Elspet and I were waiting at Melbourne airport to catch a flight, delayed by several hours, to New Zealand. The match wasn't, then, on the telly, so even in our VIP lounge we were cut off from all the latest scores. Most frustrating!

In New Zealand, the overall voluntary body is the Society for the Intellectually Handicapped (IHC) and the National Director is the indefatigable J. B. Munro, known throughout the world of mental handicap for his energy, his creativity and his ambition for those who are intellectually handicapped in New Zealand. IHC started a little after MENCAP and J. B. (as he is known, even though this is not Dallas) managed to avoid a number of the difficulties we have since encountered, particularly in the realm of fund-raising. The IHC actually has a greater income than

MENCAP (75 per cent through Government sources) but that's because everything raised on the two islands goes into one pot, whereas the Royal Society raises *its* money and local societies and Friends' groups raise *theirs*. If we added all that lot together, we would leave the IHC standing – but that's only to be expected. After all, we're somewhat bigger, in population terms!

J. B. had laid on a programme over six days which was mind-boggling. Broadcasts, televisions, interviews, meetings, visits – you name it, we did it. Plus travel. Every day we moved up the North Island, driven by a friendly IHC staff member, Jim Jones, and every night it was an official dinner, with me making an appropriate speech, of course, and a quick night's kip before we were off on the road again. Everyone was very kind though, as they had been in Australia, hospitality abounded and by the time we flew out of Auckland, sleeping most of the way home, I had put on three-quarters of a stone. It took me nearly a year to lose it, and that in spite of a very hectic few months ahead on my return to England.

My first speaking engagement took place two days after I returned, when it was my privilege to deliver the Shaftesbury Memorial Lecture to the A-level forms of Harrow School, plus other local schools and representatives from the local authorities. It gave me a great opportunity to remind all present of the appalling history of mental handicap and, at the same time, present many of the hopeful portents for the future, many of them engendered by MENCAP. The Speech Room was packed and it afforded my theatrical heart a thrill to know I was standing on the very spot where Winston Churchill had delivered many a peroration. The speech was entitled "A Tainted Wether of the Flock" and began:

Your education has been based on the 1944 Education Act. Only two years after that, in 1946, our Society came into being as the "Association of Parents of Backward Children". But before "backward children", what names did we bestow on those who did not measure up to our ideas of normality? Idiot, fool, simpleton, witling, dolt, half-wit, imbecile, driveller, cretin, moron, dunce, oaf, dullard, sot, shallow-brain, jobbernowl, changeling, dotard.

Today: mentally handicapped.

These are but a few of the labels we have attached to people who throughout history have been scorned, maltreated and excluded from society. We have much ground to make up. As Antonio says in Act IV of *The Merchant of Venice*, "I am a tainted wether of the flock, meetest for death . . ."

Then followed a distillation of that which you have read in this autobiography, ending with a reference to the pilot television programme, *People Like Us*:

People Like Us applies not only to people with a mental handicap – but also, as I have said, to some of us present in this room. People like us (in our case, people like my wife and myself) are still vast in number. Possibly over two million parents with mildly or severely mentally handicapped offspring are living in the UK. *Their* contribution to care in the community is vast and incalculable. If all those parents left their young on the mountainside, to be cared for by the state, taxes would probably double overnight. One person with mental handicap in a family costs that family (over and above state benefits) an additional £170,000 over sixty years – and that's for the basic necessities of life. Multiply that by a million plus. Multiply that by love and devotion and desperation – and then consider what you could do to help. I would suggest you could do much:

"I am a tainted wether of the flock, meetest for death: the weakest kind of fruit drops earliest to the ground."

And I think that quote sets the scene only too well for the next story about to hit the headlines.

The Guardian, Tuesday March 17th, 1987

STERILITY RULING ON GIRL WITH MENTAL AGE OF FIVE
by Peter Hildrew, Social Services Correspondent

The Appeal Court yesterday ordered that a seventeen-year-old girl with a mental age of five should be sterilized for her own good, in a case likely to have wide repercussions for the rights of mentally handicapped people.

Lord Justice Dillon, sitting with Lord Justices Stephen Brown and Nicholls, said that the retarded girl, referred to as Jeanette, was now becoming sexually aware, and that the consequences of her becoming pregnant were frightening.

Sterilization, he said, would take away a basic human right, but the loss of that right "would mean nothing to her". She had very low intelligence, could speak sentences of only a word or two, and could not be allowed out alone. She would not be able to understand what was happening to her if she became pregnant.

The Royal Society for Mentally Handicapped Children and Adults (MENCAP) said last night that the case would cause considerable concern and "must not become a charter for the indiscriminate sterilization of women with a mental handicap".

People with a mental handicap had a right to enjoy

life in all its fullness, although parental concern was also understandable.

The Times led with this:

RETARDED GIRL, 17, MUST BE STERILIZED
by Frances Gibb, Legal Affairs Correspondent

The Court of Appeal yesterday ordered that a seventeen-year-old girl with a mental age of five should be sterilized to save her from pregnancy.

Oh yes, the scene was set all right. For a right punch-up and, sure enough, it happened.

The morning those headlines appeared, I was asked to appear on both BBC *Breakfast Time* and ITV's *TV-a.m.* As I drove along in the taxi to Lime Grove at 6.30 a.m., I was wondering what on earth I could say to catch the headlines and draw attention to this particularly distressing happening. I had established MENCAP's official view on sterilization, for this had been discussed when Judge Heilbron had refused to allow the sterilization of a girl some eleven years earlier and the National Executive Committee (now renamed the National Council), under the Chairmanship of Lord Segal had minuted:

Although recognizing that the voice of the parent must clearly be heard, the committee felt unable to endorse the proposition, put forward from some quarters, that judgments in such cases should remain solely a matter of decision by parents and their immediate medical advisers . . . an "Ethical Committee" should be established to which such cases should first be referred, and this should include other relevant professional disciplines, apart from the medical profession.

In the case of Jeanette I suppose it could be claimed that others, apart from the mother and the doctors, *had* been involved for it was the Social Services Department who wished to have the sterilization performed in the first place. But it all seemed a rather cosy enclave, with an acquiescent mother (after all, Jeanette did not live at home), compliant doctors, mistakenly intentioned social workers and approving judges. I had to overcome a considerable body of indifference to Jeanette's fate also, as well as opposition from many parents of mentally handicapped girls who did not agree with our National Executive decision in 1976, and wished to be free to have their daughters sterilized, should they so wish.

All this was going through my head in the darkened taxi as we sped along Castelnau and Shepherd's Bush Road towards the TV studios. All I needed was one phrase which would make people sit up and take notice. Then it came to me, and I immediately started to scribble out this statement, finishing it in the reception area at Lime Grove. It certainly created a furore, just as I had intended, but it also contained my own personal view of the whole unfortunate incident:

Having had the opportunity to read the full court report and to reflect on the judgment, it is my belief that this decision must be seen as an infringement of basic human rights.

In my view, the reference to the fact that ". . . many years ago a risk of pregnancy would not have arisen because she would have been strictly institutionalized" has a wistful ring to it, but, happily, the world has moved on. The current policy of care in the community stresses that care must be an overriding consideration and this implies that due attention should be paid to the protection of young girls with a mental handicap in a similar situation. Care in the community also implies certain qualified risk-taking and I believe that this has been largely accepted by parents and young people with a mental handicap alike.

Other references were made in the judgment to the fact that the girl did not need protection under the Mental Health Act but that she could ". . . hope to attain the ability of a five- or six-year-old in some skills." This appears to be a subjective view and must be open to question – for no one can deny that many people with a mental handicap may appear to have an immature mental age but nevertheless have the ability to react to a number of disparate matters, including a surprising degree of self-awareness.

In the nineteenth century early educationalists assumed that all people with a mental handicap were capable of some improvement, even if they could not be cured. They did however keep alive the possibility that people with a mental handicap might not be truly human. Frequent comparisons were made with animals.

I cannot help wondering, is the girl in this case to be spayed like a bitch?

That closing phrase made headlines in every paper throughout the land. Jeanette became a cause célèbre with a vengeance and the topic of many, many articles and leaders also. I'm glad to say that the majority agreed with me. Here is but one example from the *Guardian*:

There was little talk about basic human rights in the Appeal Court this week and the law is now the weaker for it.

The decision to sterilize is bad for several reasons. It is bad because it asserts that the courts really can divide the population into those who are fit to reproduce and those who are not. That is a very large claim, against which most mental health law and policy in the past thirty years has rebelled. It is bad because its finality denies the possibility of change or improvement in the person to be sterilized. This is not a question of possible future miracles – though some people will take that possibility seriously. It is a question of preventing unwanted conception through counselling and protection, in much the same way as one would do with a child or as is already done with patients suffering from some hereditary handicaps. It is bad because it is a judgment with more than a hint of expediency about it, the expediency which says that there aren't enough social workers around to care for such people any more and she'll be eighteen in a couple of months' time anyway, and thus outside the court's jurisdiction. It is bad also because the finality of sterilization is not the only available solution. As Judge Heilbron said (in a 1976 judgment), contraception and ultimately abortion are legally available alternatives. The Appeal Court has failed to give proper consideration to such solutions. They have established a precedent which inevitably means that more sterilizations will be considered. Of course, we are still far away from a society which decides that, in the interests of progress, all black people, Labour voters, claimants and people with low IQs should be sterilized at their local Sir Keith Joseph Memorial Clinics. But we are a tiny bit nearer to it. And that is still far too near for comfort.

The *Sunday Times* offered me their Platform columns on the following Sunday and my contribution appeared under the eye-catching headline: THEIR FINAL SOLUTION.

At the beginning of the sixteenth century, Martin Luther saw handicapped babies as a personal punishment for the sins of the parents – those who did not fear God enough, who bore illegitimate children, thought bad thoughts. Indeed, in spite of his early distress over the doctrine of predestination, Luther still called for a twelve-year-old mentally handicapped boy to be thrown in the river because he was "evil".

The seventeenth-century English physician, Thomas Willis, proposed a view of degeneration and how fools could be born to intelligent parents because of the parents' behaviour – having done too much reading or studying. There might even be "somatic insults" to their bodies, through drunkenness, or excessive youth or age.

The early nineteenth century heard Edouard Seguin voicing the first ideas for the education and care of mentally handicapped people. He, and other educationalists, assumed that all "idiots" were capable of some improvement, even if they could not be cured. Nonetheless, these same educationalists kept alive the possibility that mentally handicapped people might not be truly human. Frequent comparisons were made with animals. "There is not one of any age who may not be made more of a man and less of a brute by patience and kindness."

In 1896 the National Association for the Care and Control of the Feeble-Minded was set up and began to press for the lifetime segregation of "defectives". Shortly afterwards, in 1908, the Radnor Commission arrived at the conclusion "that prevention of mentally defective persons from becoming parents would tend to diminish the number of such persons in the population; and that consequently there are strong grounds for placing mental defectives of each sex in institutions where they will be retained and kept under effectual supervision as long as may be necessary . . ."

But society had to wait until 1987, nearly 500 years after Luther, for a judgment to be handed down by three Law Lords sitting in the Court of Appeal, authorizing a sterilization operation on a ward of court – one Jeanette from Sunderland – because "latterly, it had been observed by the mother and the local authority that she was showing signs of sexual awareness and sexual drive with a risk of pregnancy."

Plus ça change, plus c'est la même chose . . .

Why is the judgment so wrong? Not simply because it authorizes an assault on this young girl's body. After all, the insertion of an IUD could be construed to be of similar physical intrusion. Not simply because it denies a basic human right – to bear children – which it does, but simply because it demonstrates a cynical exercise in expediency – the expediency of saving everyone time, money and effort, especially those who could be held responsible for her care and nurture.

There are other skeletons unlocked and falling out of the cupboard too. Luther, Willis, Seguin, Radnor – to name but a few. All their bones are once more rattling and old wives' tales are dusted down and recycled as support for those hoary old necromancers. Sexual behaviour can now be seen as promiscuity due to mental retardation, rather than a valid desire for physical and emotional contact and expression. The Eugenics Movement can rise and emphasize the need to prevent sexuality and reproduction amongst people with a mental handicap. The ghost of Adolf Hitler can wander abroad and scare us all.

As a result of this judgment, the concept of care in the community has received a severe jolt backwards. All the opponents of this humane and splendid (but woefully underfunded) policy can now be reinforced in their grotesque belief that people with a mental handicap *are* sub-human, *could* be responsible for child-molesting, *will* lower the value of properties and certainly *do* possess super-human strength.

Why do I write this? Not because one poor mentally handicapped adolescent may be allowed to suffer sterility – but simply because the legal support for such an infringement of human rights casts aside everything we at MENCAP, the Royal Society for Mentally Handicapped Children and Adults, have been working for over the past forty years. Education, housing, employment, leisure, self-advocacy, acceptance, a right to choose – all could go back to square one. In the field of leisure, our Gateway Clubs are pre-eminent. Over 45,000 members with a mental handicap attend these clubs – men and women, boys and girls alike. Many, if not all, show "signs of sexual awareness". Is the price of their involvement in the community, and with each other, to be sterilization? It could become the norm. A neat, tidy package – offering no risks or effort to all concerned.

Lord Justice Dillon, Lord Justice Brown and Lord Justice Nicholls may be just men, but are they wise? It seems they have completely failed to heed the words written by the House of Commons Social Services Committee only three years ago: "We must ensure that people with a wide range of mental disability receive care at least as good as that which they at present receive and preferably better . . . It means that the rest of the community has to be prepared to accept mentally disabled people in its midst . . . Frontiers are still relatively unexplored . . . Given the will to change aspects of present services, there is every reason to expect and encourage steady progress towards community care. But in the final analysis, the outcome will be judged next century neither by the location of care, nor by the nature of the concerned, but by the quality of care available and the extent to which individual needs are catered for."

To end with a preposition is perhaps undesirable. But I would rather read that, any day, than a judgment which authorizes a sterilization operation on a seventeen-year-old ward of court.

That is the most undesirable final word of all.

It wasn't the final solution, of course. After all that fuss, how could it be? The Official Solicitor decided to take the matter to the House of Lords but again the result was, predictably, the same. Jeanette could be sterilized. But not before the, then, Lord Chancellor – Lord Hailsham – had a go at me for raising the question as to whether or not Jeanette was to be treated like an animal, as of yore, and spayed like a bitch. I'm glad to say that the leader in the, now-defunct, *London Daily News* sprang to my defence:

INTEMPERATE LANGUAGE FROM THE WOOLSACK

What on earth was a Tory grandee whose political career has been marked by intemperate outbursts and a fierce reverence for authority of all kinds doing yesterday sitting in on one of the most delicate matters to have confronted the senior judiciary in recent times – the sterilization of the mentally retarded girl, Jeanette?

The answer: this was Lord Hailsham, exercising the right he has as Lord Chancellor to sit with the Law Lords and to present his opinions. Never a man to hold his tongue while other judges are content to sit in silence, Lord Hailsham offered the world his views about women, childbirth and medical procedure as if he were an expert.

Some of his remarks were extremely odd. He ruminated on what the girl was likely to do should she become pregnant, and on what might happen if she gave birth. He displayed all the knowledge one might expect of an old man whose main contribution from the Woolsack has been energetically to protect the restrictive practices of the legal profession. At the end of the hearing, with breathtaking disregard of his own outbursts outside the courtroom, Hailsham accused Brian Rix of MENCAP of using "intemperate" language in his passion to defend Jeanette.

Lord Hailsham is in danger of attracting the charge of double standards to the growing list of complaints laid against the Lord Chancellor.

And, of course, the bell-ringing old baron is no more the holder of that high office. What on earth would have happened if he'd gone even higher and succeeded in his attempt to become Prime Minister? It hardly bears contemplating . . . or is an intriguing question . . . depending on your point of view. I know mine.

As I mentioned, probably about 50 per cent of parents in local MENCAP societies felt that the question of sterilization should be answered by the mother and father concerned, with appropriate medical advice. There was another thorny question, too, which was causing a schism in the Society, that of community care for those leaving long-stay hospitals. Again MENCAP had pronounced on this, way back in November 1981, when it was unanimously agreed that we should stress:

i) the need to have a programme for the closure of the large long-stay hospitals;

ii) the reason why it was not possible to implement

any of the recommendations within existing resources;

iii) the problems associated with the "stateless" residents.

As Secretary-General, it was my job to press these points on all concerned, particularly the need for a planned programme for the closure of long-stay hospitals. Now a group of parents, initially from the North-West, had banded together as Rescare and called for the complete stoppage of all hospital closures. Once more we were in a confrontational situation: I, on the one hand, following the policies laid down by the parents serving on our National Council, whilst, on the other, suffering the blows from our own members, diametrically opposed to the decisions taken by their own democratically elected representatives on that Council.

It was difficult, to say the least, and gave me much cause for thought. So much so, that after a particularly rowdy National Council meeting, when everyone was going at it hammer and tongs, I decided that perhaps I would be serving the Society best if I resigned, and made no attempt to stand as Chairman. I offered this to Lord Allen and, I'm delighted to say, he refused to even think about it.

It's a hell of a problem, nevertheless, and one which will probably never be solved whilst there are articulate, passionate parents around fighting desperately for their own loved ones. The Labour Party doesn't seem to have cracked the nut of varying views, and I suspect that we, with our Protestants, Atheists, Jews, Catholics, Muslims, Humanists, Tories, Socialists, Liberals et al, never will, either.

We certainly found that "when sorrows come, they come not as single spies but in battalions", for, no sooner had we become involved in internecine sniping over Jeanette and Rescare than our Royal Patron was dragged into the fray by certain members of the media, who discovered that no less than three Bowes-Lyon nieces of the Queen Mother had been living in the Royal Earlswood Hospital in Surrey for many years – and it had always been presumed that they had died. There were reports in the *Sunday Times* Focus that no less than "five mentally defective cousins in the same generation" had in fact been born – long before genetic counselling was available. At least one niece was reputed to be still alive but in hospital, and the press had a field day. I endeavoured to damp down the flames by issuing the following statement:

Her Majesty Queen Elizabeth The Queen Mother, as the Patron of the Royal Society for Mentally Handicapped Children and Adults (MENCAP) fully supports the Society's endeavours to make care in the community a practical, humane and loving reality.

Furthermore, Her Majesty always wishes to be closely informed as to our work and never fails to express her continuing sympathy and understanding for all people with a mental handicap and their families.

I also wrote to the *Guardian*, in reply to a letter which slagged me off for being guilty of duplicity, setting one standard for the Queen Mother and another for the world at large, in the following terms, under the heading, MENTAL HANDICAP IN A DIFFERENT WORLD:

This was a situation which arose, originally, some sixty years ago, when attitudes were, alas, totally different towards people with a mental handicap and their families.

This applied, particularly, to the better-off families in the land, who were able to afford to send their mentally handicapped offspring away from home. If their "non-existence" was noted, it was often assumed

286

that the person had died and the impression was left unchallenged. Appalling, yes, but nonetheless commonplace.

To blame this situation on the Queen Mother is both ludicrous and unrealistic. By the time her nieces were presumed dead, the Queen Mother was supporting her husband in his many duties as the King of a country which was fighting for its existence in the Second World War. I think it extremely unlikely that the truth of the matter, in regard to the, then, Queen's nieces, was ever conveyed to her.

I finished with this rather over-optimistic phrase:

Let us hope that the knowledge we now have about the Bowes-Lyon family will act as a spur to services in this country. I am certain that the Royal Family will be in the forefront of this endeavour.

The *Observer* ran a profile on me, under the heading, RELUCTANT HERO WITH TWO LIVES:

Last week, a full ten years after he left the theatre, Sir Brian Rix performed before his biggest audience ever; but this time in a tragedy, not farce.

The man whose fame was built on dropping his trousers was drawn into the *Sun's* embarrassing revelation that the Queen Mother had three mentally handicapped nieces, who had been living for the last forty-six years in a Surrey mental hospital. According to *Burke's Peerage* they were dead.

As the week progressed, the drama took on the characteristics of a whodunnit. No one knew who had prematurely "killed off" the Royal nieces. The principal suspect seemed to be the absent-minded mother Fenella. The truth may never be known, as Fenella is now dead.

The revelations were particularly embarrassing to the Queen Mother because she is Patron of MENCAP, the Royal Society for Mentally Handicapped Children and Adults. Sir Brian was sucked into the controversy because he is MENCAP's Secretary-General. He rose to the Queen Mother's defence when he was accused by Penelope Mortimer, a hostile biographer of the Queen Mother, for being soft on royalty.

It was a hard week for Sir Brian, for the Bowes-Lyon affair followed closely on the scolding he got from Lord Hailsham, the Lord Chancellor, who took him to task for comparing the proposed sterilization of a seventeen-year-old mentally handicapped girl to "the spaying of a bitch".

Far from being cowed by the criticism, however, Sir Brian was in bullish mood last week and dished out as good as he got. He condemned as "utter hypocrisy the claims that the Queen Mother had let her nieces down by not being more attentive. How many elderly aunts – and the Queen Mother is eighty-seven next birthday – suddenly discovering that they have two handicapped nieces who are still alive would start visiting them? I am assured by the Royal Earlswood Hospital that when she found out the facts, she behaved in an impeccably aunt-like way."

I received a warm letter of thanks from Sir Martin Gilliatt (the Queen Mother's Private Secretary) for the stand I had taken, which I happened to believe was correct, but we were not quite finished yet. A member of a local society, Mr George Parker, let it be known that he would be attending our AGM and would attempt to force the Queen Mother to resign. The press and television turned up in force, but our Chairman, Lord Allen, disappointed them all by ruling Mr Parker's resolution inadmissible, which it was, for the necessary backing from a local society, as well as written notification, was not forthcoming. One chastened member sat down in his seat, and a dissatisfied media drifted away. It was the end of the story.

In spite of the *Observer* describing me as being in a "bullish mood", I would be less than honest if I didn't admit to approaching the 1987 AGM with a certain degree of apprehension. Jeanette, Rescare and the Bowes-Lyon women were all bubbling away, plus my thoughts of resignation. I asked Philip Allen, as Chairman, if I could make a statement and I believe this illustrated my uncertainty as to my continuing effectiveness as Secretary-General.

I came to this great movement some seven years ago, believing that I could achieve something for people with a mental handicap and their families because of the theatrical fame I had enjoyed for many years. This, perhaps egotistical, belief was backed up by the value I had seen stemming from the *Let's Go* programmes and from a very personal belief that I owed a great deal to my Down's daughter, Shelley, and the tens of thousands like her.

Over the past seven years I think much *has* been achieved. More Acts of Parliament affecting the lives of people with a mental handicap have been enacted in that short time than in the previous thirty-six years. Hardly a week or a day goes by without some positive aspect in the lives of people with a mental handicap becoming known to the world at large. Many *are* living happy and successful lives in the community. More and more *are* in open employment. Local authorities and central Government dare not move without at least giving some consideration to their

289

rights and just demands. And I'm happy to have been part of that general process of progress.

But, of course, there are doubters and bigots always waiting in the wings. By an extraordinary twist of fate these last few weeks have seen a series of events which have caused the media some joy and parents much fear. Are our hospitals being closed too quickly, allowing discharge without regard, to become a horrifying fact of life? Are the general public as uncaring and unhelpful as they were in days of yore? Should sterilization be allowed? Has the Queen Mother been party to some unfortunate cover-up? There are some who pessimistically believe that all this may be so. Their letters to me go to prove this. And they cause me much unhappiness and many a sleepless night. But there are others, many others, who believe the opposite and that the dignity and quality of a person's life must at all times be pre-eminent – even at the risk of personal vilification. I am one of those believers.

The other day I stood in Westminster Hall at the grand lobby organized to support the implementation of the Tom Clarke Act and I met, again, the very people I am talking about. This afternoon we go across to the Festival Hall to see thousands of people with learning difficulties – some mild, some severe, some profound, taking part in a heart-stopping, heart-warming exercise in love and life and laughter – the Gateway Festival.

Those very people are the reason for our existence. We must *never* give up in our efforts to eliminate for ever the use of the word "madhouse", to eliminate the myth that our sons and daughters are second-class citizens and should be put away out of sight and out of mind and never be allowed to have a recognition of their own worth and value.

I'm glad to say that this was greeted with a standing ovation. I felt somewhat better after that, and able to contemplate the months ahead with a little more tranquillity. In any event, the weeks which were left, sped by – not all of them so grim and earnest as those early spring days.

On June 23rd an advertisement, not dissimilar to one I had seen in Brixham years before, appeared in *The Times* and the *Guardian*, telling anyone who was interested that "The Royal Society is seeking a successor to Sir Brian Rix CBE, who is shortly to retire." A day later, I chaired the MENCAP Week Conference with the unpromising title "Better Joint Planning" with everyone knowing I would be leaving in the near future. Whether it was that news or the contents of the conference which inspired a packed lively affair I shall never know, but the fact remains it was one of the best MENCAP conferences I had ever attended.

Still in a light-hearted vein, I was interviewed by Ena Kendall for the *Observer* magazine under the title "A Pool of my Own" and you might be interested to read a bit of this, which appeared with a large colour photo of me, standing on the edge of the pool, clutching a fly scoop and looking for all the world like an ageing Neptune arising from the chlorine:

Sir Brian Rix's swimming pool lies under the flight path to Heathrow and his jaunty smile dims a little as his words are swamped by the noise from herds of passing jumbos. Still, as he points out, the offending planes are flying at 3,000 feet with the wheels not yet down so peering passengers are denied a sneaky peek at his aquatic prowess.

Sir Brian is a hardy fellow. From March to October he swims twice a day, once before leaving for his job as Secretary-General of MENCAP and again in the evenings when he returns. He and his actress wife, Elspet Gray, and their four children have always been a pool family. They had their first in 1960 when they lived in Roehampton and their second was installed when they moved into their present comfortable Victorian house eleven years ago. He tries to swim fourteen or sixteen lengths every day, using breast stroke – "otherwise you don't get the exercise you're after". When he and Elspet use the pool it's heated to about 75°F, boosted by another five degrees when their children and four grandchildren turn up at weekends. Shelley, their mentally handicapped daughter, now thirty-five, who comes to stay most weekends with her parents from the home where she lives, does not use the pool any more because she finds it difficult to get in and out. The children's old play house at one end has been adapted to a changing cabin and although the pool is not graded for depth "you can do a racing dive into it and that's as far as you need to go."

Sir Brian uses a scoop to get rid of flies, assorted creepy-crawlies and leaves that drift down from a nearby cherry tree whose trunk is embraced by a delightful white rose known as a Rambling Rector – a good name to come across in the garden of a man who was this country's leading *farceur* before he gave it all up in 1980 to work for MENCAP. He wears the serious streak that's supposed to lurk beneath the greasepaint in most true clowns very lightly. The perfectly timed quips come easily, delivered in that melodious actor's voice, forceful in committee or command. He has occasionally landed himself in controversy. "I don't like flak, and I didn't like bad notices in the theatre either. One of the great successes of the past seven years is that when we wanted to say something it's made the headlines, and that's what it's all about – making people conscious that there are hundreds of thousands of people with mental handicap in this country."

Now he is getting the seven-year itch and his departure as Secretary-General was signalled in July by advertisements for a successor. It's by way of being stage-managed: by the time a new Secretary-General has worked into the job, the chairman of MENCAP, Lord Allen, will have reached retiring age, and Sir Brian is keen to take over that voluntary position, "because I think my slightly higher-than-average profile can be of value".

Rix is still indelibly associated with dropped trousers, though, as he puts it, "I haven't dropped my trousers for ten years, and even then I rarely did, it was usually some other character, but it became synonymous with me. It belonged to an era when de-bagging as such was the quickest way of a man losing his dignity. People still refer to it even now, just when I'm about to make a most serious speech. But there you are, it's very pleasant to be remembered and it's been a marvellous help because I don't have to go through the rigmarole of who I am."

As a schoolboy he learnt Ovid and lines by the poet have come to be a creed: "When years and strength allow, tolerate labour; soon will come bent old age with silent foot." He has always been fortunate, he reckons, in being able to plan his next step: "I haven't made the money I should have made. Obviously, giving up the theatre wasn't necessarily a wise financial move, but I've always enjoyed my work and my family and friends and that's very lucky. I reckon I'll go on working and striving as long as I have health and strength."

Indeed, *Tolerate Labore* is now the motto on my coat of arms. Both a statement of fact, and a wish-fulfilment. The

East Riding upbringing has a lot to answer for, I suppose. As if to illustrate this, Field Marshal Lord Bramall, Her Majesty's Lord Lieutenant of Greater London, asked me out to lunch at the Travellers' Club, to enquire if I would like to become a Deputy Lieutenant and then, possibly, Vice-Lord Lieutenant. As many good works come within the ambit of the Lieutenancy, I agreed to accept this honour with alacrity. I'm glad to say, all has come about as Dwin (Edwin) Bramall foretold and I am now his number two.

Next, Laurie Marsh asked me if I would like to become a non-executive director of Soundalive, a company which offers guided audio tours of museums, exhibitions, historic houses, etc, using a specially adapted Sony Walkman. As this would happen after I retired, I accepted, on condition that a separate charitable company was formed to offer access and facilities to disabled people. Laurie agreed and eventually the Libertas Charity Group came into being, of which I am Chairman, made up of Barnardo's, Help the Aged, RNIB, RNID, Guide Dogs for the Blind, Country Landowners' Association (they've lots of properties we want to get into!), MENCAP and RADAR. Quite an impressive bunch. If we can't open a few doors, who can?

An offer came from the National Theatre to return to the boards in *Waiting For Godot*, but as rehearsals clashed with my last weeks at MENCAP, I had to refuse. Though not before I had the most excellent dinner with director Michael Rudman and actor Alec McCowen, and enjoyed dreaming about the prospect of an NT triumph. Alas, not to take place.

Now came the selection of my successor. First of all a weeding-out process, conducted by the Chairman (Lord Allen), the Treasurer (Barrie Davis) and me. Then the last six in front of the Management Committee with me acting as a sort of "prisoner's friend". It was not easy. The last shall be first, and it wasn't a simple matter to decide on who should be the first among equals.

In the end, it was agreed that "man management", with our ever-growing Society, should be the key and thus this news item appeared in *The Times* on September 24th:

ADMIRAL FOR MENCAP

Sir Geoffrey Dalton, Nato's former Deputy Supreme Allied Commander, Atlantic, is to succeed Sir Brian Rix as Secretary-General of MENCAP in November.

Sir Geoffrey, aged fifty-six, who recently retired as a vice-admiral, was chosen from more than fifty applicants. He said he had wanted a job in which he would be involved with people. "I wanted to continue being of service."

In the Royal Navy he raised money for the King George's Fund for Sailors. However, he said: "It is fair to say that I have some knowledge of charity work, but as yet no vast experience."

Sir Brian has been Secretary-General of the charity, the Royal Society for Mentally Handicapped Children and Adults, since retiring from the theatre in April 1980. His involvement stemmed from his first daughter, Shelley, now aged thirty-five, suffering from Down's syndrome. He said yesterday he was delighted with the choice of successor. He will be the Council of Management's candidate to succeed Lord Allen of Abbeydale as Chairman of the charity next April.

No gale force winds at this announcement. After all, hadn't another admiral, Sir John Cox, steered the Spastics Society through many a stormy sea over the last four years? In fact, I even missed the famous hurricane in the South of England in the October of 1987, for I was in

Harrogate making yet another speech at yet another conference.

One week before I retired, at the end of October, we held our Members' Meeting at Brighton. Seven years to the day after addressing these same members in Manchester, I gave my valedictory address. Here's how I began:

At the National Council Meeting on July 7th last, it was proposed that there would be a seven-year review of the Society's activities to be introduced by me, as Secretary-General, leading to a general discussion as to whether or not the Royal Society's aims reflect policy changes – as outlined in the seven-year review.

Now the aims of the Society, as expressed on the letterhead, are as follows: "to increase public awareness and understanding of the problems of people with a mental handicap, so as to secure provision for them commensurate with their needs". To help you assess the current correctness of those aims, my seven-year review will be followed by a brief analysis of the [recently held] local society survey. After that – the floor is yours. By a strange coincidence, this seven-year report coincides exactly with my tenure in office as Secretary-General of MENCAP – so it is both a report and a valediction. I hope, therefore, you will allow me a little more elbow room than that offered by the National Council – who suggested I should manage the whole thing in about fifteen minutes. That's rather like asking Wagner to rewrite "The Ring Cycle" as the "Minute Waltz". But I'll do my best!

Seven years, almost to the day, as Secretary-General. In the theatre, achieving a seven-year run is proof enough that you are a roaring success, at least in financial terms. I know that on this particular stage things are rather different, but I like to think the fact that I am bowing out and not being booed off means that I have done the job in a way which meets with some sort of approval. This role has been one of the most demanding I have ever undertaken; but it has also been one of the most rewarding, and one I am very proud to have played. However, for reasons that have been explained to you by the Chairman, it has been decided that this is the right moment for me to make my exit, and I'm hoping that after all this time I can still remember how to do it without bumping into the furniture or knocking over the scenery. Many of you may remember the day I first attended a Members' Meeting on Saturday, October 25th in Manchester – and some will remember my predecessor – so I don't plan to bore you with a blow-by-blow account of the whole seven years, but I do think it would be useful for us to look back over the edited highlights together, to take note of what we have achieved, where we have succeeded or failed, and how best MENCAP can move forward . . . I was going to say "after I've gone" but it sounds like a plug from one of our legal books . . . It also sounds rather too final, since of course I am not planning to cut myself off completely from an organization which has been such a large part of my life for so long. I may be handing over the helm (and who better to hand it to than a former vice-admiral?) but I shall still be doing a spot of rowing, along with the thousands of other dedicated parents, friends and professionals who have helped make MENCAP a household word and a popular cause. I would like to put my thanks to them on record now, for their support, their enthusiasm and imagination, and their sheer determination, sometimes in the face of impossible odds. The story of the past seven years is as much their story as it is mine: they have all contributed to MENCAP's growth and progress, which I'm sure must have surpassed the wildest dreams of the small band of parents who founded our organization more than forty years ago.

Then followed a lengthy résumé of all that you have read in the preceding pages, ending with this:

> ... shortly after I joined, I changed the staff management structure to band all our endeavours together into groups, under Group Directors, responding to four main committees of the National Council, with the Secretary-General in overall charge of day-to-day management of a staff for whom no praise is too high.
>
> That management will shortly be in someone else's capable hands, and I hope I have left Sir Geoffrey a good foundation upon which to build during the next few years. I believe our aims *have* changed and our horizons are even wider. I won't presume to give Sir Geoffrey my advice, but I would like to share with him – and with you – some words of encouragement from George Bernard Shaw. I find them invaluable whenever there is a chance I might be accused of being unreasonable. George Bernard Shaw said this: "The reasonable man adapts himself to the world: the unreasonable one persists in trying to change it. Therefore, all progress depends on the unreasonable man."
>
> Ladies and gentlemen, my last wish as Secretary-General is that no one in MENCAP will ever be afraid of being thought unreasonable. We have a reputation for leading the way in services for people with mental handicaps and their families and I firmly believe that it is possible for us to change the world. We are a great voluntary movement – with many marvellous members – fired by a common cause: our mentally handicapped sons and daughters.
>
> As you know, I am hopeful of being back with you

by the AGM. What on earth shall I do for the next six months? Perhaps John Milton has the answer in *Paradise Lost*:

> For solitude sometimes is best society,
> and short retirement urges sweet return.

And return I did. As Chairman of the Royal Society for Mentally Handicapped Children and Adults on Saturday, April 23rd, 1988.

But in the meantime, life went on. After all, the future is soon the present and then the past. It's all in the Epilogue. May I respectfully ask you to remain seated. The bars are not open and the performance will continue immediately.

Epilogue

"The Relapse"

Thanks to the BBC, the word "epilogue" has now assumed a different meaning for many people: that of a short religious service towards the end of the day, as opposed to the concluding part of a literary work, if I can claim such a distinction for this book.

It is in its latter (and original) sense I intend to use the word, sweeping up the loose ends of my story, as far as is possible, and giving you a picture of my first year in retirement.

Let me begin with the initial two months to Christmas 1987, for my diary entries will give you some idea of the frenetic energy I expended on time-consuming voluntary work to fill the void left at the end of my paid employment with MENCAP. Clearly the very word "retirement" conjures up pictures of carpet slippers, walking the mangy old dog, dropping in at the pub, mid-week hotel breaks at bargain prices for senior citizens, if your ancient banger of a car can get there or if you can afford the petrol. Knitted cardigans, increasingly warm underwear, gardening until lumbago gives you the excuse not to, moving to Worthing – but I needn't go on. Happily, none of these yet apply to me, but the spectre is there, summoned up by that dread word "retire", which *does* mean to withdraw or seek shelter. And at sixty-four, you are just not ready for that – why should you be? – so my solution was to fill every day with "sound and fury, signifying nothing". Well, not exactly nothing, but not exactly productive either.

After the farewell party given to me at MENCAP on the afternoon of Friday, October 30th, I drove home in my

Citroen CX Pallas IE (a gift from the Society, written-down value £1,500, lest you thought they were being profligate) for a relaxing weekend. All the kids and grand-children home for Sunday lunch was the first "relaxation". Always a delight, of course, but hardly sitting with your feet up, browsing through the Sunday papers. Monday and Tuesday off, except for drinks with John Whitney, the Director-General of the Independent Broadcasting Author-ity, at its Brompton Road headquarters and then on Wednesday, November 4th, I was away at 8.30 a.m. To visit (all day) the Bethlem Royal Hospital, in Beckenham, Kent. I was there, along with the MENCAP Medical Panel, to see the Mental Impairment, Evaluation and Treatment Service run by Dr Tony Holland, which is studying the short-term behavioural problems of people with a mental handicap.

The following day the mood changed completely. I donned my Lord-Lieutenancy hat (I was then a Deputy — my promotion to Vice-Lord Lieutenant of Greater London came on January 1st, 1988) and went to the Palace Theatre in Charing Cross Road to hand over a Queen's Award for Export Achievement to the Really Useful Group for all the sales of Andrew Lloyd Webber's productions overseas, including, naturally enough, *Cats*, *Starlight Express* and *Phantom of the Opera*. I then had lunch at L'Escargot in Greek Street, just up the road, with Loretto Lambe, to talk through the next MENCAP City Foundation grants, and who should walk in but Prince Edward, with some Really Useful Group executives. They were probably making all the final arrangements before he joined the company. Why that same company should want a Queen's Award when one of her sons would be working for them, beats me. Isn't that reward enough?

Oh, and by the way, when I say I was wearing my Lieutenancy hat, I was wearing it metaphorically. I was in a perfectly ordinary double-breasted dark blue suit. The hat and uniform came later, with my promotion, and then the famous Savile Row tailors, Gieves and Hawkes, did an absolutely splendid job for me. They even managed to trim down the stand-up collar, for I have absolutely no neck at all and I appeared to have about eight double chins when encased in those red tabs. By dint of crafty tailoring my chins are now reduced to manageable numbers. Two or three at most. To date, I have only worn the uniform twice. The first occasion was the presentation at New Scotland Yard and later the same day, at Westminster City Hall, of bravery awards, QPMs and BEMs. Some of the citations made you realize just how incredibly courageous people are. Like one old boy who foiled a bank robbery by shouting with such ferocity at the armed men, who had ordered him to lie down, that they dropped their loot and ran. Or the young student who thrust his arm into a crocodile's mouth to make it release a boy who was swimming with a group of people, in a supposedly safe river in Zimbabwe. I was honoured at being able to present such people with their awards. The second time I wore my uniform was when I stood in for Lord Bramall at Heathrow, as a member of the receiving party, to greet the Queen before she flew off on her state visit to Spain in October 1988. All the rest of the time – ordinary mufti, I promise you.

Friday, November 6th, saw me back at MENCAP, barely one week after leaving, lunching in my old office (looking very bare and ship-shape, now my dozens of pictures were off the walls) with my successor, Sir Geoffrey Dalton. It was a debriefing session really, but it was distinctly odd seeing everyone again so soon – and now with no standing in the Society at all, just as Chairman-in-waiting. The following Monday had me at the Arts Council, joining in the annual appraisal of the Royal Shakespeare Company and, when it was all over, it was very pleasant of Terry Hands to pay tribute to the original

Whitehall team – for it was that team, he said, which fired his imagination about ensemble work. Just as Richard Eyre (the new Director of the National) saw his first play at the Whitehall, too. Not bad, the two bosses of our greatest theatrical companies, enthused by that often critically despised theatrical form, basic British farce.

Next day was again work all day, and all evening too. First, the judging of the Home Carer of the Year Awards and then the presentations over dinner, with the usual speech, of course. The following morning, up early for the Lord's Taverners' Foundation Committee meeting, to make our quarterly grants (last year nearly £1 million was distributed), and then back to 105 Piccadilly to travel to Stratford-upon-Avon for a full meeting, on Thursday, November 12th, of the Arts Council of Great Britain. Except I didn't go, for Rhoda's eldest daughter, Carina (remember, Rhoda was Elspet's sister who died from cancer in 1978) was having some trouble in labour, so I stayed behind in case anyone needed a helping hand. Not with the delivery, of course. I'm happy to report that all went well and a bouncing baby boy, Tom, arrived after an unconscionably long time. This meant I was able to get up at crack of dawn to drive to Stratford after all for the Council meeting, returning on the evening of the next day.

I will race through the rest of November and December, just to show how much I was flying about to fulfil Parkinson's Law "that nature abhors a vacuum", or words to that effect. I will pause only to comment on anything which might be of interest, and see how long it takes me.

Monday, November 16th: Lunch at Windsor with the Guide Dogs for the Blind Association, followed by an evening at Grosvenor House, presenting the Otard Cognac Achievement Awards, with Frank Bough doing the commentary.

Tuesday, November 17th: Gieves for a uniform fitting. It was then I ran into the Queen's Bodyguard (returning from the non-existent state visit of the Italian President – it was cancelled), looking frightfully smart in their plumage, which they have to return to Gieves and Hawkes for safekeeping, and then lunch, once more, with Geoffrey Dalton, but this time at the White Tower in Percy Street, hosted by Helmut Rothenberg, who wanted to get to know my successor. The evening was pleasure bent, watching Liza Minelli from our comfortable debenture seats at the Albert Hall. In case you are wondering, the Victorians originally raised money for the building by selling debenture seats and boxes. This system still applies. Seats occasionally come up for sale and I was lucky enough to buy two for Elspet, as a wedding anniversary present, way back in the 1960s. We get tickets for practically everything, except private functions, but most of the time they seem to be taken by our younger son, Jonty, who loves the place and the events there. The fact that we (or, rather, I) never seem to have the time to visit must reflect badly on my sense of priorities, I fear.

Wednesday, November 18th: Meeting with Ian Brown, Director of Drama, Arts Council, at 10.00 a.m. Drama Panel at 10.45. Richard Eyre at lunch, to tell us his hopes and aspirations for the National when he took over from Sir Peter Hall, which he did nine months later. Then home to change and dinner with the Master Templars at the Inner Temple, when those august lawyers enjoy the equivalent of a legal knees-up and back to bed in time for a good night's sleep before chairing my last meeting of the Medical Advisory Panel on Thursday 19th. It was pointed out to me that if I was to become Chairman of MENCAP I could hardly be Chairman of one of the advisory bodies, also – so it was left that should that come to pass (which it did), I would have to go. A pity. I loved the Medical lot, but I suppose the argument against the Chairman of the Society having special interests is irrefutable.

Friday, November 20th, saw Elspet and me driving to

Portsmouth to interest the Mary Rose Trust, plus HMS *Victory* and HMS *Warrior*, in the yet-to-be formed Libertas Group, to allow disabled people easier access and facilities to view these magnificent relics. We were courteously received (including being piped on and off the *Victory*) and I believe some progress was made.

Monday, November 23rd, had me back at the Arts Council once more, this time chairing the Monitoring Committee for Arts and Disabled People. In the evening, again for the Arts Council, I had to visit the Almeida Theatre to see the production of Zola's *Nana*. I did not enjoy the experience, in direct opposition to the majority of critics, who had loved the production. On the contrary, I found Zola's allegory somewhat overlong and repetitive. After all, you can only copulate and dance the can-can effectively every so often, and only emote occasionally about the horrors of poverty and the decadence of the nineteenth-century Parisian aristocracy, without boredom setting in. Mind you, a drive across London to the Almeida of twenty-two miles, there and back, in the teeth of the rush hour and past beleaguered King's Cross, was hardly a fitting start for the evening's jollities. You will have gathered that the visit was just after that disastrous fire. Perhaps that's why I was so dispirited.

It was a relief to go with Elspet the following evening to Guildford and enjoy the honest vulgarity of the first night of Ray Cooney's new farce, *It Runs in the Family*, which we felt was a return to his older form of writing, more akin to *Chase Me, Comrade!* than *Run for Your Wife*, with its heavy reliance on "poofter" jokes. With the usual reservations you always have about certain scenes in a farce at a first try-out, we thought the play very funny and Ray Cooney himself and John Quayle were excellent in the leads.

Wednesday 25th was a somewhat overcrowded day with a meeting of the Executive of the Imperial Society of

Knights Bachelor in the morning, lunch with Sir Clement Freud followed by the AGM of the Stars Organization for Spastics in the afternoon. Then it was over to the National Theatre to see the first night of *Waiting for Godot* – and as this was the play which nearly tempted me back into the theatre, I thought you might be interested to read my report to the Drama Department of the Arts Council. I've written dozens of such reports, for other productions, but thought you might like to read two. Here is the first:

Rather awkward for me to comment on last night's production of *Waiting for Godot* at the National's Lyttelton Theatre for, when my retirement was announced earlier this year, I was asked if I might be interested in returning to the boards, playing in this particular piece. For all manner of reasons, I had to decline – but obviously I had read the script a number of times before reaching my decision and so was well acquainted with the work as literature, on seeing it in performance at the National.

First let me say that I think the piece has lost much of its impact and, possibly, relevance since its first London production in 1955. Many more Samuel Beckett works have seen the glare of the spotlight and the world has begun to retreat from the abyss of the nuclear holocaust and the possibility of cataclysmic loneliness. I think the production also failed to take in the relevance of those poor sad characters living just a few yards away under the arches of the Festival Hall and thereby stressed the metaphysical aspects of the play, rather than opening up its present-day opportunities. In other words, Michael Rudman plays safe and as such has produced a polished work which will be studied by students, aficionados and intellectuals. I wonder how it will appeal to ordinary theatregoers?

The first act went by with little to rivet the attention, but Act II had some moving moments – particularly towards the end – and John Alderton seized such opportunities as came his way with alacrity and expertise. Alec McCowen, brisk, bright and jolly – with distinct military overtones – stressed his companion's increasing depression with professional exactitude.

The boy, Simon Privett (or was it Simon Doe?) spoke his lines clearly and with certainty; Peter Wight's Lucky showed little sign of being an idiot savant, as I'm sure was intended by Beckett, but when fired into action spoke his incomprehensible lines with all the certainty of a senior civil servant, whilst Colin Welland overacted shamefully as Pozzo – but just about got away with it, I think.

All in all, a good, economical, curriculum-satisfying revival of this enigmatic piece. Whether it will make up the loss of audience interest caused by *The Wandering Jew* remains to be seen. My life, already I'm worried.

Well, I needn't have been. The piece was a reasonable success and all concerned were well satisfied. Except me. I would have liked to have been in it.

The next day, Thursday 26th, was spent on Soundalive and Libertas business and the day after saw me driving down to Bournemouth for the first meeting of the Advisory Board of the Abbey Life Ethical Trust. I have some illustrious companions on that Board, including Baroness McLeod (widow of Ian McLeod), Julian Pettifer who, apart from being a prominent writer and broadcaster, is a committed conservationist, Pran Sheth, the former Deputy Chairman for the Commission for Racial Equality and Guy Stringer who, until fairly recently, was the Director of Oxfam. We meet (four times a year) to monitor the Trust and advise on future policy, and a jolly little group we are, under the chairmanship of Alan Frost, who is the Director of Abbey Life Investments. We foregather, offer our views, have lunch and disperse. All very civilized and I'm glad to say the Ethical Trust is performing well.

The following week, commencing Monday, November 30th, had us staying with the Crowthers, Leslie and Jean, at their lovely house just outside Bath and attending the Monday Club Panto on that evening. The Monday Club has no affiliation to its better-known namesake at the House of Commons but it provides entertainment by and for people with a mental handicap, at a local level. Leslie Crowther is the Patron. We enjoyed ourselves enormously. More, really, than we have enjoyed some of the political knock-about provided by that other Monday Club at Westminster.

On December 2nd, just across the water from the House of Commons, I visited the cardiac department at St Thomas's Hospital. Over the years I have succumbed to the same problems which beset my grandfather, my mother, my brother and now, me. Namely, arrhythmia (irregular heartbeat) and a wonky valve. I am happy to say that digitalis, taken daily, generally keeps the arrhythmia at bay, whilst I have to have an annual check-up for the valve, to see how much it has deteriorated during the previous year. One day I suppose I might have to have a replacement, but I live in hopes. After all, my mother soldiered on to eighty-five until her heart *did* give out, and my grandfather managed a couple of years more – so there's life in the old dog yet. After my examination, it was over Westminster Bridge to the House of Lords, where David Renton was host at a luncheon to welcome my successor, Sir Geoffrey Dalton. Present (apart from Lord Renton) were a number of distinguished people, all interested in the work of MENCAP, including Earl Ferrers and his Lady, Lord and Lady Allen, Sir Geoffrey and Lady

Dalton, plus Elspet and me. After that, I trolled along to the Royal Society of Medicine in Wimpole Street, where the Steering Committee for the Forum on Mental Retardation was meeting, and then it was home. Not bad for a retired person, with heart problems, eh? Or am I just plain bloody stupid?

Then on Friday, I drove with Fred Heddell (the Director of Education at MENCAP) to the BBC studios in Bristol, where we recorded the first of the ten twenty-five-minute programmes for people with learning difficulties, *A Life of Our Own*. It went very well, particularly Gary Bourlet's appearance as a presenter of the programme and remember, Gary himself has learning difficulties. Then it was back to London, to be up early the next morning to make the opening speech at the London Hospital in Whitechapel (God, what a journey from Barnes) for a conference on dentistry for handicapped people. Unfortunately, I didn't know about the contents of the speech required until I got back from Bristol, so I sat in the back of a hire car and composed it whilst making that ghastly trip across London. In the event, I could read my scribbles and the speech went well.

At the weekend – well, on the Sunday to be precise – we had a lunch at L'Escargot, with many others, to celebrate that lovely actress Jean Anderson's eightieth birthday (Elspet had been in *Tenko* with her), leaving after that for our old friends, the Turveys, to spend a couple of nights with them in the charming village where they live, Linton, near Cambridge. Then it was back to the House of Commons to have another meeting and lunch with the PRMH (Profound Retardation and Multiple Handicap) Steering Committee hosted by Dafydd Wigley, Plaid Cymru MP for Caernarfon and father of two tragically handicapped sons, who had died only recently. Next day, December 9th, it was a meeting of the United Charities Unit Trust and the MENCAP City Foundation, whilst

Thursday, December 10th, found me in Bristol, once more, for another programme in the *A Life of Our Own* series and Friday back again in London, in Hill Street, Mayfair, at a meeting of the Knights Bachelor Charity Committee. This was followed by another uniform fitting at Gieves and a buffet lunch with the Leader of the Opposition, Neil Kinnock, in the House of Commons, where many large charities were represented. I got in by default, I suppose, for I had accepted the invitation when I was still Secretary-General and a lunch is always welcome. As Elspet said: "For better for worse, but never for lunch." I was trying to live up to that and keeping out of the house!

On Saturday, December 12th, I had to visit MENCAP, yet again, when the National Council made a presentation to me of a splendid leather armchair and footrest which relaxes me in my study, where I am writing this book. Then it was a quick drive across London to Kingston Road, Teddington, to chair the Friends of Normansfield AGM. Lunch with actors Terence Alexander and his wife, Jane Downs, on the Sunday and over to the Royal Horticultural Society's Old Hall in Vincent Square on the Monday morning to see the Chinese Ambassador open the Emperor's Warriors exhibition. Soundalive Tours were doing the audio presentation of this, so I had a vested interest.

The next day, I was out to lunch yet again – and here I will stop these diary entries. I hope they have shown you (and me) the turmoil I was in immediately after my retirement. A turmoil which led me, eventually, to accept the proposition which was put to me, quite indirectly and casually at this lunch at L'Escargot by John Chapman, the author, and the eventual director, Christopher Renshaw, that I should return to the theatre in a revival of that old Whitehall farce, *Dry Rot*. Nine months later, I did. Amazing how these gestation periods seem to be all the same in my life. I should have been born a woman . . .

Earlier in 1987, Chris Renshaw had been directing a revival of *Bless the Bride* and, wanting some new dialogue, he approached John Chapman to write it. Chris remembered John with great admiration, for the first play he had seen as a boy in London was also John's first play as an author, *Dry Rot*. Chris had subsequently moved on from Magdalen College, Oxford, into the world of opera, directing at Glyndebourne, Covent Garden, the Aldeburgh Festival, Sadler's Wells, as well as European opera houses, and also those in America and Australia. John, on the other hand, had continued to write: *Simple Spymen*, *Not Now Darling*, *Move Over Mrs Markham* (the last two with Ray Cooney), *Look, No Hans!* (with Michael Pertwee), *Oh Clarence, There Goes the Bride* being but a few of his titles. He had tended to concentrate for long periods on writing for television: *Hugh and I* (with Hugh Lloyd and Terry Scott), *Blandings Castle* (with Sir Ralph Richardson) and *Fresh Fields* (with Julia McKenzie and Anton Rodgers) spring readily to mind, but there have been many others.

So, these two met, and Chris enthused – yet again – about *Dry Rot* and how he would like to direct a revival, setting the piece in its original period of the early 1950s. John, naturally enough, was intrigued and the question as to who might play in it came up. "Well, Brian's about to retire," said one. "Let's ask him." Thus, early in November, a phone call came from John asking if I would be interested and, oh yes, would Elspet consider playing too?

As this was just after my abortive flirtation with the National, I had not yet made any decision, one way or the other, as to whether or not I might pick up my theatrical career again, even fleetingly, so I declined. John, however, suggested that a lunch with Chris Renshaw would do no one any harm, for he would like to meet me and discuss my distant memories of *Dry Rot* of thirty-odd years ago. Hence my sitting down with them on December 14th to enjoy a splendid lunch in Elena's room at L'Escargot, which, as I am sure you know by now, is in Greek Street in Soho.

No decisions were taken at that meal, other than the obvious one that if I did agree to appear, it would not be in my old part of Fred Phipps the bookie's runner, but as Alf Tubbe, the bookie himself – the part originally created by John Slater, taken over by Leo Franklyn and filmed by Ronnie Shiner. I, on the other hand, had played for 1,475 performances as Fred Phipps, plus appearing in the film. So, even after thirty-four years, a change would be as good as a rest! Anyway, I was now too old (and too heavy) for my original role, so there was no question of giving a one thousand four hundred and seventy-sixth performance.

I really forgot all about it over Christmas, having one particularly marvellous afternoon with Elspet taking our grandchildren to see the RSC production of *The Wizard of Oz* at the Barbican. My report to the Arts Council reflects this:

All right, all right! I *do* believe in fairies. And in witches – good ones from the north and wicked ones from the west. Oh yes – and I believe in wizards, too. Particularly if they come from Oz . . . no, *especially* if they come from Oz, via the RSC and the Barbican, and it's Christmas 1987 and you and your wife are accompanied by your three eldest grandchildren, all of five, four and three, and you're surrounded by other grandparents, parents and offspring, all enjoying the same childhood memories, all following the yellow brick road, and an afternoon of happiness, nostalgia, tears and laughter with Dorothy, the Scarecrow, the Tin Man, and Cowardly Lion et al. Oh, we were all off to see the Wizard, make no mistake about it – and we were all over the rainbow in the process.

Why can't the RSC always entertain so effectively

at the Barbican? After this splendid production, I'll be even more mystified the next time I lose my way in that cavernous building, wondering why I came along in the first place to see some load of old rubbish. Obviously, they *can* do it – and outstandingly well when they get it right. I must have just picked the wrong events. Ah well, I can live on memories. Next time I'm bored (or disappointed), I'll dream I'm back in Oz with Imelda Staunton, Dilys Laye, David Glover, Paul Greenwood, John Bowe, Jim Carter, Bille Brown, Tony Church, and Millie. Millie, by the way, is Toto the dog. She gets into drag, or whatever is the opposite of that, with remarkable facility – a veritable canine Vesta Tilley – and captivates all our hearts. Never act with children or animals – and there are plenty of the former about, too. Munchkins, Winkies and Flying Monkeys abound. But never once do the adult actors and actresses (or Apple Trees, or Farmhands or Poppies, or Snowflakes or Jitterbugs, or Emerald City Citizens) seem hexed by that hoary old saying. They just get on with the job, and do it beautifully, directed by Ian Judge, with choreography by Sheila Falconer, designs by Mark Thompson, lighting by Nick Chelton, orchestrations by Larry Wilcox and musical direction by Richard Brown – not forgetting the originators, author L. Frank Baum, with music and lyrics by Harold Arlen and Yip Harburg. They all deserve a *very* happy Christmas. They certainly gave me one.

And when that happy Christmas was over, a return to reality in the New Year of 1988, and yet another lunch, this time with Lee Menzies (who had agreed to produce *Dry Rot*), as well as John Chapman and Chris Renshaw. The venue, very agreeable, the Ritz on January 12th, and almost the first person I saw was Jeffrey Archer, lunching with someone else, who came over to say he had heard from Lee that I was interested in *Dry Rot* and if that was true, so would he be, as a backer. I must say I thought that very generous for, after all, he had already helped me, or rather MENCAP, through the donation of one of his short stories – so why be interested further? Quite simply, Lee Menzies had produced Jeffrey's huge success, *Beyond Reasonable Doubt*, at the Queen's Theatre, and later in the year was to become the Managing Director of the Playhouse in Northumberland Avenue, when Jeffrey Archer bought a majority shareholding in that beautifully refurbished theatre. So now you know why that highly successful author was an interested party. At the end of the lunch, I had become one also. Not only was Lee Menzies very persuasive – offering me a considerable say in the production (casting, dates, length of run, etc) – but also making an offer of 25 per cent of any profits to the MENCAP City Foundation. Of course, first those profits had to be made, but that was always a possibility.

So, I went away to think it over. A late summer production, giving me time to write this book, two weeks in Bath, sixteen weeks in the West End (probably Shaftesbury Avenue, for Lee had already sounded out Louis Benjamin, the President of Stoll-Moss Theatres Ltd, the company running the Apollo, Lyric, Queen's and Globe) and that would be that. It was very tempting. Still, it was a difficult decision and I needed time to contemplate.

It took two weeks. I consulted Elspet, the family, the Lord Lieutenant (my duties for the Lieutenancy), Lord Allen (my duties if I became Chairman of MENCAP) and my conscience. I wrote down a chart of all the pros and cons. I lay awake and worried. Two days before my sixty-fourth birthday, I accepted the offer. Why? Mainly, I think, because of the fun of being with a crowd of actors again (including Elspet), of appearing in a very funny play, hearing audience laughter and because of the challenge.

What would it be like to return to the stage after an absence of nearly twelve years in a type of part I had never played before? Would Michael Pertwee's gloomy forecast in the mid-1970s as to my box-office appeal still apply? Would my energy-level be up to the explosion of effort which is required every night in a farce? Would the critics (many of whom were now past their sell-by dates, whilst others were still mewling and pewking in their nurses' arms when I was packing the Whitehall and Garrick Theatres) be miffed that I had left the theatre and was now "condescending" to return? Would those same critics consider John's *Dry Rot* a comedy classic or look on it as a simple piece of work, hardly worth their benison? Would it really be worth my while to risk losing a nostalgic legendary reputation for a few months' return in an old play on Shaftesbury Avenue?

There were many more questions besides, but you can see why I fell. How much easier to slip quietly into a peaceful old age, partaking in good works and never again enjoying the surge of adrenalin which active employment in the theatre can bring. But how *boring*. So, on February 8th, 1988, Nigel Dempster's column in the *Daily Mail* carried this headline: "Rix, A New Case of *Dry Rot*". The cat was out of the bag and I was committed.

And there was just one other temptation I forgot to mention. "The Relapse" makes a far better heading (and story) for this Epilogue rather than, say, "Journey's End". That would have been too depressing.

Apart from assuming the chairmanship of MENCAP towards the end of April and enjoying two splendid holidays (one in March at La Gazelle d'Or in Morocco, where we met two lovely people, Jean and Matthew Gardiner, and then went on holiday with them in July to Le Mas Candille in Mougins, in the South of France, where we ate too much and I learned my lines) the rest of the spring and summer of 1988 was taken up writing this book and preparing for *Dry Rot*. An intentionally dreadful toupee to be fitted at Wig Creations, costumes to be agreed with designer Tim Goodchild, casting and auditions to be held, advance publicity to be planned with Peter Thompson – you would be amazed how much time all this took. Throw in work for the Arts Council, watching the West Indies toying with us at Lord's, attending various committee meetings for the English Speaking Union, the Lord's Taverners, the Theatre of Comedy, Friends of Normansfield, MENCAP, plus a number of fund-raising speeches for the latter, and the months sped by.

There were family matters to attend to, as well. Clearing the pool, so the grandchildren wouldn't find it green and slimy at weekends, seeing Louisa's first nights in Alan Ayckbourn's *How the Other Half Loves*, directed by Alan Strachan at Greenwich and, subsequently, the Duke of York's Theatre. Visiting the BBC Television Centre to enjoy a recording of *Colin's Sandwich* with Louisa opposite Mel Smith, and Jamie as the associate producer. Spending some Saturdays and Sundays with Shelley at home, which were fairly peaceful, for now, poor love, she is pretty inactive. Encouraging Jonathan in his writing by offering support and criticism when this seemed appropriate. Enjoying the company of our extended family, too. Fellow grandparents, in-laws, consorts, brothers, sisters, nephews, nieces, children – if we all get together (which we do only occasionally) there are over fifty of us but, luckily, we seem to gather in more manageable numbers than such an overcrowded coach party. Unhappily, one of that party shuffled off this mortal coil in February when Elspet's beloved Auntie Gertie died at St Andrews, in her ninetieth year. All the family mourned, and it left Elspet with only one living relative in Scotland, Gertie's son, Donald. Visiting (or being visited by) old friends too, like Michael Pertwee who, in 1988, recovered from two chemotherapy sessions for leukaemia (which is now in remission). He went completely bald but has now regrown a splendid thatch of hair much darker and curlier than his previous thinning, grey, lank locks. Remarkable, but not recommended by Michael as a hair-restorer. Oh yes, and listening to the nightingale which sang outside our bedroom window once nightly, and twice on Thursdays and Saturdays, all through February, March and April. Equally remarkable.

On August 10th, 1988, rehearsals of *Dry Rot* began in a club in Chiswick. Three weeks there and then the final week in the set, which had been erected at the Lyric Theatre in Shaftesbury Avenue. We were lucky, inasmuch as the Lyric had been dark for some weeks, so Lee was able to do a deal with Stoll-Moss which allowed us the luxury of working in the set before our first technical rehearsal. With a play as complicated as *Dry Rot* – collapsing stairs, sliding panels et al – such a chance was a godsend, so by the time we reached the lovely Theatre Royal in that glorious Georgian city of Bath, we had worked out how *not* to break a miscellany of legs, necks and backs.

However, for me, rehearsals – although enjoyable – were anything but straightforward. Peter Thompson is a very bright press representative and by the time we opened in Bath I had been interviewed, photographed, televised and broadcast by no less than twenty newspapers and magazines, eighteen radio and fourteen television programmes. My return to the boards was hyped up to be a theatrical second coming. The world at large knew about my lunch, my swimming pool, my dressing-room, my underpants, my family, my wife, my fears, my hopes – and on, and on – thanks to the most incredible blanket coverage, from *Wogan* to *One in Four*, from *The Times* to *Time Out*, from Gloria Hunniford to Ned Sherrin's *Loose Ends*. On our first night in Bath, Tuesday, September 6th, the entire *Around Midnight* show, on Radio 2 with Brian

Matthews, was broadcast from the stage of the Theatre Royal, after that performance was over. It was an amazing piece of PR work, and one which nearly exhausted me, such were the demands on my time. But all worth while. The Great British Public certainly knew that *Dry Rot* was being revived and that I was in it. All we needed were rave notices and we would be packed (for our advance bookings were very good), with Lee Menzies, Christopher Renshaw and John Chapman fully justified in their optimism. We didn't get such notices. They were a very mixed bag.

We should have anticipated such a reaction really, but we had such a good cast, had played to such enthusiastic audiences (and notices) in Bath, that we were perhaps lulled into a false sense of security. We had forgotten with what indifference two old farces had been received in the recent past, when they were revived: *Rookery Nook* at the Shaftesbury Theatre, presented by the Theatre of Comedy, with Tom Courtenay, Peggy Mount, Ian Ogilvie and Lionel Jeffries in the cast. Even the magic of Ben Travers's name could not save that one. Then there was *Tons of Money* at the National Theatre, and although Michael Gambon, Diane Bull, Polly Adams and Simon Cadell were on-stage, with Alan Ayckbourn directing, the same half-hearted reaction came from both critics and audience. John Chapman and I should have known better than to be optimistic, and even though we believed *Dry Rot* to be infinitely superior as a play to *Tons of Money* and more understandable to a today's audience than *Rookery Nook*, we should have cast our minds back thirty-four years to the first production of *Dry Rot*, when we, too, were received with a certain degree of superiority by the critics, even then. In fact, Kenneth Tynan simply described it in 1954 as "a play about horses, fit for donkeys". I'm glad to say that tens of thousands of donkeys poured into the Whitehall for nearly four years, braying with laughter the while. Eventually, of course, those same critics (or most of them), in Salvation Army terms, came to scoff but remained to pray and recognized the farces at the Whitehall and the Garrick as being an important part of the British theatre.

Now, however, after my twelve-year absence from farce, many of the critics were new to the genre and adopted similar attitudes to their predecessors all those years ago. Several others, veterans, who trudge night after night to the same old theatres, to write the same old column inches for the same old newspapers – namely Milton Shulman of the *Evening Standard*, Jack Tinker of the *Daily Mail*, Irving Wardle of *The Times* and Michael Billington of the *Guardian* – started again from where they had left off, i.e., Milton and Jack facing both ways, with Irving and Michael being positively indifferent, if not snide and hostile. Michael Billington even had a dig at the Arts Council and made some puerile joke about the newly ennobled Lord Rees-Mogg losing his trousers instead of me. He finished by intimating that the only worthwhile farce had to be spiced by sex, which is about as fatuous a statement as declaring that the missionary position is the only satisfactory one in the act of love-making – and it was Michael who brought up the subject, not me.

Milton admitted there were "some delights" and Jack Tinker said, "there are moments when the playing sweeps aside all resistance" and went on, "Sir Brian exploits each situation with the precision of the master farceur" and I'm not going to argue with that! A critic, new to me, Marius Brill of the *Daily Mirror*, described the play as a "corking evening out" but it was left to an aficionado of farce, Michael Coveney of the *Financial Times*, to express all John Chapman, Lee Menzies, Christopher Renshaw and I had hoped for, as a reaction to the play:

Brian Rix returned to the London stage on Wednesday after an absence of twelve years during which time he has done such dignified things as running MENCAP and chairing the Arts Council's Drama Panel.

I am relieved to be able to report that he drops his trousers and makes a right idiot of himself. He plays Alf Tubbe, a crooked bookie in a toupee of which Charlton Heston, king of toupees, would be proud. Snug and orange on Sir Brian's snowy thatch, it sits like a squirrel in a snowdrift while its master pretends to be posh. "Where was you at School?" he quizzes the smooth young secretary Danby (Robert Bathurst). "Harrow" would appear to be a final sort of reply. Rix, undaunted, squirrel hopping, counter-punches. "Same 'ere. Whereabahts in 'arrow?"

Dry Rot was John Chapman's first play and Rix's second big hit, in 1954, at the Whitehall. It is set in a country hotel near a racecourse in the early 1950s. Alf and two sidekicks have descended on a scene of post-war tranquillity to fiddle a race by switching the horses. They plan to nobble the favourite and collect ten grand by backing him to lose.

As a period piece it has boundless fascination. In terms of farce genre, it is a palpable and rather ingenious mix of Pinero's *Dandy Dick*, Ben Travers's *Thark*, and *The Three Stooges*.

Chapman's writing is that of an actor well versed in the arts of plastic mime and climactic lunacy. Christopher Renshaw's production trusts that our collective memory will respond to mention of Bessie Braddock's bloomers, Gordon Richards, and ration coupons. These old Whitehall farces dig deep in the atavistic urges of a theatre-going public for too long ignored.

They touch on a national xenophobia recharged by the war-time fear of invasion. And they employ the theatrical metaphor of a madhouse to explain away

323

simple eccentricity. The language is puerile and pun-based, with scatty derivations, but the effects are primarily visual.

Renshaw's production captures this superbly, achieving a liquid ensemble perfection in such sequences as the tapping on the wood-panelled set.

Other mime set pieces are a riding lesson on the sofa for Nick Wilton as Fred Phipps (Rix played this part in 1954), a typical Derek Royle somersault with unspilt drink as the bemused kidnapped French jockey and, finally, the famous tea sequence in which Derek Griffiths as the spindly, Teddy Boy-ish Flash Harry juggles tea-cup, sugar lumps, napkin and cream cornet while trying to maintain a carapace of social pretence as a guest way out of his social depth.

At this distance, the farce now assumes a comic resonance in the assault on old values by the new spivs of opportunism. Richard Vernon's snootily unruffled Colonel, whose castle has been reluctantly let out to rent, is England under fire. The new age, embodied by Rix, Wilton and Griffiths, is one of feigned accents, fiddles and conspiracy.

Nick Wilton's pretend jockey is passed off, under pressure, as a dwarfish piano tuner. There is no funnier or more tender, scene on the London stage than the Colonel's wife (Elspet Gray) attempting to explain that dwarfish retreat with a tale of a non-existent piano that has gone missing. Mr Vernon heaves a despondent sigh and accepts his wife's incipient madness as yet one more sign of the times.

What more can I say? Nothing, I think, except to mention the three other members of the cast, all on the distaff side, who were excellent, too – Julie Peasgood, Julie Dawn Cole and Harriet Reynolds.

The play fulfilled its season at the Lyric, with large

audiences rocking with laughter, just as in days of yore, rising to a crescendo during holiday time, half-term and Christmas, when family parties came in great numbers and recreated a facsimile of the Whitehall all those years before, except it was the children who had seen us *then*, who brought *their* children now – not forgetting parents who had become grandparents, who brought everyone along. Such occasions were joyous, on both sides of the footlights – except there are no footlights nowadays . . .

The whole experience answered many of my personal doubts. Could I still get laughs? Would an audience still come to see a play I was in? Would I find repetition as boring as I had all those years ago? The answer, to all three questions, was yes. But it was also "yes" to a lot of other questions. Would I enjoy rehearsals? Would I enjoy being with actors again? Would I enjoy hearing laughter once more? Would I enjoy the whole experience? A positive affirmative to all.

But two clouds cast a gloom over everyone for various reasons, when the play opened. The first was the untimely death of Roy Kinnear, who died as a result of an accident, falling from a horse, whilst filming *The Last Return of the Four Musketeers* in Spain. He was a friend to us all, and we were miserable at his unhappy fate, as we were all miserable for his wife, Carmel Cryan and their family, Carina, Kirsty and Rory. At a charity preview of *Dry Rot* – charities Roy had helped so much, including the Spastics Society and MENCAP – I asked the audience to stand in his memory, at the end of the show. Everyone rose immediately, the silence was deafening and many an eye was piped in the next still moments. What a loss to us all, as a friend and as an actor. He was a lovely man.

Then there was the accident that happened to me on the first night of *Dry Rot*. Halfway through the play, I had to turn and run off-stage to avoid being seen. As I turned, I thought I had been struck on the calf of my right leg by a heavy brass paperweight, which was on a nearby table, and which I thought I had caught in the sleeve of my dressing-gown. One look, and I realized that the paperweight was still in place. One step, and I realized I had torn the muscle in my leg and could no longer put my right foot to the ground. I hobbled off in great pain and then played the rest of the play clutching on to various bits of furniture, with the other actors making the moves for me as best they could. Hardly the way to face the critics – particularly as three of the funniest set pieces were all in that half of the play and all involved me, in an active role. With hindsight, I suppose we should have rung down the curtain, had me treated and then continued – but we didn't, and certainly lost quite a few laughs because of my incapacity. When the curtain finally did descend, it was immediate medical and physiotherapy attention, with many a hydrocortisone injection and many a physio session to follow. What a way to win new friends and influence old ones on the first night of a thirty-four-year-old revival, after a twelve-year break from the stage. Those people who wished me "break a leg" instead of "good luck" nearly had their way. In fact, I had torn the medial belly of the gastrocnemius muscle at the musculotondinous junction, if you must know . . .

On Armistice Day, November 11th, 1988 (or what used to be Armistice Day when I was a lad) Duncan Weldon and his wife, Janet, came to see the play and afterwards Elspet and I took them to supper at the Garrick Club. Now Duncan has come a long way since the days he worked in the theatre at Southport, where his first job was as call-boy during the visit of *Dry Rot* with Johnnie Slater playing Alf Tubbe. The farce was on a highly successful tour, whilst it was still running in London, Leo Franklyn having taken over the part of the bookie. The call-boy has long disappeared from the backstage staff, to be replaced by the ubiquitous p.a. which blares out the play over your dressing-room loudspeaker, minute by minute and night after night. At least the call-boy system was restful — assuming, of course, that the young man concerned remembered to make your call on time. If he was late, or failed to turn up at all, there was hell to pay, with yet another actor missing his or her entrance cue. Duncan Weldon is such a keen theatre buff, though, that I am sure he never committed so heinous a crime.

Nowadays, of course, he is the Managing Director of Triumph Theatre Productions, who have leases on no less than five West End theatres and are responsible, amongst other productions, for those star-studded seasons at the lovely Haymarket Theatre. Anyway, he came to see us in *Dry Rot* as an old friend, but also with an objective in mind. Over dinner, he asked me if I would be interested in directing a farce, on tour only, with Cannon and Ball early the following year. The play he had in mind was *Boeing-Boeing*, but as Cannon and Ball are extremely well-known for their broad North-country humour, they hardly seemed to fit the bill in that play's leading parts as two smart, svelte, French boulevardiers. Well, one of them is less smart and svelte than the other, but that gives you the general picture. I demurred, and dinner continued, undisturbed by any other reference to business. Which is quite right and proper at the Garrick. Later, I remember thinking that a splendid play for Cannon and Ball's talents would be Michael Pertwee's piece, *A Bit Between the Teeth*, and suggested this be considered instead. "No", came the answer. "They're keen on the title of Boeing-Boeing." So, once more, my interest waned.

Then came the dreadful disasters, involving two Boeings, at Lockerbie and Derby Airports. *Boeing-Boeing* was hardly a load of laughs now, so minds were changed and *Bit* became the flavour of the month, which was now February. Duncan and I flew to Manchester, to meet "the boys" and see the first half of their pantomine, *Babes in the Wood.* I liked them immediately (they even turned up in suits for lunch. Such deference!), and found their performances at the matinée, full of old-age pensioners (of which I was now one), absolutely impeccable. Normally, at this late stage in a pantomine run, without any kids in front, the leading comics are inclined, shall we say, to fool around. Cannon and Ball didn't and I was most impressed by their professionalism.

So, we agreed to go ahead, with *A Bit Between the Teeth* being re-titled *You'll Do For Me*, one of Cannon and Ball's catch phrases; the play's author, Michael Pertwee, also re-wrote parts of the script to suit them, added one half-dressed young lady to equal the numbers in *Boeing-Boeing*, and we were away. Rehearsals began at the end of March, and the play opened in Guildford on April 18th, 1989. Now Duncan Weldon has an arrangement with Guildford – as he used to have with that quite extraordinary town, Billingham. (I believe ICI and Shell are largely responsible for what must be the greatest square-footage of paved canine lavatory in the world. The Entertainments Centre, housing the theatre, is an island entirely surrounded by droppings, or so it was in my day. But I digress.) Duncan arranges for the theatre in question to mount the production, Triumph Theatre Productions supply some of the capital, the box-office recoups part of the costs and then the play goes on tour, or transfers to the West End, or ends in oblivion. Obviously, if the box-office takings are good, everyone is delighted, for then Guildford (or wherever) gets a subsidized production, as does Triumph – since everything has been mounted for the original venue – thus saving all concerned a great deal of money.

Well that's the theory. It doesn't always work out that way. Sometimes the box-office returns don't come up to scratch, and there are long faces all round. To everyone's amazement, this was the case with Cannon and Ball, for they are hugely successful on TV, in summer season and panto, but this was the first play they had ever done. They were super, as was the rest of the small cast; directing them was a pleasure; they got all their laughs; but the audience at Guildford stayed away in droves. Actually, many cancelled as soon as the play was advertised, not because the title put them off, but simply because Cannon and Ball had no reputation as actors, amongst local theatre-goers. To them, the well-made play, with the well-liked leading artist, the well-tried author and the well-trodden path over well-known middle-class mores is all. Variety pros are something else and, as such, must be eschewed. Mind you, you can't altogether blame Guildford. I did warn Duncan it might well turn out that way.

So, in spite of notices which said "the evening was as much a triumph [for me] as it was for Cannon and Ball" and it was a "rip-roaring success" – in fact, it wasn't. I regret to say that, despite similar raves, many other towns visited by Cannon and Ball on that tour held to the same tenets as those maintained in Guildford. Only Cardiff let down its hair in large numbers and laughed and laughed. The rest laughed and laughed, too, but did so in numbers which must have been desperately depressing to a comic duo who have much to offer. It must have been pretty depressing for Duncan Weldon as well, not to mention the Yvonne Arnaud Theatre at Guildford. But there we are. Even amongst theatre-goers class distinction still exists in our egalitarian society. A laugh in a theatre is somehow different from that experienced in a variety house or on telly. Or so it seems. Even if it's the same joke. I say, I say, I say – there's nowt so queer as folk.

So, I reach my bus-pass and my OAP with the two strands of my working life quite clearly delineated. It *is* rewarding (and fun) to make people laugh and receive such letters as these from parents, the first from Mr Denis

Couch of Saltash in Cornwall and the second from Sir Robin Day, rather nearer the corridors of power than that:

> On a recent visit to London I took my children, aged fourteen, eleven and eight to see *Dry Rot*. It was the high spot of our holiday. To see our children laughing so much was a tonic to us all ... I saw the play thirty years ago at the Whitehall ... I fell about laughing then, and fell about again last week.

And from Sir Robin:

> Thank you for your great courtesy and kindness in receiving me backstage last night with my son Alexander, after your *magnificent* performance. Alex was thrilled ... He is full of *Dry Rot* this morning, repeating many of the lines with great gusto!

It is rewarding (and sad) to read another two letters, both received by our Profound Retardation and Multiple Handicap team in Manchester:

> As parents of two small children with severe mental handicap we view the long-term future with trepidation. However, projects like this give us hope.

And from an older parent:

> Unfortunately, I am now not well enough to battle on any more. I therefore earnestly beg you all to ensure that Laura and her friends have an increased and enhanced life, which is everyone's birthright, whatever the situation. For they are disabled through no fault of their own. For my part, I thank you for all your concern.

Those two sets of letters may seem totally disconnected. But is that so? Bringing laughter to people *does* enhance their lives, of this I am certain, just as laughter and love and understanding can enhance the lives of people with a mental handicap. No man is an island, and I have been so lucky to be granted an opportunity to take part in both great enterprises. I only hope I can continue and, in the years to come, live up to the *Daily Mail* headline for the second production of *Dry Rot*: "Rix is still a farce to be reckoned with".

Deo volente.

Or, if you prefer, Kismet.

Either way, that is exactly where this tale began.

YET ANOTHER

Farewell Performance

"A farce to be reckoned with"

As if to prove that *Daily Mail* headline prophetic, immediately after I had finished this book I was pitchforked into the fray again. Once more the problem was the sterilization of an adult woman, but this time I had to battle on two fronts. One, the sterilization issue itself and its consequences for all non-emergency operations on mentally handicapped adults and two, misreporting by the BBC on the *Six O'Clock* and *Nine O'Clock Television News*. Perhaps you would like to cast your eye over the facsimile of *MENCAP News* which follows. It makes fascinating reading. Well, it does for me anyway . . .

THE MONTHLY NEWSPAPER OF
THE ROYAL SOCIETY
FOR MENTALLY HANDICAPPED
CHILDREN AND ADULTS

ISSUE No. 27 JANUARY/FEBRUARY 1989

BBC APOLOGISES TO MENCAP'S CHAIRMAN

Readers will probably be aware that a case was recently publicised when application was made for sterilisation of 'F', a 35-year-old woman with mental handicap.

We publish here MENCAP's Press Release giving our reaction to the case. We also print below the correspondence to and from the BBC and to The Times, following Sir Brian Rix's interview on the case on BBC TV News. This will explain to members and other readers how his comments were misrepresented by the BBC.

PRESS RELEASE 2/12/88

Less than two years ago, MENCAP expressed its concern, following the Jeanette Case that, in the absence of clear general guidelines, to be applied to the particular circumstances of an individual case, courts could grant third party applications for sterilisation of a person with mental handicap as a drastic form of contraception which would be unacceptable as a norm for non-handicapped people.

Sir Brian Rix, CBE, DL.

> "The response that was transmitted was in answer to the general problems of the rights of people

BBC TV 6 o'clock and 9 o'clock News, and these were edited to such an extent that my contribution was not only a nonsense but had no relevance to the points that were being made. The response that was transmitted was in answer to the general problems of the rights of people with a mental handicap, and taken out of context, became utter nonsense. It was a clear demonstration of the lack of basic editorial values, such as accuracy, impartiality and fair-mindedness.

Endeavours are being made to obtain a transcript or audio tape of the full interview, but in any case I should be grateful if you would look into this matter so that the record can be put straight.

I think, as Chairman of MENCAP, that it is my duty to inform our membership, many of whom will not have seen the 1 o'clock News, about the inaccuracy of the report I refer to.

I would like the opportunity to reproduce part of my letter, together with any response you

o'clock News was as follows: "Can I just ask for a short answer, a response to society's view that mentally handicapped people should be sterilised. What do you think of that view?"

To which I replied: "Appalling, it's Victorian - it's earlier than Victorian. It is treating them purely as chattels. It is treating them really as not worthy, second-class citizens, not worthy of consideration."

On both the 6 o'clock and 9 o'clock News this last answer appeared after the Official Solicitor had expressed his views regarding the sterilisation of 'F' and, whilst the camera showed shots of Mencap's office, Joshua Rosenberg's voice-over said "But Sir Brian Rix, who's Chairman of the mental health charity, Mencap, is worried about the implications for other cases". Then the camera came on to me, with the answer given above.

Such a juxtaposition is clumsy and unforgivable and totally misleading, and I must ask that you address this case with the

332

It is ironical that on the day following your interview with Brian Walden on ITV, when you agreed that BBC journalism had been inaccurate and biased in the past but that it now has "a new style" and changes are being made "on a grand scale", that I have to bring the following to your attention.

On Friday, December 2nd, following the announcement in the High Court that a decision had been made with regard to the sterilization of a mentally handicapped woman, I was interviewed for BBC *News at One* and Radio 4 *PM* and afforded an opportunity of stating fully MENCAP's views on this important issue. The television interview was live and the Radio 4 *PM* interview edited: both were totally accurate in their content.

In addition, I recorded an interview for inclusion in the BBC TV *Six O'Clock* and *Nine O'Clock News*, and these were edited to such an extent that my contribution was not only absurd but had no relevance to the points which were being made. The response that was transmitted was in answer to the general problems of the rights of people with a mental handicap, and taken out of context, became utter nonsense. It was a clear demonstration of the lack of basic editorial values, such as accuracy, impartiality and fairmindedness.

Endeavours are being made to obtain a transcript or audio tape of the full interview, but in any case I should be grateful if you would look into this matter so that the record can be put straight.

I think, as Chairman of MENCAP, that it is my duty to inform our membership, many of whom will not have seen the *One O'Clock News*, about the inaccuracy of the report to which I refer.

I would like the opportunity to reproduce part of my letter, together with any response you may make, with a view to clarifying the situation, and I attach for your information a copy of the official press release issued by MENCAP.

Letter from John Birt, BBC to Sir Brian Rix 14/12/88

Thank you for your letter of 5th December.

We owe you an apology. We should have made clear that we were looking for a brief summary of MENCAP's position that could be included in a wider report. In addition, due to pressure of time, there was indeed some confusion about the context in which you gave the reply which was actually broadcast. This was recognized after the *Six O'Clock News* and an improved version was broadcast in the later bulletin. There is no doubt, however, that on this occasion we failed in our intention to give viewers a clear account of MENCAP's views on this issue.

I am very sorry that you were the victim of what I consider – in my experience – to be a rare occurrence.

Envoi to the Paperback Edition

And, truthfully, this *is* the last word. On April 6th, 1989, a letter went from the Secretary-General of MENCAP, Sir Geoffrey Dalton, addressed to the Right Honourable, The Lord Mackay of Clashfern – in other words, the Lord Chancellor. It accompanied a report which had sprung from a MENCAP/Royal Society of Medicine conference on "The Legal, Medical and Ethical Issues of Mental Handicap". This conference had been proposed before I retired, but I was still invited to attend and was delighted when an independent working party was convened as a result, with my successor in the chair.

The report, entitled "Competency and Consent to Medical Treatment", was delivered for the Lord Chancellor's consideration between two important dates. On February 3rd, 1989, the Court of Appeal had ruled on the case (the sterilization of "F") which had caused the spat between myself and the BBC, followed by a further ruling in the House of Lords on May 4th. The sterilization of the woman in question was allowed, but no less than eight judges made noises which seemed to indicated that MENCAP's long-held views on this issue were beginning to strike a responsive chord in the ears of those concerned with the well-being and protection of people with a mental handicap. Sterilization is only one aspect of the much wider issue of consent to treatment by people who cannot speak for themselves, and MENCAP's aim is to secure for them the right to have or to reject treatment, as far as possible, on the same basis as everyone else. This means ensuring that the interests of an individual are paramount, and all the evidence for and against the treatment proposed is considered and all the legitimately interested parties heard, before the decision is taken on what is best for that person in that situation at that time.

The report to the Lord Chancellor suggests that to achieve this we shall need, in varying combinations according to the seriousness of the particular issue: legislation; guidelines for professionals and others involved; and "ethical committees" for the more serious cases. The right to have necessary treatment, and the right to refuse unnecessary treatment, are among the most precious rights we have; and it is worth going to a great deal of trouble to secure this equality for people with a mental handicap.

In the February Court of Appeal hearing two very important points were made. The first by Lord Justice Butler-Sloss: "It is not suggested in this case, nor could it be, that sterilization should be performed on those unable to consent for eugenic or purely social reasons. Such reasons would be totally abhorrent and unacceptable."

The second point was quoted by Lord Donaldson, from an earlier judgment by Lord Brandon in 1984. This suggested that the common law might well be the umbrella for all such difficult cases: "The common law, however, while generally immutable in its principles, unless different principles are laid down by statute, is not immutable in the way in which it adapts, develops and applies those principles in a radically changing world and against the background of radically changed social convention."

Furthermore, in the House of Lords' ruling in May, Lord Griffiths pointed to a greater need for certainty, and hence the need for either amending legislation or a judicial response which moves the common law forward. As long ago as the sixteenth century, soon after Martin Luther had passed his pitiless judgment on that unfortunate mentally handicapped boy, the renowned jurist, Sir Edward Coke, wrote: "Reason is the life of the law, nay the common law itself is nothing else but reason."

Well, we had to wait 400 years for that to be argued in the Court of Appeal and the House of Lords on behalf of people with a mental handicap, and there is another hopeful sign on the horizon. The Lord Chancellor has reacted to all this pressure by asking the Law Commission to examine the whole question of consent for people unable to consent on their own behalf. The Commission will make positive recommendations. It seems we will not have to wait another 400 years before reason, in all things, prevails.

Do you know – I think there's hope for us yet.

November 1st, 1989.

Index

Abbey Life Ethical Trust, 310
Abbey Life Investments, 311
Abortion Bill, 250, 251
Academy Theatre, Johannesburg, 119
ACAS, 264
Achurch, 111
Ackland, Joss, 93
Acts of Parliament, 144, 150, 239–40, 248–9, 251, 264–5, 289
Adams, Polly, 321
Addenbrooke's Hospital, Cambridge, 69
Adelaide, 272
Adult Training Centres, 140, 149–50
Advisory Group on Disability (Prince Charles's), 159
Agra, 241, 242
Air India, 113
Albert Hall, 232, 307
Albery, Ian, 75, 90
Albery Theatre, 56–7
Aldeburgh, 314
Alderton, John, 112, 310
Aldwych Theatre, 65, 136
Alexander, Terence, 41, 313
Alas Smith and Jones, 99
Allard, John, 178
Allen, Lord, 145, 160, 180, 195–6, 240, 247, 266, 270, 271, 285, 288, 293, 294, 295, 311, 317
Allied Dunbar, 178, 212
All That Jazz, 88
Almeida Theatre, 308
Alton, David, 169, 248, 249–50, 251, 255

Ambassadors Theatre, 56, 58, 73–4
Amsterdam, 123
Anderson, Jean, 312
Anderson, Jon, 174
Andrews, Eamonn, 91–2
Annie Get Your Gun, 102
Apollo Theatre, 317
Archer, Jeffrey, 316–17
Argentina, 209
Arlen, Harold, 316
Armstrong, Donald, 75
Around Midnight, 320
Arthur, Dr Leonard, 165, 166, 169
Art of Coarse Acting, The, 69
Art of Coarse Moving, The, 98
Arts Council of Great Britain, 24, 34, 116, 267, 305, 306, 307, 308, 315, 319, 322; Drama Panel, 267–8, 307, 309–10, 323
Ashcroft, Dame Peggy, 13, 231
Asher, Jane, 73
Association of Chief Police Officers, 239
Association of County Councils, 229, 266
Association of Parents of Backward Children *see* MENCAP
Aston, Sir Christopher, 159
Astoria Theatre, 56, 58, 73, 75–81
Atkinson, Sir Alec, 262
Atkinson, Dorothy, 205
Atkinson, Rowan, 174, 192
Attenborough, Sir Richard, 65–6, 231, 263

Attenborough Report on Arts and Disabled People, 24, 262
Attlee, Clement, 11
ATV *see* Central TV
Auckland, 273
Aukin, David, 90
Australia, 62, 109, 123, 137, 256, 271–3, 314
Avengers, The, 93
Ayckbourn, Alan, 66, 136, 319, 321

Babes in the Wood, 8, 327–8
Backstage Productions, 80
Bacon, Francis, 244, 251
Bader, Sir Douglas, 239
Bain, Romany, 210
Baker, Kenneth, 160
Balderton Hospital, Newark, 220
Ball, Bobby, 327–9
Banana Ridge, 89
Bannen, Ian, 67
Bannerman, Kay, 35
Banstead, 220
Baraitser, Michael, 247
Barbados, 96, 97
Barber, John, 36, 37–9
Barbican Theatre, 315, 316
Barclaycard, 112
Barclays Bank, 144, 178
Barclays Unicorn Group, 178
Barker, Felix, 33, 37
Barnardo's, Dr, 178, 236, 294
Barnsley Junior Chamber of Commerce, 193
Baron, Lynda, 98
Barratt, Ray, 96
Barrie, J. M., 64
Barrington, Jonah, 27
Barrington, Ken, 112
Barson, Roger, 272
Barton, Jack, 196–7, 199
Bass, Alfie, 98
Bath, 311, 317, 320
Bathurst, Robert, 323
Baum, L. Frank, 316
Beatlemania, 76, 80
Beatles, 76, 80, 94
Beckenham, 304

Beckett, Samuel, 309, 310
Bedfull of Foreigners, A, 66
Bedser, Alec, 129
Bedser, Eric, 129
Belfast, 173, 207
Belgrano, 178
Benjamin, Joanne, 61, 63, 66, 69, 72, 123, 145
Benjamin, Louis, 317
Bentley, John, 241
Berkoff, Stephen, 60
Bernhardt, Sarah, 70
Berry, Rex, 88, 113
Best of Friends, The, 67
Bethlem Royal Hospital, 304
Better Services for the Mentally Handicapped, White Paper, 1971, 150, 153, 154, 222
Beyond Reasonable Doubt, 317
Bickmore, Dr. G. H., 5
Bicknell, Professor Joan, 117, 162–4
Billingham, 328
Billington, Michael, 84–6, 322
Billy Rose Theatre, New York *see* Trafalgar Theatre, New York
Birmingham, 160, 219, 222, 234
Birt, John, 333
Bit Between the Teeth, A, 37, 38, 39, 327–8
Blackadder, 192
Blackman, Honor, 241–3
Blackpool, 185, 237
Bland, Peter, 39
Blandings Castle, 314
Bless the Bride, 314
Blick Rothenberg and Noble, 178
Blunkett, David, 229
Boardman, Jules, 68–9
Bob Hope Classic, 226
Boddey, Martin, 226
Bodies, 73, 74
Boeing-Boeing, 327–8
Bolam, James, 74
Bolton, Guy, 35
Books for Students Ltd, 233
Bootham School, 5, 94, 116
Bottomley, Peter, 264
Boucicault, Dion, 123

Bough, Frank, 306
Bourge, Paul, 214
Bourlet, Gary, 100, 312
Bournemouth, 122, 310
Bowe, John, 316
Bowes-Lyon family, 286–8
Bowring, Peter, 184
Boxcar Willie in Concert, 82
Boycott, Geoffrey, 196
Braddock, Bessie, 232, 323
Braden, Bernard, 231
Brain, Lady, 25
Bramall, Field Marshal Lord
    Edwin, 294, 305
Brandon, Lord, 336
Brasher, Chris, 227
Breakaway Girls, 117
Breakfast Time, 230, 276
Brearley, Mike, 96
Brechin, Anne, 205
Bridgetown, Barbados, 97
Bridlington, 8, 9, 10, 127
Briggle, Stockton, 69, 70
Brighton, 296
Brill, Marius, 322
Bristol, 199, 312, 313
British Airways, 113, 123, 237
British Broadcasting Corporation
    (BBC), 14, 26, 27, 28, 31, 32,
    43, 63, 71, 94, 98, 99–100,
    111, 116, 152, 160, 169, 170,
    184, 206, 216, 231, 238, 262,
    276, 303, 312, 319, 332–3
British Caledonian, 237
British Medical Association
    (BMA), 105, 253
British Rail, 176
British Shoe Corporation, 75
Brixham, 3, 84, 116, 119, 121,
    124, 134, 291
Broadway Theatre, 56, 58, 61–3,
    66
Brooke, Harold, 35
Brown, Bille, 316
Brown, Ian, 307
Brown, Richard, 316
Brown, Lord Justice, 275, 282
Broxbourne, Lord, 145
Bruce Forsyth Classic, 225

Bryan, Dora, 83
Bryden, Ronald, 33
Buckingham Palace, 99, 101, 159,
    180
Bull, Diane, 321
Burke's Peerage, 287
Burton, Martin, 234
Butler, Professor Neville, 199
Butler, R. A., Lord, 189
Butler-Sloss, Lord Justice, 336

Cadell, Simon, 321
Cairo, 242
Caernarfon, 312
Calendar, 182
Callaghan, James, 30, 100
Calvert, Phyllis, 74, 232
Cambridge, 69, 312
Cambridge Theatre, 73, 81
Camden Council, 63
Campaign, 214
Campbell, Janet, 143
Campbell, Professor Stuart, 250
Cannon, Tommy, 327–9
Canterbury, Archbishop of, 145
Canterbury Tales, 82, 85
Capital Radio, 66, 73, 77
Cardiff, 16, 202–3, 329
Care in Action, White Paper,
    1981, 222
Care in the Community, White
    Paper, 1981, 222
Carlisle, Mark, 159–60
Carman, George, 166
Carnegie Council, 24
Carrington VC, 67
Carshalton, 140
Carter, Jim, 316
Casson, Sir Hugh, 216
Caterham, 164
Cats, 304
Catweazle, 43
CBI (Confederation of British
    Industry), 185
Central Association for Mental
    Welfare, 259
Central Television, 164, 197
Centre Point, 75
Chaffee, Senator, 201

Chalker, Lynda, 190
Channing, Carol, 82–4, 86
Chapman, Betty, 242
Chapman, John, 11, 29, 31, 34, 87, 93, 136, 242, 313–14, 316, 318, 321, 322, 323
Charity Commissioners, 116
Charity Projects, 174
Charles, Prince of Wales, 159, 172, 180, 181, 215–16
Charley's Aunt, 137, 192
Charlton, Jane, 174
Chas and Dave, 174
Chase Me, Comrade!, 32, 55, 93, 118, 234, 308
Cheeseman, Peter, 103
Chef and Brewer, 225
Chelton, Nick, 316
Cheshire, 152
Chicago, 73
Chichester, 137
Chorus Line, A, 263
Christie, Agatha, 74
Chu Chin Chow, 13
Church, Tony, 268, 316
Churchil, Donald, 32, 40
Churchill, Winston, 273
Clapsaddle, Joe, 70
Clarke, Brian, 89
Clarke, Kenneth, 110, 220, 221, 225, 229, 234, 237
Clarke, Tom, 264–5, 290
Classic Cinemas, 55, 58, 59, 61, 62, 63
Cleese, John, 112
Cleveland, 219
Clore, Sir Charles, 81
Clore Foundation, 205
Clouds, 73
Club, The, 60
Clywd, 152
Coke, Sir Edward, 336
Cole, Julie Dawn, 324
Colin's Sandwich, 99, 319
Collins, Mike, 119
Comedy Theatre, 14
Commission for Racial Equality, 310
Commonwealth Institute, 194

Community Care Campaigners, 236–7, 244
Confederation of Health Service, Employees, (COHSE), 104
Conservative Party Conference, 237
Conti, Tom, 73, 81, 88, 89
Cook, Jeanne, 118
Cook, Peter, 96
Cooney, Linda, 77–9, 118
Cooney, Ray, 31, 32–3, 34, 42, 44, 55, 56, 58, 64, 65, 66, 70, 72, 73, 74, 75–6, 77–9, 80–81, 84, 86–9, 90–91, 93, 119, 239, 308, 314
Cooney-Marsh Theatres, 44, 55–89, 100, 116, 117, 118, 122–3, 145
Cooney Productions, Ray, 70, 72
Cooper, Felicity, 33
Copenhagen, 122
Corfu, 112
Cornwall, 330
Coronation Street, 43
Costello, Elvis, 174
Cottingham, 4
Couch, Denis, 329–30
Country Landowners' Association, 174, 178, 294
Courtenay, Tom, 73, 321
Coutts, 177
Coveney, Michael, 123, 136–7, 322–4
Covent Garden Opera, 314
Cowper, Richard, 152
Cox, Sir John, 236, 237, 295
Coy, Charlotte (grandchild), 172, 203
Coy, Christopher, 171
Coy, Elizabeth, 171
Coy, Jolyon (grandchild), 172, 204, 244
Coy, Jonathan (son-in-law), 137, 171–2, 204, 244
Coy, Dr Peter, 171
Craven, Gemma, 81
Creez, The, 43, 93
Cribbins, Bernard, 87
Crichton-Brown, Sir Robert, 270

341

Crisp, Quentin, 69
Croft, Michael, 63
Cromwell, Oliver, 30
Crosby, Bing, 77
Crossroads, 43, 197–8
Croton, Gordon, 100
Crowther, Jean, 95, 97, 112, 272, 311
Crowther, Leslie, 35, 91, 94–5, 97, 84, 292, 311
Cryan, Carmel, 325
Cuckoo in the Nest, 136
Cummings, James, 143, 205
Curry, Tim, 90

Daily Gleaner (Jamaica), 51
Daily Graphic and Daily Sketch, 27
Daily Mail, 318, 322, 331, 332
Daily Mirror, 322
Daily Telegraph, 36, 37–9, 170
Dalton, Sir Geoffrey, 295, 298, 305, 311
Dandy Dick, 323
Daneman, Paul, 70
Dangerous Corner, 67
Davidson, Frank, 272
Davies, Tudor, 145
Davis, Barrie, 294
Dawson, Anna, 35
Day, Alexander, 330
Day, Sir Robin, 216, 225, 330
Day Services – Today and Tomorrow, 262
Dear Daddy, 74
Delfont, Lord, 27, 90
Delhi, 241–2
Dempster, Nigel, 318
Denbosch, 123
Dench, Dame Judi, 231
Denison, Michael, 232
Denny, Frank, 199, 247
Denton, Charles, 197
Derbyshire, 219, 222
Devil's Disciple, The, 172
Devon, 219
Devonshire, Duke of, 202
DHSS *see* Health and Social Security, Department of

Dial Rix, 28
Diamond Riding Centre, Carshalton, 140
Dickens, Charles, 184
Diddisham, 152
Diener, Joan, 82
Dillon, Lord Justice, 275, 282
Dilston Hall, 212
Dionne, quins, 35
Disabled Persons (Sevices, Consultation and Representation) Act 1986, 265, 290
Dish Ran Away, The, 11
Disraeli, Benjamin (Earl of Beaconsfield), 140, 141
Djanogly, Raphael, 175
Dominion Theatre, 75
Donaldson, Lord, 336
Don Juan, 172
Don't Just Lie There, Say Something, 37, 93
Douglas, Hazel, 136
Douglas, Wallace, 38, 42, 93
Dover, 123
Down, Colin, 215
Downs, Jane, 41, 313
Down's syndrome, 16, 22–3, 24, 165–6, 169, 197–8, 260, 289, 295
D'Oyly Carte Company, 23
Dracula, 82, 103
Drake, Alfred, 82
Drake's Drum, 82
Drury Lane Theatre, 83, 86
Dry Rot, 11, 29, 32, 34, 118, 313, 314, 316, 317, 318, 319, 320–31
Dublin, 173
Duchess Theatre, 74
Duck Variations, 60
Duet for One, 73
Duffield, Vivien, 205
Duke of York's Theatre, 56, 58, 64–73, 85, 90, 101, 319
Dury, Ian, 174
Dybwad, Professor Gunner, 208
Dyer, Charles, 32
Dyfed, 152

Eagle Has Two Heads, The, 13, 71
East, 60
East Lynne, 6
Eastwood, Clint, 63
Edinburgh, 199
Edinburgh Festival, 69, 84, 85, 90
Edrich, Bill, 129–30
Edrich, John, 129–30
Education Act, 1944, 273
Education Act, 1970, 23, 26, 264
Education and Science, Department of (DES), 159–60, 204, 224
Education Reform Bill, 159, 160
Edward, HRH, Prince, 304
Edward, My Son, 13
Egypt, 242, 263
Elements of a Comprehensive Local Service for People with Mental Handicap, 228
Ellis, Frederick, 261
Elton, Lord, 190
Elvis, 73, 75, 76, 77, 80, 122, 123
EMI, 81
Emmerdale Farm, 7, 44
Empire Theatre, Nottingham, 13
English Speaking Union, 177, 178, 319
Ennals, David, 105, 109, 223
ENSA (Entertainments National Service Association), 6
Entertainment Wise, 118
Entertainments Centre, 328
Epsom College, 129, 130
Equity, 26, 49, 80
Esher, 146–7
Essex, University of, 192
Eugenics Movement, 281
Evans, David, 175
Evans, Nigel, 164
Evans, Richard, 197
Evans, Stuart, 184
Evening News, 33, 37, 46
Evening Standard, 34, 76, 322
Evening with Quentin Crisp, An, 69
Exton, Clive, 32, 93

Eyre, Richard, 90, 104, 238, 306, 307
Ezra, Sir Derek, 183, 185

Fairbrother, Pauline, 145
Falconer, Sheila, 316
Falkland Islands, 178, 209, 238
Farjeon, Herbert, 74
Farmfield Hospital, Surrey, 220, 221
Farr, Derek, 35
Fawlty Towers, 35, 68, 117
Featherstone, Norman, 96
Fenn-Smith, Clive, 178
Ferrers, Earl, 311
Festival Hall, 309
Festival of Britain, 14
Feydeau, Ernest, 30, 38
Fielding, Harold, 58, 90
Financial Times, 123, 136, 322–4
Firbank, Ann, 14
Fire Angel, 90, 91, 97
Fisher, Thomas, 105
Fishko, Robert, 69, 70
Flavin, Tim, 241
Fleet Hospital, Lincolnshire, 220
Flood, Gerald, 74
Flowers, 62
Folkestone, 158
Follies, 81
Fontana, 127, 192
Foot, Alastair, 35
Ford, John, 233
Forsyth, Frederick, 242
Forum on Mental Retardation of the Royal Society of Medicine, 250, 312
Fosse, Bob, 88
Fountain Hospital, London, 260
Fourth Protocol, The, 242
Fowler, Norman, 220, 224, 237
Fowlie, Dr Hector, 105
Fox, Dame Evelyn, 259
Fox, Paul, 98
France, 137, 318
Franklyn, Leo, 29, 35, 92, 315, 326
Franklyn, William, 91
Fraser, Prof. William, 199, 247

Fresh Fields, 314
Freud, Sir Clement, 309
Fringe Benefits, 39, 40–42, 43, 45, 56, 98
Frost, Alan, 311
Frost, David, 96
Fryd, Felicity, 259
Fryd, Judy, 142, 145, 228, 258–61

Galletley, Roger, 144
Gambon, Michael, 321
Gardiner, Jean, 318
Gardiner, Matthew, 318
Garner, Rex, 87
Garrick Theatre, 28, 29, 36, 37, 95, 111, 142, 174, 318, 322
Gavin, Nikki, 146–7
Georgiades, Carina, 110, 306
Georgiades, Evie, 137
Georgiades, Jessica, 110
Georgiades, John, 110, 137
Georgiades, Rhoda, 110–11, 137, 306
Georgiades, Zoë, 110
Geraldo, 94
Gerard, Ronald, 175
Gibb, Frances, 276
Gielgud, Sir John, 67, 69, 101, 231
Gieves and Hawkes, 305, 306–7, 313
Gilbert, Jimmy, 98
Gilbert and Sullivan, 102
Gilliatt, Sir Martin, 134, 171, 288
Glamorgan, 152
Globe Theatre, 317
Glover, David, 316
Glyndebourne, 314
Goa, 242
Goddards Green Hospital, Hassocks, 220
Godspell, 82
Gone with the Wind, 61
Good, Jack, 76, 77
Good, Margit, 77–9
Goodchild, Tim, 319
Goodman, Lord, 208
Gorbachev, Mikhail, 201

Gover, Alf, 128
Gow, Dr Lyn, 272
Grade, Lord, 55
Grand Magic Circus, Le, 82
Grant, Peter, 184
Grant, Russell, 230, 234, 235
Gray, Dulcie, 232
Gray, Elspet *see* Rix, Elspet
Grease, 80
Great American Backstage Musical, The, 60
Green, Benny, 216
Green, Michael, 69, 98
Greenwich Theatre, 319
Greenwood, Paul, 316
Greenwood Theatre, 63
Griffiths, Charlie, 96
Griffiths, Derek, 324
Griffiths, Sir Eldon, 202, 336
Gruby, Gary, 266
Guardian, 3–4, 16, 33, 60, 84–6, 119, 214–15, 218–25, 253–4, 269, 275–6, 278–9, 286–7, 291, 322
Guide Dogs for the Blind Association, 178, 294, 306
Guildford, 308, 328, 329
Guinness, Sir Alec, 231
Guinness/Distillers, 185
Guthrie, Robin, 116
Gwynedd, 152

Hailsham, Lord, 283–4, 288
Hair, 81–2
Half Life, 67–8, 101
Hall, Sir Peter, 101, 307
Hall, Wes, 96, 97
Hambro Life (now Allied Dunbar), 178, 212
Hamilton, Les, 185
Hampshire, 219, 222, 224
Hancock, Tony, 117
Hands, Terry, 305
Harburg, Yip, 316
Harding, Jacki, 72, 73, 145
Hard Times, 184–5
Hare, Robertson, 65
Hargreaves, Kenneth, 248
Harper, Gerald, 96

Harris, Anita, 70
Harris, Rolf, 101
Harrison, Gilbert, 39
Harrogate, 6, 94, 296
Harrow School, 273
Harry Secombe Classic, 226
Harvey, Ray, 111
Haslam, Sir Robert, 183–4
Hassocks, 220
Haymarket Theatre, 64, 327
Headingley, 51
Health and Human Services,
    Department of (USA), 201
Health and Social Security,
    Department of (DHSS), 104–7,
    150–51, 153–6, 190, 204, 205,
    217, 218–25, 229, 262
Health Education Council (HEC),
    198–9
Hearne, Gordon, 177
Heath, Edward, 16
Heath, Ted, 94
Hedda Gabler, 67
Heddell, Fred, 143, 312
Heginbotham, Chris, 214, 236
Heilbron, Judge, 276, 279
Hello, Dolly, 82–4, 86–7
Hello Mum, 99
Help the Aged, 294
Hencke, David, 217–21
Henderson, Dickie, 91, 95, 101,
    226, 245
Henderson, Gwyneth, 245
Henley Business College, 185
Henry, Wendy, 135–6
Henry IV, Part I, 184
Henshall, Harry, 107, 108
Her Majesty's Theatre, 81, 90
Hermelin, Rolf, 143–4, 148, 190,
    265
Hertfordshire, 219, 222
Hester Adrian Research Centre,
    161
Heston, Charlton, 323
Hildrew, Peter, 275–6
Hillards, 244
Hiller, Dame Wendy, 231
Hilton, Tony, 32
Hitler, Adolf, 214, 281

Hobson, Harold, 33, 36
Hobson, Valerie, 157–8, 243
Hogg, Dr James, 161
Hogg's Back, 93
Holbeach, 220
Holden, William, 210
Holland, Mary, 144, 146, 148,
    200, 205, 263, 265
Holland, Dr Tony, 304
Hollis, Peter, 267
Holman, Molly, 45
Holt, Kenneth, S., 247
Holt, Thelma, 239
Home Carer of the Year Awards,
    306
Home Farm Trust, 214
Home Office, 115
Hong Kong, 137
Hopkinson, David, 178
Hordern, Sir Michael, 231
Horne, Kenneth, 28
Hornsea, 5, 128
Hospital Consultants and
    Specialists Association, 105
Howard, Trevor, 232
Howe, Edward, 145
Howe, Sir Geoffrey, 178, 208,
    256
Howerd, Frankie, 193
How the Other Half Loves, 66,
    319
*How to Succeed in Business
    Without Really Trying*, 81
*How to Survive in an Occupied
    Country*, 117
Hugh and I, 314
Hull, 49
Hull, University of, 192
Humberside College of Higher
    Education, 192
Hume, Cardinal Basil, 245, 251–4
Humphries, Barry, 216
Hunniford, Gloria, 320
Hylton, Jack, 27

Ibsen, Henrik, 67
Iceland, 201
I Have Been Here Before, 67
Ilkley, 7, 8

Imperial Society of Knights Bachelor, 270, 308–9, 313
Independent, 171
Independent Broadcasting Authority (IBA), 66, 304
Independent Development Council for People with Mental Handicap (IDC), 141, 159, 228, 236
India, 240–42
Indian Airlines, 242
Ingram, David, 206
Inland Revenue, 177, 255–7
Innes, Neil, 174
In One Ear, 99
Instant Sunshine, 69
Institute of Directors, 185
Intel, 177
International League of Societies for Persons with Mental Handicap, 142, 208–9, 263
International Television Association, 202
International Year of Disabled People (IYDP), 158–9, 180, 191, 195
Inverness, 127
Invitation to Remember, An, 231
in vitro fertilization, 245–54
Ipi Tombi, 81
IRA, 174, 206
Ireland, Northern, 152, 173, 206
Irma la Douce, 82
Irreversible Brain Damage, 69
Israel, 113
Is Your Honeymoon Really Necessary?, 65
It Runs in the Family, 308
ITV, 27, 28, 32, 181, 216, 276, 232

Jackson, Glenda, 90, 232
Jackson, Gordon, 232
Jackson, Richard, 69
Jacobs, David, 91, 210–11
Jacobs, Pat, 210
Jaipur, 241, 242
Jamaica, 51, 210
James, Sid, 29

Jane Steps Out, 14
Jason, David, 66
Jay, Peggy, 195
Jay, Tinker, 58, 74
Jay Report, 195
Jeanette, 163, 275–6, 277–9, 281, 283, 285, 289
Jeans, Ronald, 67
Jeffries, Lionel, 321
Jenkin, Patrick, 150, 153–5
Johannesburg, 119
Johannessen, Finn, 123
John, Elton, 96
Johnson, Frank, 208
Johnson, Professor Malcolm, 205
Johnson, Vivienne, 39
Johnson Over Jordan, 67
Johnston, Brian, 26, 91, 171, 204, 231
Joint Stock Theatre Company, 99, 117
Jolliffe, Sir Anthony, 179–80, 207
Jolly, Dr Hugh, 240
Jones, Griff Rhys, 174, 192
Jones, Jim, 273
Jongh, Nicholas de, 60
Joseph, Sir Keith, 160, 204–5, 279
Joseph P. Kennedy Junior Foundation, 200, 201
Journal of Mental Deficiency Research, 199, 246–7, 252
Judge, Ian, 316

Keep Fit Association, 232, 235
Kemble, Vivian, 231
Kemp, Lindsay, 62
Kendal, Felicity, 73, 192
Kendall, Ena, 291–3
Kennedy, Joe, 200
Kennedy, John F., 201
Kennedy, Robert, 201
Kennedy, Rosemary, 201
Kennedy Institute of Ethics, 201
Kent, HRH The Duchess of, 63
Kent, University of, 103, 117, 206
Kent County Constabulary, 201
Kenton, Stan, 112
Kentucky Fried Chicken, 114

Kenya, 208, 210
Keyser, David de, 73
Kidner, Gerald, 105
Kilburn Empire, 13; see also
    Broadway Theatre
King, Philip, 28, 31
King Lear, 13, 148
King's Hall, Ilkley, 7
Kingsley, Charles, 270
Kinnear, Carina, 325
Kinnear, Kirsty, 325
Kinnear, Rory, 325
Kinnear, Roy, 46, 112, 325
Kinnock, Neil, 313
Kirman, Brian, 247
Kismet, 82, 331
Kominowski, Bogdan, 77

Labiche, Eugène, 30
Labour Party, 185, 285
Laburnum Grove, 67
Laker, Jim, 127, 128–9
Lambe, Loretto, 145–6, 161, 304
Langdon-Down, Dr John, 22, 23,
    24, 25, 107, 169
Langdon-Down, Norman, 25
Landen, Dinsdale, 73
Langham, Chris, 174
Last Return of the Four
    Musketeers, The, 325
Latham, Richard, 412
Lau, Patrick, 137
Lawlor, Dr Terence, 105, 106,
    107, 109
Lawrence, D. H., 152
Lawrence, Jean, 238
Lawrence, John, 238
Lawrence, Robert, 237–8
Lawson, Nigel, 30, 179, 255, 258
Laye, Dilys, 316
Lee, Christopher, 232
Lee, George, 120–22, 134, 141,
    142–3, 146, 147, 148, 261
Leeds, 181
Leggett, David, 221
Leicester, 165
Leighton, Alan, 144, 196, 201
Let My People Come, 58
Let's Get It Straight, 201

Let's Go, 99, 111, 140, 143, 184,
    289
Let Sleeping Wives Lie, 35, 36,
    95, 268
Levene, Philip, 32
Leventon, Annabelle, 90, 91
Levin, Angela, 215
Leyland, Richard, 77
Libertas Charity Group, 294, 308,
    310
Lieutenancy of Greater London,
    294, 304, 317
LIFE, 165, 245, 249
Life of Our Own, A, 100, 143,
    206, 262, 312, 313
Lillee, Dennis, 59, 30
Lincolnshire, 219, 220, 222
Linton, 312
Little Hut, The, 14
Littler, Emile, 27
Little Willie Junior's Resurrection,
    59, 60, 82
Littlewood, Joan, 34
Liverpool, 261
Living Like Other People, 228
Livingstone, Ken, 216
Lloyd, Hugh, 314
Lloyd Webber, Andrew, 304
Logan, Fergus, 264
Logan, Jimmy, 38, 39
London Daily News, 283–4
London Hospital, 312
London Marathon, 227
London Mask Theatre, 67, 71
Look, No Hans!, 314
Loose Ends, 320
Lord, Basil, 29, 117–18
Lord's Cricket Ground, 96–7,
    137, 204, 226, 238, 319
Lord's Taverners, 49, 112–13,
    121, 226–7, 234, 306, 319
Love in a Mist, 28
Lowe, Arthur, 67
Lowry, Sir Pat, 264
Lufton, 174
Lumley, Joanna, 93
Lunatic Fringe, The, 69
Luther, Martin, 280, 281, 336
Lynn, Ralph, 65

Lyric Theatre, 317, 320, 324
Lyttleton Theatre, 309

McCormack, Mary, 161
McCowen, Alec, 294, 310
MacGillivray, R. C., 247
McGiven, Cecil, 28
MacGregor, John, 179
McKenzie, Julia, 314
Mackintosh, Cameron, 90
McLeod, Ian, 310
McLeod, Baroness, 310
McLoughlin, Jim, 272
Madden, Cecil, 26, 28
Maggie, 82
Mail on Sunday, 215
Major, John, 237
Mamet, David, 60
Manchester, 146, 148, 161, 192,
    208, 234, 263, 296, 297, 330
Manderson, Anne, 137
Manderson, Tim, 13, 71, 94, 95,
    137
M&G Investment Managers, 178
Mansfield, Katherine, 152
Mansfield, Mike, 231
Margate, 9
Margolis, Mike, 70
Marks, Alfred, 91, 137
Marre, Lady, 181
Marriott, Anthony, 35
Marsh, Jean, 88
Marsh, Laurie, 44, 55, 57–8, 59,
    62, 63, 68, 75, 81, 84, 87, 88,
    294
Martin, George, 94
Mary Rose Trust, 308
Master Templars, 307
Matthews, Brian, 320–21
Matthews, Francis, 98
M. Butterfly, 81
MCC (Marylebone Cricket Club),
    49, 51, 238
Melbourne, 272
MENCAP, 81, 89, 115, 116, 123,
    124, 173–5, 193, 209, 210,
    239, 243, 270, 273, 317, 323,
    325, 332, 335; advert for
    Secretary-General, 3, 16–17,
120; origins, 21, 142, 258–61;
    Parents Committee, 109;
    Homes Foundation, 109, 143,
    145, 151, 203; Management
    Committee, 121, 133, 146, 271,
    294, 295; offers post to Rix,
    133–6; Rix joins as Secretary-
    General, 137–42; Gateway
    Federation, 139, 143, 144 202,
    207, 227, 282, 290; City
    Foundation, 141, 146, 176–7,
    178–9, 184, 205, 304, 312,
    317; local societies, 141, 145,
    149, 244, 273; staff, 142–8;
    Trustee Visitors' Service, 143;
    membership, 144; Profound
    Retardation and Multiple
    Handicap Project (PRMH),
    146, 161–2, 234, 263, 312,
    330; Unit Trust, 146, 178, 180;
    Medical Advisory Panel, 148,
    199–201, 240, 246–7, 250,
    252, 265, 304, 307; Members'
    Meetings, 148–51, 153, 155,
    166, 296, 297; YNG
    NGHYMRU (in Wales), 152;
    Conference: 'Better Services for
    the Mentally Handicapped –
    When?' 153–5, 156; and Pirates
    Spring, 157–8; and IYDP,
    158–9; Week, 162, 169–70,
    204–5, 227, 262, 291;
    Conference: 'Right from the
    Start '81', 162–4; and mentally
    handicapped children, 165–9;
    fund-raising, 178–85, 207,
    211–12, 225–8, 230–34, 244,
    264, 270; becomes Royal
    Society, 180–1; appeal, 181–3;
    and Mental Health
    (Amendment) Bill, 186–90;
    new HQ opened by Queen
    Mother, 191; Business Supplies,
    191; and Young and Rubicam,
    194–5, 197–8; and
    Teignmouth, 213–15; and the
    National Development Team,
    217–25; publications, 228,
    258–63; and Storytime,

230–32; and in vitro
fertilization, 245–54; and
charitable giving, 254–7;
fortieth anniversary, 258,
261–7; Ad Hoc Leisure
Committee, 262; and
sterilization, 275–84, 332–7;
and community care, 284–6;
AGM 1987, 288–9; advert for
new Secretary-General, 291;
appoints Sir Geoffrey Dalton,
295; and Rix's last weeks and
retirement, 295–303; appoints
Rix Chairman, 299
*MENCAP Famous Faces
Collection, The*, 215–16
MENCAP News, 332
*Mental Handicap – Partnership in
the Community?*, 263
Mental Handicap – Progress,
Problems and Priorities, White
Paper, 1980, 222
Mental Health Act, 1959, 150,
187–90
Mental Health Act, 1983, 190,
278
Mental Health (Amendment) Bill,
186–90
Mental Impairment, Evaluation
and Treatment Service, 304
Menzies, Lee, 316–17, 321, 322
Merchant of Venice, The, 90, 274
Mercier, Sheila *see* Rix, Sheila
Mermaid Theatre, 62, 73, 86, 89
MGM (Metro Goldwyn Mayer),
83
Michaels, Louis, 39, 64
Middlefield Hospital, Solihull, 220
Middlesex, 96
Miles, Lord, 62–3, 73, 90, 231
Miles and Miles, 71–2
Mills, Sir John, 226, 231
Milton, John, 140, 299
MIND, 159, 214, 236
Mind Your Language, 72
Minelli, Liza, 307
Misérables, Les, 91
Mitchell, Julian, 67–8
Mitchell, Stephen, 226

Mittler, Professor Peter, 208–9
mongolism *see* Down's syndrome
Monroe, Marilyn, 232
Montagu, Helen, 80
Moore, Mary Tyler, 88
Morecambe, Eric, 118
Morley, Robert, 89, 232
Morocco, 318
Morris, Colin, 11, 31, 34
Morris, Dr David, 199–200, 247
Mortimer, Penelope, 288
Mosey, Don, 204
Mougins, 318
Mount, Peggy, 321
Mousetrap, The, 29, 55, 65, 73
Move Over Mrs Markham, 314
Moxon, Michael, 172
Much Ado About Nothing, 172
Munro, J. B., 272
Murray, Braham, 91
Murry, Colin Middleton, 152
Murry, Helen Middleton
(daughter-in-law), 152, 153,
203, 241
Murry, Jackie Middleton, 152
Murry, John Middleton, 152
Murry, Ruth Middleton, 152
Murry, Violet Middleton, 152
Music, Music, Music, 77
Myatt, Edward, 177–8, 180
My Fair Lady, 102
My Farce from my Elbow, 4, 12,
16, 39

Nairobi, 208
Naked Civil Servant, The, 69
Nana, 308
Nangle, Jock, 180
Nap Hand, 35
Napley, Sir David, 270
National Association for the Care
and Control of the Feeble-
minded, 280
National Council for Voluntary
Organizations, 256
National Development Team for
the Mentally Handicapped
(NDT), 217–25

National Health Service, 22, 104–7, 110, 154, 156, 217–25, 263

National Health Service Act, 1946, 105–6

National Health Service Act, 1977, 106

National Playing Fields Association, 226

National Rubella Council, 216

National Service, 6, 7, 11

National Society for Mentally Handicapped Children *see* MENCAP

National Theatre, 68, 136, 172, 238, 294, 306, 307, 309, 314, 321

National Westminster Bank, 115

National Youth Theatre, 40, 63

Neagle, Dame Anna, 82, 231

Neal, Harry, 143

Nederlander, James, 87–8

Newall, Paul, 180

Newark, 114, 115, 220

New Horizons, 227

News of the World, 37

New Statesman, 33

New Theatre, Cardiff, 16

Newton, Tony, 110

New York, 56, 58, 64, 76, 80, 82, 87, 88, 113–14, 210–11, 263

New Zealand, 124, 271, 272–3

Next Steps, 228

Nicholls, Lord Justice, 275, 282

Nicholls, Phoebe, 89

Nicholson, Emma, 237

Nightmare Abbey, 67

Noble, Larry, 11, 29, 72, 93

Noble, Michelle, 72

Norman, Betty, 199

Norman, Elisabeth, 247

Normansfield, Friends of, 25, 60, 107–9, 114, 175, 234, 313, 319

Normansfield Hospital, Teddington, 21–6, 104–9, 117, 121, 175, 187

Northamptonshire, 111

Northumberland, 212

Norwich, 175–6, 177

Norwich, Lord Bishop of, 186

No Sex Please, We're British, 35

Nothing but the Truth, 8

Not Now, Darling, 73, 87, 89, 314

Nottingham, 11, 12, 104, 114, 192, 199

Nottinghamshire, 219, 220

Nottinghamshire Constabulary, 114

Nureyev, Rudolf, 33

Nursery World, 259

Observer, 33, 111, 166, 215, 287–9, 291–3

Office of Health Economics, 263

Official Secrets Act, 217, 218, 219, 224, 225

Ogilvie, Ian, 321

Oh Boy, 76, 77

Oh, Calcutta, 58

Oh, Clarence, 314

Old Vic, Stoke-on-Trent, 103

Oliver, John, 144

Olivier, Laurence, Lord, 231

One for the Pot, 31, 32, 55, 118–19, 120

100 Guinea Club, 175, 227

One in Four, 320

Only Fools and Horses, 66

On the Move, 99

On Your Toes, 235, 241, 243

Open University, 148, 192, 205, 263

Opera House, Harrogate, 94

O'Reilly, John Boyle, 160

Orwell, George, 235

Oslo, 122, 123

Otard Cognac Achievement Awards, 306

Oval, the, 127, 128, 129

Ovid, 293

Owen, Dr David, 244

Owens, Miss, 115

Oxfam, 310

Oxford, 6, 229, 234, 314

Oxford Playhouse, 136

Padgate, 6

Palace Theatre, 235, 241, 304

Palin, Michael, 193
Palma, Majorca, 114
Paradise Lost, 299
Parents' Voice, 258–61
Parker, George, 288–9
Parker, Thane, 67
Parkinson, Michael, 96
Parlophone, 94
Parnell, Val, 27
Parsons, Ian, 272
Parsons, Nicholas, 91, 112
Pascoe, Peter, 145
Patch, Wally, 11
Paterson, Bill, 89
Patrick, Nigel, 74
Paul, Roger, 180
Payne, Harry, 108
Peacock, Marjorie, 145
Peasgood, Julie, 324
Peg's Paper, 9
Pelling, Clive, 144
Pennock, Lord, 183
People First, 206
People Like Us, 262, 274
Pertwee, Maya, 46
Pertwee, Michael, 31, 35, 36, 37, 38, 42–3, 46, 65, 93, 94, 314, 318, 319–20, 327–8
Pertwee, Roland, 65
Peter Pan, 65
Pettifer, Julian, 310
Phantom of the Opera, 304
Philip, Duke of Edinburgh, 180, 226
Phillips, Alan, 143, 144
Phillips, Leslie, 89, 232
Phillips, Sian, 70
Pilkington, Antony, 184
Pinero, Sir Arthur, 323
Pink String and Sealing Wax, 65
Pirates Spring, 157–8, 213
Plaid Cymru, 312
Plain English Campaign, 202
Plank, David, 165
Plaskett, Freddie, 264
Player, Dr David, 198
Playhouse, 317
Playhouse, Nottingham, 104

Police and Criminal Evidence Act, 1984, 239–40
Portsmouth, 308
Posner, Geoffrey, 114
Postman's Knock, 28
Powell, Enoch, 160, 245, 248, 251, 252, 253
Powys, 152
Pratt, Oliver, 247
Presley, Elvis, 76, 77
Price, Alan, 174
Price, John, 112
Price, Richard, 231
Price Waterhouse, 33
Priestley, J. B., 67, 136
Primrose, David, A., 247
Princes Theatre *see* Shaftesbury Theatre
Privett, Simon, 310
Proby, P. J., 76–7, 123
Profumo, David, 158
Profumo, John, 157, 243
PROGRESS, 248
Protheroe, Brian, 60
Pryke, Della, 162
Punch, 40, 42, 98
Pursuing Quality, 228
Puss in Boots, 63
Pym, Chris, 205

Quayle, Sir Anthony, 231
Quayle, John 308
Queen Elizabeth Hospital, Banstead, 220
Queen, HM the (Elizabeth II), 99, 100, 102, 159, 180, 238, 269, 305
Queen Mother, HM The, 134–5, 145, 171, 191, 261, 266, 286–8, 290
Queen's Award for Export Achievement, 304
Queen's Theatre, 317
Questors Theatre Company, 69

RADAR, 159, 294
Radioactive, 99
Radio Society of Great Britain, 117

Radio Times, 117
Radley, Malcolm, 114
Radnor Commission, 280, 281
RAF, 6, 94
Rainworth, 220
Raise the Titanic, 55
Ramsden, Christine, 174
Ramsden, Dennis, 98, 174
Ramsden, Nico, 174
Rank Organization, 75
Ransom Hospital, Rainworth, 220
Rathbone, Elfrida, 259
Rattigan, Terence, 136
Rawsthorne, Anne, 70–71, 72–3, 76, 80, 86, 89
Raymond, Paul, 33
Reading, Donna, 39
Reagan, Nancy, 230
Reagan, President Ronald, 201
Really Useful Group, 304
Rees-Mogg, Lord, 322
Regent Street Polytechnic, 58, 59, 61
Regent Theatre, 56, 58–61
Reid, David, 145
Reluctant Heroes, 11, 12, 14, 26–9, 31, 32, 268
Reno, 82–4
Renshaw, Christopher, 313–14, 316, 321, 322, 323
Renton, Lord, 124, 133, 134, 145, 159, 190, 195, 196, 202, 240, 271, 311
Rescare, 285, 289
Reynolds, Harriet, 324
Reynolds, Sir Peter, 184
Rice, Tim, 90
Richards, Sir Gordon, 323
Richardson, Sir Ralph, 314
Riding for the Disabled, 23
Right from the Start '81 (MENCAP report), 162
Rimmer, John, 272
Ring, The, 59
Rio de Janeiro, 263
Rittner, Luke, 267, 268
Rivals, The, 197
Riviera, 137

Rix, Ben (grandchild), 153, 203, 204
Rix, Brian: birth, 4; childhood, 4–6; and mother, 4–5, 39, 92; and father, 4–5, 6, 7, 8, 22, 39, 92; sits Oxford entrance exam, 6; and RAF, 6–7; tours with Donald Wolfit, 6; in repertory, 6; demob, 6; becomes actor-manager, 7; in *Nothing but the Truth*, 8; in *Babes in the Wood*, 8; meets and marries Elspet, 9–10; at Bridlington, 9–11; in *Reluctant Heroes*, 11–12; at Nottingham, 12–14; television appearances, 14, 26–8, 32, 91–7, 98–100, 111, 116, 181–3, 216, 230–31, 277–8, 312, 313, 320; and birth of daughter Shelley, 15; and discovery that Shelley has Down's syndrome, 16; and Shelley's admittance to Normansfield Hospital, 21; and Friends of Normansfield, 25, 60, 107–9, 114, 175, 234, 313, 319; and fund-raising, 25–6, 178–85, 202, 206, 211–12, 225–7, 230–34, 244, 264, 270; and the press, 27, 36–9, 40–42, 45–6, 84–6, 135, 165–6, 186–90, 195–6, 197–9, 214–15, 217–25, 246–7, 249–52, 253–8, 267–8, 276, 278–84, 285–9, 291–2, 295, 318, 320, 322–4; and contract with BBC, 28; in *Dry Rot*, 29, 320–31; and birth of daughter Louisa, 29; and birth of son Jamie, 29; and birth of son Jonathan, 30; in *Simple Spymen*, 29; on farce, 30–31, 136–7, 322; in *One for the Pot*, 31; and *This is Your Life*, 32, 91–7; in *Chase Me Comrade!*, 32; moves to Garrick Theatre, 34; in *She's Done it Again*, 35–6; in *Don't Just Lie There, Say Something*, 37; in *A Bit*

Between the Teeth, 37–9;
returns to Whitehall in *Fringe
Benefits*, 39–46; acrimonious
correspondence with Michael
Pertwee, 42–3, 46; and cricket,
49–51, 96–7, 112–13, 127–30,
204, 226–7, 238, 272, 319; as
Theatre Controller with
Cooney-Marsh, 55–122; and
Regent Theatre, 58–61; and
Broadway Theatre, 61–3; and
Duke of York's Theatre, 64–73,
90; and Ambassadors Theatre,
73–4; and Astoria Theatre,
75–7, 80–81; and Shaftesbury
Theatre, 81–2, 83–7; and
Trafalgar Theatre, New York,
82, 87–8; receives CBE,
100–102; and Sherrard Report,
104–7; as disc jockey, 111; as
budding property developer,
114–15; first application to
MENCAP, 120–2; appointed
Secretary-General of MENCAP
133–6; first days in job,
137–42; and MENCAP staff,
142–8; MENCAP Medical
Advisory Panel, 148, 199–201,
240, 246–7, 250, 252, 265,
304, 307; first Members'
Meeting, 148–51; and Jamie's
wedding, 152; and
grandchildren, 153, 172,
203–4, 244, 304, 315, 319;
and MENCAP conference,
'Better services for the Mentally
Handicapped – When?', 153–6;
and Pirates Spring, 157–8; and
IYDP, 158–9; and IDC, 159,
228; and MENCAP conference,
'Right from the start '81',
162–4; and *Silent Minority*,
164–5; and mentally
handicapped children, 165–9;
and MENCAP Week, 1980,
169–70; and social events,
1981, 171–93; and honorary
degrees, 192; and Young and
Rubicam, 194–5, 197–8; and

Crossroads, 196–8; and
Gateway, 202, 227, 290; and
MENCAP Homes Foundation,
203; and MENCAP Conference
1982, '16 . . . And then what?',
204–5; and the Open
University, 205–6; and Lord
Mayor's Appeal, 207, 211–12;
at International League of
Societies for Persons with
Mental Handicap conference,
208–10; and Teignmouth,
213–15; and the National
Development Team, 217–25;
and Storytime, 230–2; and
Community Care Campaigners,
236–7; in India, 240–42; and
in vitro fertilization, 245–54;
and charitable giving, 254–8;
and MENCAP 40th
anniversary, 258, 261–7;
knighthood, 269–70; plans to
become MENCAP Chairman,
270–1; in Australia and New
Zealand, 271–3; and
sterilization (Jeanette case),
275–84, 332–7; and
community care, 284–6; at
MENCAP 1987 AGM, 288–90;
last weeks as MENCAP
Secretary-General, 294–9; first
months of retirement, 303–13,
considers returning to the
theatre, 313–15, 316–18;
becomes chairman of
MENCAP, 299, 318
Rix Elspet (née Gray), 3, 9–10,
11, 14–15, 16, 21, 25, 29, 33,
35, 43, 44, 81, 82, 84, 92, 93,
94, 95, 97, 98, 101, 103, 109,
110, 111, 112, 117, 119, 120,
123, 127, 133, 137, 149, 171,
175, 177, 187, 192, 200, 207,
210, 217, 225, 235–6, 238,
240–42, 243, 245, 263,
268–70, 272, 274, 291, 306,
307, 312, 313, 314, 315, 317,
324, 326
Rix, Jack (grandchild), 153, 204

Rix, Jamie (son), 29, 93, 99, 103,
  117, 123, 128, 152–3, 199,
  203, 206, 241, 269, 319
Rix, Jonathan (son), 30, 44, 92,
  93, 95, 101, 102–3, 113, 117,
  127, 128, 199, 307, 319
Rix, Louisa (daughter), 29, 66,
  81–2, 89, 96–7, 98, 99, 103–4,
  117, 137, 171, 199, 203, 204,
  244, 269, 319
Rix, Malcolm (brother), 4, 5, 93
Rix, Nora (sister), 5, 93
Rix, Sheila (sister), 5, 6, 44, 91,
  93–4, 118
Rix, Shelley (daughter), 15–17,
  21–2, 25, 29, 103, 116, 117,
  149, 187, 194, 248, 289, 292,
  295, 319
RNIB (Royal National Institute
  for the Blind), 159, 294
RNID (Royal National Institute
  for the Deaf), 159, 294
Road Haulage Association, 264
Roberts, Professor Gwyn, 199
Robinson, Emmott, 51
Robson, Dame Flora, 231
Rodgers, Anton, 314
Rooden, Matty van, 146, 147
Roof Over My Head, A, 98
Rookery Nook, 321
Rose, 73
Ross, James, 143
Rossi, Sir Hugh, 215, 237
Rothenberg, David, 178
Rothenberg, Helmut, 178, 180,
  183–4, 307
Roundhouse Theatre, 62
Rowland, Toby, 84
Rowntree, Richard, 116
Rowntree Memorial Trust,
  Joseph, 116
Royal Commission Report, 1957,
  150
Royal Court Theatre, 99
Royal Earlswood Hospital, 286,
  288
Royal Exchange Theatre,
  Manchester, 91

Royal Shakespeare Company
  (RSC), 268, 305, 315
Royal Society of Medicine, 312
Royal Star and Garter Home, 239
Royle, Derek, 93, 136
RSPB (Royal Society for the
  Protection of Birds), 178
Ruddigore, 23
Rudman, Michael, 294, 309
Run for Your Wife, 91, 308

Sachs, Andrew, 35, 91
Sadler's Wells Theatre, 314
St Andrews, 319
St Anne's-on-Sea, 73
St George's Hospital, London,
  117, 162
St Lawrence's Hospital,
  Caterham, 164
St Lucia, 124
St Martin's Theatre, 74
St Paul's School, 103
St Thomas's Hospital, London,
  311
Salford, 219, 222
Saltash, 330
Sanctuary, Gerald, 144
Sandilands, Jo, 135
Sands, Bobby, 173
San Francisco, 82, 84
Santa Fe, 77–80
Saunders, James, 73, 74
Saunders, Ernest, 185
Saunders, Sir Peter, 29, 55, 58,
  65–6, 72
Savoy Theatre, 24, 56, 58, 73, 86,
  89
Sayle, Alexei, 174
Scanlan, Charles, 177
Scarlett, John, 105
Scott, Terry, 66, 314
SDP (Social Democratic Party),
  244
Seagulls Over Sorrento, 14
Searle, Mr, 15–16
Secker and Warburg, 4
Secombe, Sir Harry, 226, 231
Segal, Lord, 135, 245, 276
Seguin, Edouard, 280, 281

Selsey Bill, 26
SERPS (State Earnings Related Pension Scheme), 262
Sexual Perversity in Chicago, 60
SFX Band, 174
Shaffer, Anthony, 75
Shaftesbury Memorial Lecture, 273–4
Shaftesbury Theatre, 56, 58, 69, 73, 81–7, 321
Shakespeare, William, 13, 90, 142, 148, 172, 184, 207, 274
Shapiro, Alexander, 247
Shaw, George Bernard, 172, 298
Shaw Theatre, 63
Sheffield, 219, 222
Shennan, Vicki, 145
Shepley, Michael, 226
Sheridan, Richard, 197
Sherrard, Michael, 105
Sherrard Report, 108, 109, 110, 111, 116
Sherrin, Ned, 320
She's Done it Again, 35, 37, 93
Sheth, Pran, 310
Shiner, Ronnie, 29, 118, 315
Shiv Films, 61
Shotter, Winifred, 65
Shriver, Eunice Kennedy, 201
Shulman, Milton, 322
Shylock, 90
Silent Minority, 164–5, 224
Sim, Sheila, 232
Simmons and Simmons, 177
Simon, Dr Gerry, 219
Simple Spymen, 29, 31, 32, 136, 314
Sinden, Donald, 87, 232
Singapore, 236
Singleton, Roger, 236
Sisson, Sir Roy, 184
Six of Rix, 28
Slater, Betty, 231
Slater, John, 29, 230–31, 315, 326
Sleuth, 75
Slough, 261
Slough Project, 143, 161
Smith, Mel, 99, 174, 192, 319

Snagge, John, 226
Snowdon, Lord, 159, 207
Snowdon Council, 159
Society for the Intellectually Handicapped (IHC), 272–3
Society of West End Theatres (SWET), 57
Solihull, 219, 220, 222
Solly, Ken, 143, 144
Solo, 192
Somerscales, Bob, 70
Somerscales, Tom, 70
Something's Afoot, 74
Sondheim, Stephen, 81
Sony, 202, 294
Sorrento, 264
Soundalive Tours, 294, 310, 313
South Africa, 81, 119
South-West Thames Regional Health Authority, 105
Spain, 114, 305, 325
Spain, Bernie, 162
Spastics Society, 148, 159, 214, 236, 237, 295, 325
Special Olympics, 141, 202
Spina Bifida Association, 91
Spinechiller, 69–70
SPUC (Society for the Protection of the Unborn Child), 245, 249
Stafford-Clark, David, 99
Stafford-Clark, Max, 90, 99
Stamina, 228, 262
Stand by Your Bedouin, 35, 55
Starlight Express, 304
Stars Organization for Spastics (SOS), 95, 121, 225–6, 309
Staunton, Imelda, 316
Stealey, Vic, 262
Stephenson, Pamela, 174
Stern, Jan, 247
Stevens, Peter, 68
Stevens, Shakin', 76
Stewart, Ed, 96
Stoke-on-Trent, 103
Stoll-Moss Theatres, 64, 84, 90, 317, 320
Stone, Richard, 43, 46
Storytime, 231–2, 235
Strachan, Alan, 319

Strategy for Mental Handicap in Wales, 152
Stratford, Brian, 247
Stratford-upon-Avon, 306
Streets of London, The, 123
Stringer, Guy, 310
Stross, David, 94
Sudbury, 266–7
Suffolk, 266–7
Sun, 101, 287
Sunday Express, 45
Sunday Night at the London Palladium, 28
Sunday People, 136
Sunday Telegraph, 103, 185
Sunday Times, 33, 36, 215, 279–83, 286
Sunderland, 281
SUNFUND, 270
Surrey, 127, 128, 129–30, 146–7, 219, 220, 221, 222, 224, 259, 286, 287
Surrey County Cricket Club 1979 Year Book, 127, 130
Surrey Young Cricketers, 103, 127
Sutton, 219, 222
Suzman, Janet, 67
Swainson, Capt Anthony, 175, 227
Sweet and Low, 74
Sweeter and Lower, 74
Sweetest and Lowest, 74
Sydney, 123, 272
Sylvaine, Vernon, 31, 35
Syms, Sylvia, 232
Syros, 137

Tahoe, Lake, 84
Taylor, David, 263
Taylor, Jean, 263
Taylor, Weston, 37
Teignmouth, 158, 213–15
Teignmouth News, 213
Tenko, 235–6, 312
Tennent, H. M., 73, 80
Test Match Special, 112
Tewson, Jane, 174
Thames Television, 98

Thark, 323
Thatcher, Denis, 234–5
Thatcher, Margaret, 182, 207–8, 235, 269
Theatre Knights (and Dames), 231
Theatre of Comedy, 72, 75, 81, 87, 91, 239, 319, 321
Theatre Royal, Bath, 320–21
Theatre Royal, Nottingham, 11, 12–13
Theatre Royal, Stratford East, 123
There Goes the Bride, 314
They're Playing Our Song, 73, 81, 87
This is Your Life, 32, 91–6
Thompson, Mark, 316
Thompson, Neville, 133–4, 145, 169, 178
Thompson, Peter, 319, 320
Thorson, Linda, 60
Three Stooges, 323
Ticketmaster, 68
Tilley, Vesta, 316
Time and the Conways, 67
Time Out, 320
Times, The, 36, 113, 119, 170, 186–90, 195–6, 197–9, 208, 246–7, 248–52, 254–8, 267–8, 276, 291, 295, 320, 322
Tinker, Jack, 322
Titmus, Fred, 96
Tivoli Theatre, Copenhagen, 122
Todd, Richard, 232
Tons of Money, 136, 321
Took, Barry, 42, 98
Torbay, 213
Torquay, 244
Tour, Frances de la, 73
Trade and Industry, Department of (DTI), 177
Trafalgar Square Theatre *see* Duke of York's Theatre
Trafalgar Theatre, New York, 56, 58, 82, 87–8
Travers, Ben, 31, 65, 89, 136, 321, 323
Triumph Theatre Productions, 39, 66, 327, 328
Trueman, Freddie, 193, 204

Trumpington, Baroness, 237, 262
Tumbledown, 238
Tumbledown, 239
Turner, Joan, 90
Turvey, Bill, 94, 312
TV-a.m., 276
20th Century Coyote, 174
Two Into One, 91
Tynan, Kenneth, 321

Udwin, Hymie, 119
Udwin, Rene, 119
Unborn Children (Protection) Bill,
   245, 248, 252, 253
United Charities Unit Trust, 178,
   312
United Nations Charter of Human
   Rights, 168
United States of America, 56, 58,
   64, 69, 76, 88–80, 82–3, 87–9,
   113, 200–201, 210–11, 261,
   263, 265, 314
Uproar in the House, 35

Vamp, The, 63
Vaughan, Dr Gerard, 190, 237
Vaughan, Sally, 72, 145–6
Vernon, Richard, 324
Victory, HMS, 308
View from the Boundary, 204

Wagner, Richard, 296
Waiting for Godot, 294, 309–10
Walden, Brian, 332
Wales, 16, 151–2, 202–3, 312
Wales, HRH Princess of, 172,
   180, 215–16
Wallace, Philip Hope, 33
Walmsley, Jan, 205
Walsh, Dermot, 11
Wandering Jew, The, 310
Ward, Linda, 205
Wardle, Irving, 36, 322
Warnock, Lady, 246
Warnock Report on Human
   Fertilization and Embryology,
   245, 247, 253–5
Warnock White Paper, 248, 249,
   251, 253–5

Warrington, 6
Warrior, HMS 308
Warwick University, 113, 117
Warwickshire, 219, 222
Washington, 200, 201, 265
Watford, Gwen, 73
Watson, Basil, 169, 211
Watt, Tommy, 94
Webb, Marti, 60
Weill, Hanna, 198–9
Weill, Nina, 197–8
Weinberg, Sir Mark, 178
Weldon, Duncan, 39, 42, 90,
   326–9
Weldon, Janet, 326
Welland, Colin, 310
Welsh Office, 152
Wertheimer, Alison, 214
Wesker, Arnold, 90
Wessex Regional Health
   Authority, 224
West End Managers' Association,
   26, 86
West Indies, 272, 319
West Germany, 256
Westminster Theatre, 67, 71
West Sussex, 219, 220, 222, 224
Whelton, Michael, 144
White, Jo McLaren, 261
White, Michael, 82, 90
Whitehall Theatre, 11–12, 26, 28,
   29, 30, 32, 33, 34, 35, 39, 40,
   56, 72, 92, 93, 98, 111, 120,
   136, 142, 156, 171, 174, 216,
   234, 255, 257, 306, 313, 318,
   321, 322, 323, 325, 330
Whitehouse, Christopher, 253,
   254
White House, 201
Whitelaw, Lord, 258
Whiteley, Richard, 193
White Rose Players, Harrogate, 6
Whitfield, June, 66
Whitnall, Tim, 76
Whitney, John, 77, 304
Whixley Hospital, N Yorkshire,
   220
Who Killed 'Agatha' Christie, 74

Whose Life Is It Anyway?, 73, 86, 88–9
Wig Creations, 319
Wight, Isle of, 110
Wight, Peter, 310
Wigley, Dafydd, 312
Wigley, Dr Guy, 162
Wilcox, Larry, 316
Wilkes, Angela, 215
Wilkinson, Colm, 91
Williams, Austen, 169
Willis, Rear-Admiral, 214
Willis, Thomas, 280, 281
Wilson, Harold, 100
Wilson, Peter, 231
Wilson, Renée, 231
Wilton, Nick, 324
Windsor, 306
Winter Gardens, Bournemouth, 122
Winterton, Ann, 254
Winterton, Nicholas, 254
Wisdom, Norman, 87
Wise, Ernie, 118
Wizard of Oz, The, 315–16
Wogan, 320
Wolfit, Donald, 6, 7, 12
Woman, 135
Woman's Weekly, 206
Wonnacott, Linda, 164
Wood, Charles, 238
Woolley, Alys, 105
World at One, 225

World at Their Fingertips, 116
Worm's Eye View, 11, 14, 29, 118
Wow Show, The, 99
Wright, Jimmy, 117
Wright, Sir Oliver, 201
Wymark, Olwen, 268
Wyndham's Theatre, 57, 75
Wynne-Parker, Michael, 177–8, 179, 180
Wynne-Parker Financial Services, 178

Yeldham, Peter, 40
Yeo, Tim, 214
York, 5
Yorkshire, 127, 196, 219, 220, 222
Yorkshire County Cricket Club, 130
Yorkshire League (cricket), 49
Yorkshire Personality of the Year, 1981, 193
Yorkshire Television, 98, 181–3
You'll Do For Me, 328
Young, Sir George, 150, 237
Young, Marion, 146, 147
Young and Rubicam, 194–5, 197–9, 209
Young Variety, 63
Yvonne Arnaud Theatre, 329

Zimbabwe. 305
Zola, Emile, 308